BREAK THE WHEEL

BREAK THE WHEEL

ENDING THE CYCLE OF POLICE VIOLENCE

KEITH ELLISON

12

TWELVE

NEW YORK   BOSTON

Twelve
Hachette Book Group
1290 Avenue of the Americas, New York, NY 10104
twelvebooks.com
twitter.com/twelvebooks

First Edition: May 2023

Twelve is an imprint of Grand Central Publishing. The Twelve name and logo are
trademarks of Hachette Book Group, Inc.

The publisher is not responsible for websites (or their content) that are not owned
by the publisher.

The Hachette Speakers Bureau provides a wide range of authors for speaking
events. To find out more, go to hachettespeakersbureau.com or email
HachetteSpeakers@hbgusa.com.

Twelve books may be purchased in bulk for business, educational, or promotional
use. For information, please contact your local bookseller or the Hachette Book
Group Special Markets Department at special.markets@hbgusa.com.

Library of Congress Cataloging-in-Publication Data has been applied for.

ISBNs: 978-1-5387-2563-4 (hardcover), 978-1-5387-2565-8 (ebook)

Printed in the United States of America

LSC-C

Printing 1, 2023

For Gigi and Darnella

CONTENTS

FOREWORD BY PHILONISE FLOYD

As I sat down to write this, I had just watched the video recording of Tyre Nichols getting punched, kicked, pepper sprayed, tased, medically neglected, and ultimately killed by five Memphis police officers. It stirs painful memories for me and my family. It transports us right back to that moment when we learned what had happened to George Perry Floyd, my brother.

Tyre, like my brother (whom we called Perry), also called for his mother. He was also an unarmed Black man. Like Tyre, my brother had a lot to live for and a life filled with friendship, love, and meaning. Like my brother Perry, Tyre was taken away from us all too soon. And like my brother, Tyre was killed because of a nationwide and historic problem involving police brutality.

It's not just Minneapolis and it's not just Memphis; it's all over the country. In my own hometown of Houston, we have serious problems, and you can probably say the same thing for nearly every city in America. And just as the murder of Tyre Nichols at the hands of five Memphis police officers stirred painful memories for me and my family, it stirred painful memories for a nation that has now witnessed another tragic killing at the hands of those people who are trained to ensure our safety.

Will it ever end?

After Perry was killed, I became a spokesman for police reform, and it's not a role I ever sought or wanted. But I turned my pain into purpose.

In fact, those of us who have lost loved ones to police violence are all part of a club to which we never wished to belong.

I learned a few things along the way. I learned that this problem of police brutality is not confined to the United States. I learned that the problem of armed government agents using deadly force against unarmed civilians affects victims at local, national, and even international levels. We witness it in every American city, and you can find it in China, Iran, London, and Peru. Perhaps this is why the world rose up when my brother died with Derek Chauvin's knee on his neck. Perry has become an international symbol of police violence, and a symbol of resistance to that violence.

I pray that Tyre Nichols's family will see a vigorous prosecution of the five Memphis officers involved in his death, and I hope that everyone who stood around and did nothing will be fired. These two things— quick disciplinary action and an aggressive prosecution—are the only things that are sure to bring police brutality to an end.

I know some will call for more training, and good training is important. But the men who killed George Floyd—Derek Chauvin, Tou Thao, Thomas Lane, and Alexander Keung—were all well trained. How come their training did not tell them what was so obvious to the civilians who stood by screaming, videotaping, and begging the officers to just stop? How come the training of the Scorpion Unit in Memphis did not stop those officers from ganging up and beating an unarmed and innocent person to death?

In my brother's case, a nine-year-old witness, wearing a T-shirt with "Love" written across it, knew that Perry was in serious distress. But the officers' training in CPR and racial sensitivity did not compel them to prevent what was obvious to a nine-year-old girl. We need something more basic than training. The Memphis Scorpion Unit was supposed to be a well-trained elite unit. So much for that. What we need is decency. What we need is accountability.

I'm glad to write this foreword for Keith Ellison's *Break the Wheel* because accountability is exactly what he and his team delivered. Days after my brother was killed, my family and I asked Minnesota Governor Walz to appoint Ellison to lead the prosecution of the officers who killed my brother. We had lost faith in the established system. It wasn't personal, but we did not believe the system would handle the case properly. I knew it was going to be a tough case, regardless of the video evidence. The "not-guilty" verdicts of the officers who beat Rodney King in 1992 were not far from my mind. But Ellison took the case, assembled a team, and delivered accountability for my family and the nation.

So many of us want to believe that George Floyd's death was not in vain, and that something good would emerge out of our family's tragedy. In fact, I am writing a book of my own for the benefit of every family and community that is faced with police violence. I hope that book and this one will offer truths that will make a difference: *Break the Wheel* is a blueprint for holding police accountable and a must-read.

With the tragic killing of Tyre Nichols, we see that the officers were fired quickly, and indicted, and the videotape of the tragic incident was released immediately. It's hard to believe this would have happened without Ellison's example in seeking justice for my brother.

This is progress, but it's not enough. As I write this foreword, the George Floyd Justice in Policing Act has not been passed, but many cities, police departments, and states have taken meaningful action. The Biden administration has acted by executive order. These are small steps, but meaningful steps. In the end, we need a societal change. We need to break the wheel of injustice, as Ellison says. My family and I are committed for the long run.

Chapter 1

"MAMMA! MAMMA! I'M THROUGH!"

My phone woke me up at 4:45 a.m. It was lighting up, begging my attention. Still half asleep, I swung my feet to the side of the bed and reached for the phone. I hoped I wouldn't wake my wife.

I thumbed the glowing screen to find out what was going on.

My twenty-five-year-old outreach coordinator, Keaon Dousti, had left an urgent message about a video. I touched the face of my iPhone, and the video began to play.

"Mamma! Mamma! I'm through!" shouted the Black man trapped under the knee of a Minneapolis police officer. The officer appeared to be riding on top of the man struggling under the weight of three Minneapolis cops. The man cried and yelled "I can't breathe" many times in the first part of the video. His face twisted in agony and he cried out in pain, "My stomach hurts, my neck hurts, everything hurts."

I couldn't believe how long the video was running, how long this torment continued. And I recognized the location: Cup Foods at 38th Street and Chicago Avenue. This is the heart of working-class South Minneapolis. It's across the street from where Hamza, a Palestinian immigrant, fixes my car.

I know this area well. In 1997, just three blocks south of 38th and Chicago, fifteen-year-old Lawrence Miles Jr. was shot in the back and nearly bled to death in an open field next to the apartment complex where he grew up. The shooter was Minneapolis police officer Charles Storlie. Why was Miles shot? He was playing tag with his friends using BB guns.

Long before I ever ran for office, I was working in a private practice as an attorney, and Miles was my client. His case taught my legal partners and me just how tough it could be to sue the police for the deprivation of civil rights and unreasonable and excessive force. In 2002, the jury found in favor of Officer Storlie.

This was a devastating loss for Lawrence Miles. Now forty years old, he still suffers from the physical injuries he sustained twenty-five years ago. Despite our best efforts, he never received any compensation for his injuries.

Incidentally, Storlie is the same officer who shot and nearly killed undercover Minneapolis officer Duy Ngo in 2003. Ngo was lying on the ground after being shot by another suspect and was completely disarmed and disabled when Storlie shot him. Ngo, a Vietnamese American working with the controversial Minnesota Gang Strike Force, was scheduled to report the very next day to his U.S. Army Reserve unit to deploy to Afghanistan, where he would serve as a combat medic. After years of being ostracized by his department and enduring more than twenty-five surgeries due to the shooting, Ngo committed suicide in 2010.

As I watched the glowing screen of my cell phone, I didn't know the man who was being killed, but I knew this story. I was viscerally aware of this recurring tale.

Philando Castile was a beloved lunchroom manager at an elementary school in Saint Paul, Minnesota, when he was killed at a traffic stop in 2016 by St. Anthony police officer Jeronimo Yanez. Castile had committed no crime and had tried to comply with Yanez's commands, but he was dead nonetheless. Diamond Reynolds, Castile's girlfriend, livestreamed the aftermath of the shooting, and the squad video caught the shooting itself in horrifying detail.

The case of twenty-four-year-old Jamar Clark, who was killed by Minneapolis police officers eight months before Castile, was less clear-cut. He had a felony conviction at nineteen and a Domestic Violence No Contact order in place when he was killed outside a party in North Minneapolis.

Clark's shooting and death happened just blocks from where I sat in my home watching this video in the early morning hours of May 26, 2020. Still, in Clark's case, the woman who got the order against him told a journalist he was "a kind, nurturing man," and he seemed to be turning his life around. He was "no angel," as they say, but he was certainly no demon, either. Eyewitnesses to his death gave wildly conflicting accounts.

Clark's girlfriend had gotten into a fight at the party, so they left. But she was hurt, and someone called an ambulance. While she was sitting in the ambulance, Clark went to check on her. He somehow got into an altercation with the officers on the scene—Mark Ringgenberg and Dustin Schwarze. They said they shot Clark after he grabbed for an officer's gun. But witnesses said Clark was handcuffed on the ground when the police shot him.

In the end, Hennepin County attorney Mike Freeman declined the charges against Ringgenberg and Schwarze. DNA testing revealed traces of Clark's genetic material on an officer's gun. This could have been the result of inadvertent touching during the struggle, or it could corroborate the officer's story. Who knows? For the purposes of making a case, though, it was a bagful of reasonable doubt. In the absence of other information, it made charging the officers impossible. It was not, however, an exoneration.

Mike Freeman said, "His DNA is all over that gun and he had no business having his hand on that gun, which is why they shot him [and] which is why I didn't prosecute them."

I have worked with Freeman. He's a friend and a committed civil servant. Like all of us in public life, he has gotten more than his share of criticism, both deserved and undeserved. But to the ears of many who heard his statement, it was another in the relentless series of examples of the system not caring about the lives of Black people—that Clark's life didn't rate. Under Minnesota law, Freeman would be in charge of the Floyd murder case, too.

———

In the dark of my bedroom, the video dragged on, and the man's suffering was palpable. His struggle to survive was obvious as he cried out for a breath, for his mother.

"Mamma!" he cried. The officers were immune to the man's suffering. Their demeanor was casual and routine. They appeared unconcerned and even nonchalant. The cop with his knee on the Black man's neck stared out at the people filming him, defiant and impassive. The officer continued scraping and rubbing the man's face into the hard asphalt surface of Chicago Avenue.

I didn't know this officer, but I recognized something in him.

Maybe it was what could be seen in Officer Timothy Loehmann, who shot and killed twelve-year-old Tamir Rice at a playground. The African American boy had a pellet gun, and the 911 caller had said the gun was likely not a real firearm.

Loehmann's personnel records were released after the shooting. He had been hired by the Cleveland Police Department even after his supervisors at the Independence Police Department described him as emotionally unstable. They said he had an "inability to perform basic functions as instructed" during a weapons training exercise. Cleveland PD admitted to not looking into Loehmann's personnel file during the background check.

I sat at the edge of the bed, unable to stand under the weight of what I was watching. It wasn't just the brutality and human suffering captured on the video, but the cycle it represented. There are names we all know: Freddie Gray, Trayvon Martin, Michael Brown. There are those known locally, the ones killed by Minneapolis police: Terrance Frank-lin, Fong Lee, Alfred "Abuka" Sanders. Unfortunately, there are more we will never know—all part of a repeating cycle of in-custody deaths, protest and unrest, lawsuits, and study commissions and recommenda-tions. This is the wheel of policing in America that we're stuck in. It has been going on for more than 100 years. Civil rights leader Bayard Rustin once said, "The only weapon we have is our bodies, and we need to tuck them in places so the wheels don't turn."

The wheel Rustin had in mind was the system of Jim Crow segrega-tion, but it is connected to the wheel that spins between officer-involved deaths and inaction. They both spin along, a cycle of injustice going 'round and 'round. Sixty years after Rustin, haven't we seen that it's not enough to just stop the wheel? Isn't it time to actually break it? Isn't it time to get a new set of wheels that roll toward liberty and justice for all? But we don't have that in the United States at this time.

And on May 26, 2020, I was watching the wheel grind a man's face into the street.

Floyd was wearing a tank top that exposed his shoulder while it was scraped and rubbed raw against the pavement as the police pressed him into it. One officer on Floyd's neck, a second officer pushing down on his back while the third held Floyd's legs, preventing him from turning his body to get a breath. A fourth officer, a stout Hmong man, stood guard, taunting the people assembled. "If he's talking, he's breathing," he declared to the people insisting that the Black man, under the weight of this man's colleagues, could not breathe.

The people on the video witnessing the horror taking place weren't buying it. A young Black man, whom I thought I recognized, yelled back, "You're sayin' that's okay? You're sayin' it's all right what he's doing?" Then he yelled, "Check his pulse." He joined a chorus of furious onlookers, including a young white woman who told the officers she was a firefighter.

I couldn't look away from the horror that was unfolding, and I was shaken by the sheer length of time the abuse continued.

Then the officer standing guard said in a singsongy voice, "That's why you don't do drugs, kids!"

I hadn't moved. I wasn't dressed yet. I couldn't bring myself to peel my eyes away even for a second. These cops were so brazen. I thought, *They don't give a damn who is even watching.* As the clip continued to play before me, gripping me as if I were standing there with the other onlookers, a warm droplet fell from my cheek onto the phone. *It never ends.*

The young Black man yelled again, "Check his pulse, check his pulse, Thao."

He seemed to know the officer standing guard, or maybe he just read the officer's name plate on his shirt.

Then I realized how I knew this fellow. I had known him for years, though I hadn't seen him recently. His name was Donald Williams. When he was a child, he was one of the neighborhood kids on the wrestling team with my sons Jeremiah and Elijah.

About two and a half minutes into the video, the body of the man on the ground went limp. His voice gradually became thicker and slower, making fewer and fewer comments. Eventually, he stopped saying anything. His eyes closed, and he was just motionless. Still, the officer, who had disregarded the pleas of the suffering man, kept his full body weight on his knee, wedged into the space between the man's head and shoulder.

Donald Williams and the others kept yelling for the officer to get off the man, and to check his pulse.

The yelling, I knew, would get louder.

There were protests after the Jamar Clark killing in 2015. Protesters set up a camp around the Minneapolis Police Department's Fourth Precinct Station. Hundreds occupied it around the clock for more than two weeks. My son Jeremiah, a local artist and activist, got involved. One night, he was on the protest line, hands in the air, chanting, "Hands up, don't shoot." Suddenly, an officer shouldered a gun and aimed it at Jeremiah's head.

A friend of mine, a young east African immigrant, snapped a photo of the moment and tweeted it, noting in the caption that cops were even aiming guns at a congressman's son. The position I held then, my job, was irrelevant, though. The problem was that my son, clearly unarmed and peacefully protesting, had a gun aimed directly at him. The photo made my blood run cold, and then boil.

It was a quieter kind of change, but the Clark tragedy affected us all. Jeremiah was inspired to make a difference. Today, Jeremiah is a Minneapolis City Council member representing the North Side, which has been the scene of more injustices than just Clark's killing.

Watching the video that morning, I was reminded of the tweet that exposed the threat to my son's life. It was a sudden, crisp understanding of what is meant when people talk about the "digital revolution." It occurred to me: If I was waking up to this video, then so were millions of other people. And if it made me this upset and confused, then we would see protests at least as big as those following the Clark killing.

I was transported back to memories of the town where I was born—the site of the 1967 Detroit uprising. I was three and a half years old then. According to my dad, the Detroit police raided an unlicensed, after-hours bar on the west side near West Grand Boulevard and 12th Street, known as a "blind pig." These informal bars started during Prohibition, but blind pigs continued to thrive well after that period. They offered an alternative to white-owned bars in the racially segregated Detroit of the 1960s, which didn't have "Whites Only" signs, but they didn't really need them, either. Everybody knew where they were and were not welcome—segregation northern style.

There had been years of tragic clashes between the police and the Black community in Detroit. On July 23, 1967, the conflict exploded into one of the deadliest. It was one of the most destructive riots in American history, lasting five days, and surpassing the scale of Detroit's 1943 race riot, twenty-four years earlier.

In 1967, I was too young to understand the smoke billowing from burning buildings or windows being smashed, but I remember seeing military vehicles rolling past our house. At three, I stood on my tiptoes, looking out a window in my house on Ilene Street near Outer Drive, watching soldiers in military vehicles. An older brother, Brian, has reminded me that we lived close to the Eight Mile Armory. Maybe we saw the National Guard heading to the affected areas. My brothers and I didn't see any protesting or looting, but we were aware of it.

Forty-three people died in the Detroit riot in 1967, but the civil disturbances of that era created a negative effect on the economy of Detroit that continues to this day. The riots accelerated white flight and suburbanization; and while the unrest probably did not have much effect on the decisions by Ford, GM, and Chrysler to abandon Detroit, it did not help. Mostly, it scarred the collective psyche of the people who endured it, like me.

As I watched the cell phone video that morning, I wondered what the children of Minneapolis would remember from the coming days.

When I was that young, I could sense how stressed and worried my parents were. Our dad was a physician, and Brian and I both remember him pulling long hours because of the troubles. I could feel my mom's fear and anxiety. I remember, too, my mother ordering us to hide under the bed when something outside scared her.

Thinking back on those Detroit days, I couldn't ask my mom what had prompted her fear. She passed away due to COVID-19 on March 26, 2020. It was exactly two months to the moment I was watching this cell phone video.

My mom witnessed the hardships of African Americans. Her dad was an NAACP leader in Natchitoches, Louisiana. She would recount how crosses were burned in front of their home; how her dad was prohibited from buying gasoline by the local store owners sympathetic with the Ku Klux Klan; and how he had received racist and terroristic telephone calls through the night. Callers said things to my grandmother Doris like, "We got that n— —r tied up to a tree. He ain't gonna make it home—ever." Even though my grandfather made it home, the threats affected my mom, and they affected me vicariously.

My mom would have been outraged at what happened to George Floyd.

My mother was among the 100,000 recorded deaths caused by COVID-19 by late May 2020. I was still grieving, and my four brothers were, too. We couldn't bury her properly because of the pandemic restrictions. We couldn't have a church service; we were only able to have the funeral home and the grave site.

As her casket was lowered into the ground, my oldest brother, Leonard, and I had to stand back while my brothers, Tony and Eric, stood at the graveside with Brian, who is a Baptist minister.

By the end of May 2020, I'm sure that perhaps 100,000 families shared the same sorrow, and everyone living through this moment was frustrated and sick of the quarantine. The health and safety restrictions connected to COVID-19 had people anxious and ready to get out.

And now another Black death under the wheel. A dam broke under the weight of people's worry, anxiety, grief, and isolation and let them spill onto the streets. And COVID-19 wasn't the only thing—we were ramping up for a historically divisive presidential election.

That early morning of May 26, 2020, I suspected there would be an enormous group of people protesting, and I was afraid we were on the cusp of chaos—but not only from the protesters.

One night during the Jamar Clark protests, at about 10:45 p.m., a group of four men, three wearing masks, were hovering around the camp outside the Fourth Precinct. But they were not joining the protest. Rumors had been circulating of possible attacks by white supremacists, so several guys working security around the protest asked the men to identify themselves.

They asked the men why they were wearing masks. The three masked men refused to answer, so the protesters demanded they leave. At that moment, one of the men turned and opened fire. Five men doing protest security were shot. Fortunately, all of them survived.

The most significant charges to come out of the incident were leveled at Allen Lawrence Scarsella, twenty-three, who was charged with riot and five counts of second-degree assault. Daniel Thomas Macey, twenty-six, Nathan Wayne Gustavsson, twenty-one, and Joseph Martin Backman, twenty-seven, were charged with second-degree riot. One of the injured protesters later reported that he heard one of the masked men use the word "n——r." During the trial, more evidence surfaced indicating the shooter and his friends were white supremacists. They were convicted.

I knew that dramatic acts of brutality often spark chaos, and I worried that the horrific incident playing on my cell phone might spark unstable people. For example, I thought of Micah Xavier Johnson, an African American man who felt compelled to respond to the murders of Philando Castile in Minneapolis and Alton Sterling in Baton Rouge, Louisiana.

On July 7, 2016, in what can only be described as a bias-motivated crime, Johnson ambushed a group of police officers in Dallas, killing five and injuring nine others. Two civilians were also wounded. It was the deadliest attack against U.S. law enforcement since September 11, 2001. It was terrifying to consider what violence this video might inspire.

Nearly eight minutes into the video, with the man lying still on the ground, the officer finally lifted his knee, but only due to the paramedics telling the officer to get off. The video continued, though.

Staring at the screen of my phone, watching paramedics roll the limp body onto a stretcher, I said without looking at my wife, "Oh my God! Moni, you need to see this..."

I could feel her turn over and knew she was looking at me, "Huh?" (My Mónica is a light sleeper.)

"Hun, you need to see this!" I said.

"What is it?" Her Colombian accent lilted from the other side of the bed.

"This man...they're murdering him right on video." I was probably louder than I realized.

Without pause, her tone quickly changed. "No, I don't want to see that. I don't want to see another person killed. Uh-uh. No thank you." She turned her body away as she pulled the blanket over her head.

I didn't push. She had seen enough. Colombia, my wife's birthplace, is the country with the second largest internally displaced population in the world, behind Syria. Having grown up in Medellín, she was no stranger to state violence, narco violence, and rebel violence. She—like too many people in Minneapolis, the U.S., and the world—didn't need to see the horror to know it was happening. They have seen enough violence and brutality. She has seen way too much.

But I was transfixed by the screen of my phone as I turned back to the video. I restarted it and rewatched the police officer, whose name I didn't yet know, defiantly stare back at the bystanders who pleaded with him to stop hurting the man under his knee; to get up and check his pulse. Still, the officer kept kneeling on the man's neck, rocking back and forth.

I was watching a murder. I knew it in my heart. As a lawyer, however, I know very well it isn't murder until a jury says so.

There was a time when I would have jumped out of bed and run out into the streets with my neighbors to protest the injustice and yell "No justice, no peace!" Now I am the Minnesota attorney general, and that kind of moral certainty is a privilege I gave up when I took my oath of office. Not only did that oath oblige me to take a calm, objective approach to the evidence, but the years had changed me as well. When I became an elected public official in 2003, maybe even a little before that, I began to understand that I needed to be more deliberate, gather more facts, and make decisions that factored in the perspectives of all of the people I represent. By the time I became the Minnesota attorney general, I was acutely aware of the need to be just and fair, but also to be perceived that way.

I set aside my fears, tears, anger, and sorrow as I turned my attention to the days ahead. I knew this tragedy was going to demand my attention one way or another.

The tragedy in this case did not follow the expected path. The first time the system held a Minneapolis police officer accountable was when a Black officer shot and killed a white woman while on duty in 2017. But the prosecution of Mohamed Noor was just, and appropriate: He had shot and killed an unarmed person, with no reasonable basis for using that level of force.

The stakes were high. The outcome rested as much on public perception as fact. My friend Mike Freeman, the local prosecutor, was going to face, fair or unfair, challenges from the public to his credibility on prosecuting excessive force after his unartful comments about the Clark case.

I began to set the stage in my mind. I was quite certain that as news hit the street, the activists would be out fairly soon. Who could blame them? I believe that peaceful protest helps move the needle of progress. It's also a right guaranteed by the First Amendment.

Several organizations in the Twin Cities were actively working on the problem of police violence. For example, Families Supporting Families Against Police Violence was founded by Toshira Garraway. Her fiancé, Justin Teigen, was found dead in a trash dumpster in 2009 after he was stopped by St. Paul police. Communities United Against Police Brutality was founded by Michelle Gross, a nurse by training, who has been working on police accountability for forty years. My former staffer Miski Noor is co-lead for the active Black Visions Collective.

I knew these groups, along with less structured elements of the Minneapolis political scene, would organize protests, make demands, and raise pressure on public figures to act. I also knew they had seen a lot and heard a lot of long-since-broken promises. They were frustrated and demanded "transformation." Talk of "reform" was not welcome in many circles in the Twin Cities.

I assumed that I'd get calls from legislators, perhaps the governor, and the commissioner of the Minnesota Department of Human Rights, Rebecca Lucero, who used to work on my congressional staff. During the Obama administration, when the Jamar Clark investigation was going on, I took calls from leaders in the U.S. Department of Justice and other places.

I assumed that this horrific example of abuse would draw the U.S. DOJ's attention, even with Donald Trump in the White House.

I watched the man, whose name I still did not know, go limp another time. In both law and politics, it is so easy for human life to become faceless and unknown. As I gamed out the different legal and political demands made by this killing, I knew I needed to hold on to the human tragedy at the center of it.

I don't remember how many times I watched the video that morning. It made no sense to me. I couldn't understand it. I watched it as a man of faith, as a Minnesotan, as a father, as a Black man, as the ranking officer of Minnesota's justice system, as an activist, as a husband, as a lawyer, as a human being. The video shocked me, but I can't claim it surprised me. It blew my mind, and it was numbingly familiar. It was like nothing I had seen, yet identical to countless experiences I have witnessed in which people found themselves on the business end of state violence.

For a moment, I was transported back to 1967 Detroit, and I was a child again, watching a conflict I couldn't foresee or understand.

Then a calming thought came into my mind. We were facing a *human* crisis, and it could be understood and confronted. The work was in learning, coming to know, and holding on to our shared humanity.

So I got up and headed to the bathroom to start my day. I knew I had to talk to the leaders in my office: chief of staff Donna Cassutt and chief deputy John Keller. I knew we were going to act. I knew what I wanted to add to the cause of justice, but I also knew that if I wasn't careful, I could add to the chaos. I didn't want to move emotionally but rather effectively.

I don't know what time it was, but we started early. I was texting my staff that we had to meet virtually.

I was working at my dinner table. My wife is a serious coffee drinker, and she set a hot cup beside me as the meeting began. I looked at the computer screen, containing little square video images of my team members, and asked, "What do we know?"

Keaon, who had seen the video on Facebook the night before, told me the details first. He had screen-recorded it and posted it on Twitter at 1:14 a.m. By 1:47 a.m., Mukhtar Ibrahim, a journalist at *Sahan Journal*, had DM'ed Keaon and remarked, "This is so brutal. Did it happen tonight? Do you know who took the video?" Keaon confirmed that the events in the video had occurred the night before and sent Ibrahim the Facebook link.

Ibrahim then sent Keaon a copy of Minneapolis Police Department spokesman John Elder's press release describing a sad but otherwise unremarkable situation of an inebriated man dying in a "medical incident." The video and the press release were so different that Keaon and Mukhtar wondered whether they were describing the same incident. Mukhtar then retweeted the video. The tweet generated 13.7 million views.

Keaon followed with the facts. The man's name was George Floyd. He was forty-six. He had worked as unarmed security at a few spots I knew well: the Conga, El Nuevo Rodeo, the Salvation Army. He was from Houston, Texas.

John Stiles, the communications director at the Minnesota attorney general's office, chimed in that we already had media calls coming in. He asked me what I wanted to say.

John pushed the voice-recording icon on his phone, and I started talking, free style. This is how we often develop statements.

I said, "George Floyd mattered. Somebody loved him. His life was important. It had value. He lost it yesterday in an encounter with law enforcement that once again raises pain and trauma for so many people."

Then I began to describe what I had seen on the video earlier that morning. I tried to capture the horror of it and the apparent indifference of the officers to Floyd's suffering. I mentioned the onlookers who were so disturbed that they pleaded for the officers to stop, but they also pulled out their cell phones to record the trauma they were witnessing.

I also noted that only a few weeks before, the public safety commissioner, John Harrington, and I had completed our working group on police-involved deadly force encounters. The working group had met for about a year. With the help of working group members— police, civil rights activists, people from the disability world, philan- thropists, and prosecutors—we put together a report with twenty-eight recommendations.

But what was it all for? I thought. It struck me that all this effort put forth by John and me was to prevent the kind of tragedy that unfolded in that video.

No statement could capture how I was feeling. I didn't know whether I was sad or mad or what. I felt like screaming and crying, but I didn't do either. I started organizing. I was outraged, and I knew deci- sive action was needed.

I encouraged people who were also infuriated by George Floyd's death to protest but to do so safely by observing COVID-19 pandemic protocols. I expressed my condolences to the family of George Floyd.

At that time, I didn't know Floyd's beautiful family, including his little daughter Gigi, his brothers and sisters, and so many others, not to mention his girlfriend, Courteney Ross.

I also had no idea what was coming, but I was ready for it. I thought the attorney general's office might launch an investigation into the Min- neapolis Police Department's pattern of unconstitutional policing. It never occurred to me that we would assume control of the prosecution within less than a week.

I had a full schedule that Tuesday morning, but before eleven a.m., the national news was ablaze. We were on for a two-thirty interview with MSNBC and an evening interview with Lawrence O'Donnell.

But it was still morning. As attorney general, I had to say something. John Stiles was ready with a draft statement, and we went over it, line by line. We published it around midday. I tried to stick with my schedule, but it had to give way to what was unfolding: a media onslaught. Our prepared state- ment wouldn't be enough, so I had to get ready to speak directly to the public.

I went back to the statement of the Minneapolis police spokesman, John Elder, to get ready for my interviews. Under the heading "Man Dies After Medical Incident During Police Interaction," the police department's statement read: "On Monday evening, shortly after 8:00 p.m. officers...responded to...a forgery in progress. Officers were advised that the suspect...was under the influence. He physically resisted officers. Officers were able to get the suspect into handcuffs and noted he appeared to be suffering medical distress. Officers called for an ambulance. He was transported to Hennepin County Medical Center by ambulance where he died a short time later...No officers were injured in the incident."

The statement was unbelievable. No mention of force. No mention of Floyd's begging for a breath of air. No mention of the people who assembled on the scene and pleaded for his life. No mention of Derek Chauvin's knee on Floyd's neck. Though shocking in what was omitted, the statement was typical in many ways. Officers responded to the scene to deal with a criminal who died "somehow." Over and done, and on to the next. The statement was callous and cold, and it seemed like an attempt to deceive the public.

The MPD initially characterized Floyd's death as a result of "medical distress."

As soon as I had watched the video that morning, I knew things were going to get bad, but the coming days saw all my worst fears manifest into reality. Protesters took to the streets in such large numbers that they overwhelmed all efforts to organize them. At night, the crowd outside the Third Precinct police station, where the officers involved in Floyd's death were based, was a tangle of strong political convictions and a riotous atmosphere. Activists and community members with deep commitments to justice stood shoulder to shoulder with people getting drunk off booze raided from liquor stores. Sometimes, they were the same people.

Minneapolis police responded with ham-fisted shock-and-awe techniques. Stories emerged of journalists blinded by rubber bullets. A video circulated on social media of officers spraying tear gas from the window of a squad car as they passed groups of random pedestrians in broad daylight. Another video appeared of officers dressed like soldiers, launching tear gas at citizens sitting quietly on their front porches.

Rumors spread like wildfire. Organized white supremacists were patrolling the streets with semiautomatic rifles and burning neighborhoods; rudimentary bombs were being planted in alleys and gas stations; and antigovernment extremists and white supremacists were dressing as protesters, causing destruction to discredit the movement.

Even now, some years later, it's hard to say what was true. For instance, one of the most unbelievable rumors turned out to have a kernel of truth. The "Umbrella Man" was said to have been dressed as a stereotypical "black-bloc antifa" when he smashed the windows of an auto parts store near the Third Precinct. Turns out he was captured on video, and the public soon discovered his ties to white supremacist organizations.

It wasn't an isolated incident, either. Three men associated with the far-right "Boogaloo Boys" traveled to Minneapolis from Texas and were later arrested for firing shots into the Third Precinct to "cause chaos." They were ultimately convicted.

The worst damage occurred in the immediate area on Lake Street around the Third Precinct in South Minneapolis. The damage spread up and down the street for miles; the station still stands, burned out and empty, as I write this. A lot of small-business owners who had nothing to do with what happened to Floyd, some of whom would have been sympathetic to the outrage, lost their businesses and their livelihoods. A lot of them were immigrants and people of color whose means of survival and hard-earned wealth were destroyed. They were victims, too, and I expressed my sympathy for them.

Destruction fell across the city, though. North Minneapolis stores on West Broadway were attacked, and even parts of St. Paul suffered damage.

On May 29, 2020—four days after Floyd's murder—Minnesota governor Tim Walz gathered leaders from all over the community and asked for a restoration of peace. I joined him at a press conference calling for everyone to obey a curfew he was putting in place.

"I'm going to be real clear: We need your help to comply with the curfew," I said. "Straight up. If anybody's unclear about what we're asking for, that is what we're asking for."

I went on:

We know that the noble, just aims of the protesters are righteous and good. But we also know that some evil elements are literally interfusing themselves with the protesters to destroy and cause arson so that the whole community will have a low opinion of the protests. Because they're not for justice for Mr. Floyd, they're against it. And they know that if we protest righteously and peacefully and justly, public sentiment will rise up to support our demands. So they want to stop that.

So we need people to help us…You can go on social media, you can protest there, you can do all these things. But to be on the street after eight o'clock means we can't get you separated from the bad people. So we know you're brave, we know you're strong, we know you'd never compromise on justice, we know you're righteous, and we believe in what you're doing—but we need to be able to stop the burning and the looting and the destruction.

I noted that one officer, Derek Chauvin, had "been arrested: charged with murder." Even though I had not yet been assigned to the case, I informed the people that "complaints are [commonly] amended, charges could be increased, there could be something added, there might be other people who will be charged as well, we're at the beginning of this… The wheels of justice are moving, and now they're moving swiftly. But we need you to help us, make sure that justice is done."

Still, despite the rioting and unrest, there was something amazing happening. Communities across the city pulled together. Community groups and leaders convened meetings so neighbors could organize.

People listened. During the day, massive groups, mostly peaceful, were on the streets. Volunteers swept up broken glass and helped small businesses cover windows in plywood. Food was distributed to the hard-hit, working-class area whose grocery stores were severely damaged, looted, or burned to the ground. After the curfew went into effect, very few people were on the streets.

Nighttime in Minneapolis was eerie. Once curfew went into effect the streets were quiet—downtown, uptown, midtown, north, south. Neighbors sat on their porches, keeping each other company and watching for signs of trouble.

Truly sophisticated patrols were organized: Volunteers monitored social media and acted as dispatchers for "rapid responders" who drove around to investigate threats. My adult sons, Jeremiah and Elijah, patrolled our Northside neighborhood to protect it from agent provocateurs like the Umbrella Man and the Boogaloo Boys, who were exploiting the chaos to foment their sick version of an Armageddon.

However, the damage inflicted on Lake Street remains. One of my favorite restaurants, Gandhi Mahal, was burned to the ground, as were other small businesses and housing developments.

Given my role as attorney general, the chaos spilled over into my job. By May 28, there was a sense of urgency and panic among elected officials that things were spinning out of control. Politics aside, leaders feared that the mass gatherings could turn into COVID-19 super-spreader events. There was a lot of worry about whether calm could be restored to the streets, but you can't set politics aside for long when you work in the government.

I heard through the grapevine that Hennepin County attorney Mike Freeman and the U.S. attorney, Erica McDonald, were negotiating a possible state-federal joint resolution of Officer Chauvin's case. I wasn't on the case, so everything I knew about the resolution came from the newspapers and rumors.

That day, I watched as Freeman and McDonald held a press conference to make an announcement. It didn't start on time: a bad sign. Finally, McDonald took the podium, with FBI Special Agent-in-Charge (SAC) Rainer Drolshagen and Mike Freeman standing six feet away per social distancing rules. The day was windy, and McDonald's hair was being tossed around. She lowered her mask and began.

She said she had hoped there might be a "development" to tell the press, but there wasn't. Probably a good place to stop, but she continued with a short briefing, giving ample assurances that the federal government was dedicated to seeking a just outcome. She noted that the federal government was reviewing the case with an eye to possible criminal civil rights violations.

Next, FBI SAC Drolshagen shared the number for the FBI tip line. Then Mike Freeman took the mic.

Things went fine at first. Freeman expressed empathy for George Floyd and shared a little about the investigation. Then he said, "There is other evidence that does not support a criminal charge."

The press grabbed Freeman's line. It freaked people out. That line became the news, and it carried into the weekend. It would be the only thing anyone remembered about the press conference.

I could only shake my head.

Politics 101: Only have a press conference when you have something to say. It's better to cancel and leave the reporters wondering, rather than stepping in front of cameras without anything to go from. Freeman and McDonald are smart, trained professionals. They knew better than to have a pointless press conference, especially in an environment when reporters are desperate for anything to report—anything at all. Nonetheless, everything was utter chaos. The streets were full of protesters, and the COVID-19 restrictions were making people nuts. There was bound to be a gaffe.

Freeman's comment was inarticulate, and he is certainly not the only one who made a mistake that day. He was trying to say there was still a lot of evidence coming in, and some of it would cast Floyd in a negative light. The toxicology report had already revealed methamphetamine and fentanyl in Floyd's bloodstream. Of course, drug use isn't a capital offense and doesn't justify the officer's actions, but it could diminish the jury's regard for the victim and affect the outcome of the case.

Freeman understood that convicting a police officer is extremely hard, even with video evidence. He was likely trying to lower expectations, but it was an unforced error. The medical examiner had already given an initial assessment, and it was clear—George Floyd died from "cardiopulmonary arrest caused by law enforcement subdual restraint and neck compression."

Freeman had already charged Chauvin with third-degree murder and second-degree manslaughter in Floyd's death, but it wasn't enough. After his comments in the Clark case, many in the public already assumed he would slow-pitch the Chauvin prosecution. That night, the MPD's Third Precinct station on East Lake Street went up in flames.

The next day, a Friday, county attorney Freeman asked me if I'd be willing to team up with him to prosecute the people who killed George Floyd. I agreed. Additionally, I received a letter from ten legislators representing Minneapolis in the state House who asked Governor Tim Walz in a letter to transfer the case to my office. "Unfortunately," the letter read, "our constituents, especially constituents of color, have lost faith in the ability of Hennepin County attorney Mike Freeman to fairly and impartially investigate and prosecute these cases." I had not lost faith in Freeman, however. In fact, he was the only one to successfully prosecute a police officer for killing someone while on duty. Despite what some in the community might think, I knew that Mike Freeman and the Hennepin County attorney's office were effective and professional, and we were going to need their help. There's one rule for successfully prosecuting any high-profile police shooting: Find a way to use the help available to you, all of it.

On May 31, Governor Walz asked me to lead the prosecution.

This occurrence was nothing short of surreal for me. Thirty-one years before, in 1989, a botched drug raid in North Minneapolis had claimed the lives of two elderly Black Minnesotans, Lillian Weiss and Lloyd Smalley. I had led a group to the Minnesota state capitol to deliver the results of a petition drive demanding that Governor Rudy Perpich instruct Attorney General Hubert H. Humphrey III to select a special prosecutor to investigate the deaths. Our group held a press conference outside the attorney general's office to announce our demands and deliver the petitions. While there, we debated with the former state human rights commissioner, Stephen Cooper, on camera over the authority of the governor and attorney general to conduct these investigations regarding Weiss and Smalley.

It was 1989, and I was somehow making time to lead civil rights marches, despite being a third-year law student with a new wife, a baby, and another one on the way. I didn't graduate at the top of my class, but I made it through.

I was fired up for civil rights, and I was demanding justice. Now, thirty-one years later, I was the attorney general, and people were demanding that I be appointed to investigate George Floyd's death. Would anything be different?

It was a Sunday. Governor Walz and I had a few conversations about what it might mean for me to take over. I told him I would need my team, and I needed to speak to them first.

I checked in with John Keller, the chief deputy, and Donna Cassutt, the chief of staff. I spoke with David Voigt, the deputy AG for public safety, and Matt Frank, the managing attorney for the criminal prosecution group. We huddled and we talked. Could we do it? We didn't exactly have a huge prosecution division. In fact, we had only three full-time prosecutors.

But how could we say no? I called the governor and told him yes, the Minnesota attorney general's office was ready to get to work. The city was burning, and we could help put the fires out.

Chapter 2

THE FOUR COPS

To Protect with Courage
To Serve with Compassion

Those words are displayed on the side of every police car in the city of Minneapolis.

The requirements to be a Minneapolis police officer are high. Recruits must have at least an associate's degree or five years of continuous law enforcement or military experience to be considered for employment. The Minneapolis Police Academy provides a sixteen-week training course and focuses on skills such as patrol operations, procedural justice, defensive tactics, and medical responses, including CPR. It also focuses on mental illness and crisis intervention. The academy training covers interaction with the public, community relations, and ethics, in addition to other skills.

After successful completion of the police academy course and passing the Peace Officer Standards and Training (POST) licensing exam, recruits go through additional field training and experience. This includes six months of on-the-job training and evaluation in various situations. The officers are evaluated during shifts on days, nights, weekends, and holidays, one-on-one with a field training officer, while responding to 911 calls, and more. After four months at the police academy and another six months of field training, officers also receive ongoing police officer training. All officers receive yearly in-service training on a variety of subjects including leadership, DUI enforcement, peer support, gun range, and more. Recruits then graduate to the role of police officer, earning a patrol assignment.

During her tenure as mayor of Minneapolis (2014–2018, a period that saw the officer-involved death of Jamar Clark), Betsy Hodges implemented several additional training steps. Officers were required to value and protect the lives of both officers and suspects. The Hodges policy imposed a duty to intervene when officers see another officer using excessive force, to render first aid quickly to suspects, and to report possible misconduct. In addition, officers were required to undergo implicit bias and procedural justice training.

Implicit bias training helps officers become aware of their inherent biases to prevent those biases from guiding their decision-making. Procedural justice training teaches officers how to treat residents fairly and to ensure residents are being heard at all times, whether or not they get a ticket or are arrested.

All this training and education begs a serious question: Does it work? Well, apparently, not on everyone. But one thing is for sure: It makes it difficult for any officer so well trained to claim that he or she just didn't know proper procedure.

On the night of May 25, 2020, Third Precinct MPD officers Derek Chauvin, Tou Thao, J. Alexander Kueng, and Thomas Lane were on regular duty, and their shifts would be anything but regular.

It was a beautiful Memorial Day—seventy degrees and sunny. Around the intersection of 38th and Chicago, folks were out, walking, talking, hanging out, and stopping by the corner store for snacks, cigs, or whatever. Cup Foods was the kind of place where people hung around inside and outside. It's located at a busy intersection in South Minneapolis.

For me, it was a racially mixed, working-class community—not upscale, not poor, though some people certainly are low income. For the officers, 38th and Chicago was "Bloods territory."

Officer Thao gave statements and later testified in a federal criminal civil rights case about his inherent bias about that area. That night, dispatch had actually called him off because they said the situation was under control. He proceeded to the scene anyway. "From my experience Cup Foods is hostile to police," Thao said. No doubt this attitude shaped the way he and fellow officer Derek Chauvin approached the scene.

Floyd and his Houston homeboy, Morries Hall, had stopped by Cup where they were semiregulars. Hall was getting a refund on a laptop that didn't work right. Floyd, on the other hand, was bouncing around the store, smiling, joking, and picking up some small items. He grabbed a banana and cigarettes for about ten dollars and change. Teenage store clerk Chris Martin later testified at the trial that Floyd seemed "a little high" but wasn't disturbing anyone. After Floyd tendered a twenty-dollar bill and completed his purchase, he walked out of the store in no apparent hurry.

Martin, nineteen at the time, took the bill from Floyd and examined it as he was trained to do. It looked a little funny to him, so he held it up to the light. It was counterfeit.

Martin said at the Chauvin trial that he thought Floyd didn't know the bill was fake. Cup Foods owner Mahmoud Abumayyaleh said the same thing in a public statement: "As a check-cashing business, this is a routine practice…the police ask the patron about the bill to trace its origin. It's likely that George Floyd didn't even know he had a fake bill."

A Minnesota statute prohibits *knowingly* passing counterfeit money. It's a crime to intentionally "defraud, possess, or utter with intent" counterfeit United States currency "having reason to know" that the currency is counterfeit. This Minnesota statute is written in a typically legalistic way, but one thing is clear: You must *know* that it's a fake bill. You can't be charged if you accidentally pass one. Intent is an essential element of the offense, and without proof of intent, there is *no crime*.

Video footage outside the store showed Floyd, Hall, and another friend, Shawanda Hill, in no rush. They were just sitting in a dark blue 2000 Mercedes on the south side of 38th Street, parked next to a local restaurant called the Dragon Wok, which had a security camera picking up the whole scene.

Inside the store, the teens decided to take up the issue of the fake bill with the fellow in the Mercedes. Per store policy, the teenage store clerks approached the purveyor of the fake twenty to see if the customer, a recognizable regular, after all, would either return the goods or pay for them with a different bill. The young clerks walked over to the car and attempted to discuss the problem. When they didn't get any response from Floyd, Hill, or Hall, the clerks went back into the store.

After a second attempt, they decided to call the police. The 911 operator summarized the conversation she had with the clerk succinctly: "So, this guy gave a counterfeit bill, has your cigarettes, and he's under the influence of something?"

"Something like that," said the clerk.

Rookie officers Thomas Lane and Alexander Kueng promptly arrived at the scene in squad 320. Both officers had recently completed their academy training and were cleared to operate on their own. In fact, according to their records, Lane and Kueng joined the MPD in February 2019, completed the academy in August 2019, and became full officers in December of that year. Minneapolis officers must serve a year on probation and work with a field training officer. Chauvin was Kueng's field training officer (FTO). Neither Lane nor Kueng had a record of using excessive force.

The officers were well trained and should have been ready to handle this fake twenty-dollar-bill case. Kueng's bodycam footage showed him and Lane entering the store and talking with store clerks. One clerk can be heard telling officers that they got a fake bill from the driver who was seated in "the blue car over there."

As the officers walked toward the Mercedes, they had to wait for the traffic to clear before they could cross the street. During this time the occupants of the dark blue Mercedes never attempted to take off. Somehow, it never occurred to the officers that a person knowingly passing fake bills might not want to hang around.

Bodycam footage shows Lane walking to the driver's side of the car, while Kueng approaches the passenger side. The passenger door is already open when Kueng encounters Morries Hall, who immediately turns his body sideways and swings his legs out onto the sidewalk.

Hall appears relaxed. He is wearing red sweatpants with blue and white stripes down the side, and a red baseball cap. With dreadlocks under his red cap and wearing square-framed glasses, Hall tells Kueng: "I'm cool. He's giving us a ride. It's his friend's car. Her name is…I forgot her name. But I know it. It's his coworker."

Kueng asks, "What brought you here?"

"I was here to buy a laptop, but it didn't work so they gave me my change back," Hall explains.

Audible through Kueng's video, Lane's voice is elevated and he sounds increasingly angry. Hall visibly tries to move away from Lane's escalating exchange. Kueng says, "Stay right there."

Lane can be heard shouting, "Show your hands! Show your fucking hands!"

Lane's bodycam shows him approaching Floyd on the driver's side, knocking on the window with a black metal flashlight, startling Floyd. Lane, every bit as tall as "Big Floyd," continues to bang on the vehicle's window to get the driver's attention.

Floyd, obviously surprised, attempts to open the car door to accommodate the officer speaking to him. Lane firmly orders him to stay in the car. Floyd complies, and then Lane shouts, "Let me see your other hand!" At this point, the officer's Glock 9mm comes out, tilted sideways gangster-style, pointed straight at Floyd's face.

"Let me see your other hand!"

Floyd complies, pleading, "I didn't do nothing!" Floyd repeats "Please don't shoot me, Officer" multiple times.

The bodycam footage shows a man who looks confused and terrified, with his hands up. Floyd begins trying to calmly communicate with the officer: "I'm sorry. What did we do, though?"

In response, Lane yells, "Put your hand up there. Put your fucking hand up there. Jesus Christ, keep your fucking hands on the wheel."

Lane shouts, "Show me your other fucking hand!" He's still threatening Floyd with the gun.

Floyd continues to demonstrate submission, in an apparent attempt to calm the officers through compliance. "I'm sorry!" Floyd tries to explain that he's anxious about having a gun pointed at him because he got shot before. Lane ignores Floyd's explanation.

"Hands on top of your head," Lane commands.

Floyd complies. The bodycam displays his submission. Floyd continues to beg the officer to de-escalate the situation: "Please don't shoot me!"

The officers order the occupants, including Floyd, out of the vehicle.

"Please, please," says Floyd as he is being cuffed and arrested. There is still no inquiry from the officers about what Floyd knows about the twenty-dollar bill.

"Hands behind your back!" shouts Lane.

Kueng, by this time, has come around to the driver's side and yells, "Stop resisting."

Floyd pleads, "I'm not. I'm sorry, Mr. Officer. I'll get on my knees or whatever."

Shawanda Hill and Morries Hall are not suspected of passing the fake twenty at this point, yet Kueng and Lane forcibly detain them without any explanation. Hill is still allowed to retain her phone, and Kueng's bodycam shows her talking with someone to arrange a ride to take her away from the scene.

Kueng asks Hill and Hall why Floyd is acting "squirrely" and "weird." Hill says, "He gots a thing going on, I'm telling you, about the police." She points to her head while twirling her finger in a circular movement, suggesting that Floyd has some sort of mental issue. "He has problems all the time when they [the police] come. Especially when that man [Lane] put that gun like that."

Kueng demands Floyd's name. Floyd gives his name immediately, demonstrating lucidity and awareness. The officers detain Floyd, seating him, handcuffed, on the ground against a storefront wall. Kueng asks, "Do you have ID on you?"

"I have it at home," Floyd says.

"What is your name?" Kueng asks.

"George. George Perry Floyd. I don't know what's going on," Floyd pleads again.

Kueng: "Spell it for me?"

Floyd: "G-E-O-R-G-E."

Kueng: "Last name?"

Floyd: "Floyd. F-L-O-Y-D."

Kueng: "Date of birth?"

Floyd: "October fourteenth, '73."

As is clear from the videoed dialogue, Floyd is cooperative. He never becomes belligerent. He never curses. Still, Kueng responds in a hostile and uncooperative way. Floyd can't win here, no matter how much he pleads, submits, or even begs.

It's about this time that Minneapolis Park Police officer Peter Chang arrives. Kueng turns to Chang and asks: "Do you mind doing me a favor? Can you run this for me?" Kueng hands Chang a piece of paper with Floyd's correct name on it.

"Man," says Kueng to Floyd, "do you know why we're here?" This is the first time in this encounter that anyone asks Floyd anything about the fake twenty.

"Why?" Floyd asks.

"We're here because it sounds like you gave a fake bill to individuals in there," says Kueng. "Do you understand that?"

"Yes."

"And do you know why we pulled you out of the car?" Answering his own question, Kueng says, "Cuz you was not listening to anything we told you."

"Because I didn't know what was going on," says Floyd.

Kueng never asks Floyd whether he knew the bill was fake, even though without intent there's no offense. Kueng didn't even try to ask Floyd a question aimed at determining where the bill came from.

Throughout this encounter, Floyd addresses the officers as "sir" and "Officer," and says "sorry" and "please." At no point does he curse the officers, threaten them, or verbally spar with them. Kueng accuses Floyd, who appears frightened throughout the incident, of resisting arrest, but at no point does either officer say what the arrest was for.

Meanwhile, Officer Chang runs Floyd's name for warrants. There are none.

So, based on the report of a fake twenty-dollar bill, Floyd had a gun stuck in his face, was cursed at by a police officer, was handcuffed behind his back, and was forced to sit on the concrete sidewalk with his back against a storefront wall—with no attempt to find out what he knew about the fake twenty-dollar bill.

Even so, things were about to take a turn for the worse.

Officer Kueng pulls Floyd up to his feet, and Kueng and Lane march him toward squad 320. As they're walking, Lane and Kueng ask Floyd if he's on drugs. Floyd denies it.

When Kueng suggests that Floyd is acting "erratic," Floyd replies, "I'm scared, man!"

Kueng notes that Floyd has "foam around your mouth"—implying drug use. But Floyd explains that he was "hooping," slang for playing basketball. (Incidentally, the defense's retained expert, David Fowler, stated in his medical examiner report that "hooping" is street slang for the practice of sticking drugs up your anus. Defense attorney Eric Nelson was too smart to ask Fowler about this bit of his "expert" medical conclusion.)

At this point, there is incomplete evidence of a crime, given that offering counterfeit currency requires proof of intent, and officers have yet to obtain anything to indicate Floyd knowingly offered a counterfeit bill. The officers know Floyd's full name. They know he is unarmed. They suspect he might not be sober. They know he hasn't tried to run away or avoid them, which would suggest consciousness of guilt. They know he's being cooperative. And they know something else: He suffers from anxiety. He expressed tremendous anxiety about having a gun pointed at his face. Despite these circumstances, and the range of options available to them, the rookie officers opt to force him into squad 320.

The squad car is parked on Chicago Avenue with the driver's side at the curb in front of Cup Foods. Lane and Kueng bookend Floyd, who is still cuffed, and perp-walk him across 38th Street to the squad. When Floyd realizes that the rookie officers plan to jam his huge frame into the tight and confined space of squad 320, he becomes alarmed and struggles to maintain balance. The bodycam video shows Floyd falling to the ground.

Kueng snaps, "Stand up! Stop falling down! Stand up! Stay on your feet and face the car door."

In an anguished and desperate tone, Floyd says, "I'm a claustrophobic man, please, man, please. I just want to talk to you." To which Lane says, "No!"

Kueng says, "You ain't listening to nothing we're saying; so we're not going to listen to nothing you saying."

Floyd pleads again, "I'm claustrophobic." True to Kueng's word, the officers are not going to listen to anything Floyd is saying—or what any bystanders might say, either.

"Please, man. Don't leave me by myself, man, please. I'm claustrophobic, that's it."

"Well, you're still going in the car," declares Kueng.

Officers search Floyd again to make certain he has no weapon or contraband. Now they are certain that he is not armed and has no outstanding warrants for his arrest. They know, at worst, he is facing charges of a nonviolent misdemeanor. Officers could have issued Floyd a ticket and a court date.

Then, despite his pleading, officers still push Floyd into the driver's side of squad 320. Floyd at first delays his compliance but finally agrees; he manages to follow these orders with great difficulty. He says, "I'm going in, Mr. Officer, I'm going in. Man, I'm scared as fuck."

He adds, "Let me count to three and I'm going in, please." And then Floyd goes into squad 320.

That's when Derek Chauvin shows up on the scene. It's 8:16 p.m. Thao, with four years on the force, is with him.

Though Chauvin does not have a higher rank than any other officer on the scene, the others accede to him because of his seniority. As the video shows, Chauvin doesn't bother asking many questions. The first recognizable words from Derek Chauvin are at 8:18 p.m.: "Is he going to jail?"

Kueng replies, "He's under arrest right now for forgery."

Floyd overhears the exchange and yells in surprise, "Forgery for what? For what?"

The nineteen-year veteran and FTO doesn't ask anything about the forgery. He is not curious about the alleged forged bill or what Floyd may know about it. He goes right in with force. No managerial sensibility. He's a hammer and every problem is a nail.

Until this moment, despite numerous uses of coercive force (cursing him, sticking a gun in his face, handcuffing him, arresting him, refusing to listen to him, ignoring his anxiety and claustrophobia, trying to lock him in the squad car), Floyd still doesn't appear to understand why he is being arrested. There is no evidence of intent, without which there is no crime, and no probable cause for a crime.

After Floyd is pushed into the squad, he continues to plead with the officers. He says "I can't breathe" multiple times. "I'm going to die in there," he cries.

Lane goes to the passenger side and begins to pull Floyd through the squad. All the while, Floyd is yelling in pain until it appears he is all the way through the squad and about to fall out the other side.

The officers decide to pull him out the passenger side. This is when Lane says, "Just take him out and MRE." MRE is maximum restraint equipment, also known as the hobble or hogtie, in which the person is bound at the hands and the feet.

At 8:19, the four officers pull Floyd out of the passenger's side of squad 320, and so begins the last nine minutes and twenty-nine seconds of George Floyd's life.

This series of events would end George Floyd's life, devastate his family members' lives, and ruin the lives of the officers. The decisions made at 8:20 p.m. that night would result in a teenager uploading a video that would spark a national social protest movement and propel legislation by state, local, and federal governments.

And something else would change, too: American history. Polls in the summer of 2020 estimated that between 15 and 26 million people joined one of the many George Floyd demonstrations, which made the protests the largest in the history of the United States. The tragic murder of George Floyd offered the possibility that a critical mass of the American public was ready to take decisive action to end state-sponsored violence against African Americans and all Americans.

Chauvin leads the effort to snatch Floyd out of squad 320, and all the officers except Thao physically force Floyd onto the ground.

Initially, Floyd seems to fall out of the squad and onto the ground on his left side, cuffed, with officers all around him. If he had stayed in that position, he might have survived. Unfortunately, within seconds, officers force Floyd into a prone position, facedown on his chest, with his hands cuffed behind his back.

The nine minutes and twenty-nine seconds begin.

Chauvin kneels on Floyd's neck. Kueng—who told Floyd he would not listen to him—presses his hands down onto his back, and Lane gets on top of his legs. Thao—calling himself a "human traffic cone"—stands between Floyd and his three colleagues and the sidewalk, where people are beginning to gather.

The situation has already caught the attention of Charles McMillan, a sixty-one-year-old man, who urges Floyd, a man he did not know, to "get up and get in the car, man!" McMillan tells Floyd, "You can't win. Get in the car, man."

In response, Floyd says, "I can't. I can't. I am not trying to win."

McMillan, who later testified at trial, described himself as being "nosy" when he first stopped his car outside Cup Foods that day.

Floyd was yelling in pain before Darnella Frazier saw him. In fact, it was his suffering that caught her attention. Darnella was with her nine-year-old cousin, Judeah Reynolds, that Memorial Day evening. Judeah wanted some snacks, and the two cousins decided to grab some at the corner store. That's when Floyd being tortured caught Darnella's attention.

This is right about the time that Darnella raises her phone and begins the video that would impact the world.

The video opens with Floyd already lying facedown on the ground. The transcript of the video does not and cannot reflect the abject horror of being there. There were multiple witnesses. Donald Williams, a professional mixed martial artist, was probably the most vocal. Another teen, Alyssa Funari, stopped her car when she saw the scene. She also started filming what took place. Genevieve Hansen, an off-duty Minneapolis firefighter, begged to help. The video itself can't capture what these people must have felt. Nonetheless, here is the transcript of the Darnella Frazier video.

[0:00–0:19] [Officer Chauvin's knee is on the neck of Mr. George Floyd. Officer Thao circles the police vehicle and stands in front of Mr. Floyd.]

[0:00–0:19] **Floyd:** "Ah. Ah. I can't breathe. Ah."

[0:19–0:40] **Floyd:** "Please. Please, I can't breathe. Please, man. Please. Somebody help me. Ah. Ahhh. Ahhh. Ah."

[0:40–0:42] **Floyd:** "I can't breathe."

[0:43–0:46] **Charles McMillan:** "Bro, you got him down. Let him at least breathe, man."

[0:45–0:47] **Floyd:** "I can't breathe. I can't breathe. Ahhhh."

[0:47–0:48] **Charles McMillan:** "I've been trying to help him out, man."

[0:48–0:50] **Thao:** "So, he's breathing?"

[0:50–0:56] **Floyd:** [inaudible]

[0:57–0:58] **Chauvin:** "Relax."

[0:55–0:58] **Floyd:** "I can't breathe. My face."

[0:59–1:00] **Charles McMillan:** "Just get up."

[1:02–1:03] **Thao:** "What do you want?"

[1:03–1:08] **Floyd:** "I can't breathe. Please, the knee in my neck. I can't breathe, shit."

[1:08–1:11] **Charles McMillan:** "Bro, get up, get up in the car, man."

[1:11–1:12] **Floyd:** "I will."

[1:12–1:13] **Charles McMillan:** "Get up, get in the car."

[1:13–1:14] **Floyd:** "I can't move."

[1:17–1:18] **Floyd:** "Mamma."

[1:18–1:19] **Charles McMillan:** "Get up, get in the car."

[1:19–1:21] **Floyd:** "Mamma. I can't."

[1:21–1:25] **Charles McMillan:** "Give him the opportunity to get in. Brother, I'm talking to you, you can't win."

[1:25–1:26] **Floyd:** "My knee."

[1:26–1:28] **Charles McMillan:** "You can't win, man."

[1:27–1:29] **Floyd:** "My neck. I'm through."

[1:29–1:31] **Charles McMillan:** "I know you're on his neck. You didn't listen."

[1:32–1:58] **Floyd:** "Ahh. I'm claustrophobic. My stomach hurts."

[1:58–2:00] **Chauvin:** "Uh-huh."

[1:58–2:00] **Floyd:** "My neck hurts."

[1:58–2:00] **Chauvin:** "Uh-huh."

[1:58–2:00] **Floyd:** "Everything hurts. Ah. I need some water or something. Please. Please. Ahhh. I can't breathe, Officer. Ahhh. Ahhh. I can't breathe, Officer. They gonna kill me, man. Ahhh, ahhhh."

[1:58–2:00] **Charles McMillan:** "Brother, get off his neck, man."

[2:00–2:02] **Alyssa Funari:** "His nose is bleeding. Like c'mon now."

[2:02–2:04] **Charles McMillan:** "That's wrong right there to put their feet on his neck."

[2:04–2:05] **Alyssa Funari:** "Look at his nose."

[2:06–2:08] **Charles McMillan:** "You can't put your feet right on his neck."

[2:09–2:12] **Floyd:** "I cannot breathe. I cannot breathe. Ahhhhh."

[2:13–2:15] **Donald Williams:** "Oh, he's a tough guy. He's a tough guy, huh."

[2:15–2:16] **Thao:** "What's that?"

[2:16–2:18] **Donald Williams:** "He's a tough guy. He's not even resisting arrest, bro."

[2:19–2:20] **Alyssa Funari:** "His whole nose is bleeding."

[2:22–2:23] **Donald Williams:** "He ain't doing nothing."

[2:23–2:25] **Floyd:** "They gonna kill me. I can't breathe."

[2:25–2:26] **Alyssa Funari:** "How long y'all gotta hold him down?"

[2:26–2:28] **Thao:** "That's why you don't do drugs, kids."

[2:29–2:30] **Donald Williams:** "This ain't about drugs, bro."

[2:30–2:31] **Alyssa Funari:** "Y'all gotta put y'all—"

[2:34–2:35] **Donald Williams:** "He is human, bro."

[2:35–2:36] **Alyssa Funari:** "His nose."

[2:36–2:38] **Donald Williams:** "At least put him in the car."

[2:39–2:40] **Thao:** "We tried that for ten minutes."

[2:40–2:47] **Donald Williams:** "That's some bum ass shit. That's some bum ass shit, bro. Y'all know that. Y'all sitting there with your knee on his neck, bro."

[2:40–2:47] **Floyd:** "Ahhh. Ahhhhhh. Ahh. Ahh. Ahh."

[2:47–2:48] **Thao:** "He's talking, he's fine."

[2:48–2:55] **Donald Williams:** "Bro, he ain't fine. Bro. It's like a jiu-jitsu move. You, you trapped on his breathing, right there, bro."

[2:55–2:56] **Thao:** "Okay, all right."

[2:56–3:01] **Donald Williams:** "You don't think that's what it is, bro. You don't think anybody understands that shit right there, bro. I trained at the academy, bro. That's some bullshit, bro."

[3:02] **Thao:** "You don't understand."

[3:03–3:05] **Donald Williams:** "Right, that's some bullshit, bro. That's bullshit, bro."

[3:05] **Floyd:** "Please."

[3:06–3:08] **Donald Williams:** "You fucking stopping his breathing right there, bro."

[3:08–3:09] **Floyd:** "I can't breathe."

[3:09–3:11] **Thao:** "Okay. He's talking. It's hard to talk when you can do that."

[3:11–3:32] **Donald Williams:** "Bro, what—get him off the ground. You're being a bum right now. Get him off the ground, bro. You can get him off the ground. You're being a bum right now. He enjoying that. He enjoying that shit. He enjoying that shit. He a fucking bum, bro. He enjoying that shit right now, bro. You could've fucking put him in the car by now. He's not resisting arrest or nothing."

[3:32–3:33] **Alyssa Funari:** "Is he talking now?"

[3:33–3:36] **Donald Williams:** "You're enjoying it. Look at you. Your body language is [inaudible]. You fucking bum."

[3:36–3:39] **Alyssa Funari:** "Bro, get the fuck off of him."

[3:39–3:40] **Darnella Frazier:** "It's the whites, they love—"

[3:40–3:53] **Donald Williams:** "Bro, you already know that. Bro, I trained with half of these bum ass dudes at the academy, bro. You know that's bogus right now, bro. You know it's bogus. You can't even look at me like a man because you're a bum, bro. He's not even resisting arrest right now, bro."

[3:53–3:54] **Alyssa Funari:** "His nose is bleeding."

[3:54] **Darnella Frazier:** "He's passed out."

[3:55–4:06] **Donald Williams:** "You're fucking stopping his breathing right now, bro. You think that's cool. You think that's cool, though. What's your—what's your, Officer, what's your badge number, bro. You think that's cool right now, bro."

[4:06] [Mr. Floyd is no longer moving or talking.]

[4:09–4:11] **Darnella Frazier:** "You going to call the police on another police."

[4:12–4:21] **Donald Williams:** "You think that's cool though, bro. You're a bum, bro. You're a bum for that. You're a bum for that, bro. You get mad. You're just sitting there. Stopping his breathing right now."

[4:21–4:23] **Bystanders 2 and 4:** "Look at him!"

[4:23–4:24] **Darnella Frazier:** "What the fuck!"

[4:24–4:26] **Donald Williams:** "You 'bout to go out right now, bro."

[4:25–4:26] **Darnella Frazier:** "Look at him."

[4:27–4:28] **Alyssa Funari:** "Get off of him!"

[4:27–4:29] **Darnella Frazier:** "What is wrong with y'all?"

[4:30] [Officer Chauvin takes out and shakes mace from tactical belt.]

[4:30–4:32] **Alyssa Funari:** "What the fuck. He got mace. He got mace."

[4:32–4:34] **Donald Williams:** "I'm not scared of you, bro. You're a pussy ass dude, bro."

[4:34–4:36] **Alyssa Funari:** "He cannot breathe."

[4:35–4:37] **Darnella Frazier:** "Call 911. Call 911."

[4:41–4:43] **Donald Williams:** "Bro, look. You can check on him. He's not responding right now."

[4:43–4:45] [Genevieve Hansen approaches from other side of street from behind Thao. Thao moves closer to Chauvin.] **Thao:** "Back off! Back off! Get off the street."

[4:47–4:53] **Donald Williams:** "He's not responsive right now! He's not responsive right now! He's not responsive right now, bro."

[4:53–4:54] **Genevieve Hansen:** "Does he have a pulse?"

[4:54–4:56] **Donald Williams:** "No, bro, look at him! He's not responsive right now, bro."

[4:56–4:57] **Genevieve Hansen:** "Check for a pulse right now, please. Check for a pulse."

[4:57–4:58] **Donald Williams:** "Bro, are you serious."

[4:58–4:59] **Genevieve Hansen:** "Check for a pulse right now."

[4:59–5:00] **Donald Williams:** "Bro, look at you—"

[5:00–5:02] **Genevieve Hansen:** "Let me see a pulse!"

[5:02–5:04] **Donald Williams:** "Is he breathing right now, check his pulse!"

[5:04–5:06] **Thao:** "How long are we going to have this conversation?"

[5:06] **Donald Williams:** "Check his pulse."

[5:06–5:07] **Thao:** "Okay."

[5:07–5:09] **Donald Williams:** "Check his pulse, Thao. Thao, check his pulse, bro."

[5:09–5:10] **Thao:** "Yeah. Okay."

[5:10–5:14] **Donald Williams:** "Thao, check his pulse, bro. You bogus, bro."

[5:14–5:15] **Thao:** "Don't do drugs, guys."

[5:15–5:21] **Donald Williams:** "Don't do drugs? Bro. What is that. What do you think that it is? So you call what he doing okay?"

[5:21–5:22] **Thao:** "Get back in the street."

[5:22–5:25] **Donald Williams:** "You call what he doing okay? You call what he doing okay? You call what you, he doing okay?"

[5:25–5:26] **Thao:** [walks to Genevieve Hansen] "Are you really a firefighter?"

[5:27–5:28] **Genevieve Hansen:** "Yes, I am. For Minneapolis."

[5:28–5:29] **Thao:** "Okay, then get on the sidewalk."

[5:30–5:31] **Genevieve Hansen:** "Show me a pulse!"

[5:31–5:32] **Donald Williams:** "You, you think that's okay? Check his pulse."

[5:32–5:33] **Genevieve Hansen:** "Check his pulse right fucking now."

[5:33–5:34] **Thao:** "Get back on the sidewalk."

[5:34–5:37] **Donald Williams:** "Check his—the man ain't yet, bro. The man ain't moved yet, bro."

[5:37–5:38] **Thao:** "Where, where [are you a firefighter]?"

[5:38–5:39] **Genevieve Hansen:** "Minneapolis!"

[5:40–5:41] **Thao:** "Okay."

[5:41–5:45] **Donald Williams:** "Bro, you're a bum, bro. You're a bum, bro. You're definitely a bum, bro."

[5:45–5:47] **Genevieve Hansen:** "Check his pulse right now. Check his pulse. Tell me what his pulse is."

[5:47–5:49] **Donald Williams:** "Check the pulse. Bro, he has not moved, not one time."

[5:50–5:54] **Nabil Abumayyaheh:** [a Cup Foods employee] "He's off crack right now. He's highly obese."

[5:54–5:56] **Donald Williams:** "Go back in the store. Go back in the store right now, bro. You don't understand…"

[5:56] **Cup Foods Employee:** "No, no, I'm the rea—"

[5:57–6:01] **Donald Williams:** "Okay, that's cool. Go back in the store, bro. Go back in the store, bro. He's not fucking moving!"

[6:01–6:04] **Cup Foods Employee:** "I see that, I see that. I'm trying to help y'all out."

[6:04–6:10] **Donald Williams:** "Bro, bro. You don't need to help me out, bro. I know your parents, I know everybody that owns this store. You don't need to help me the fuck out, bro. He's not fucking moving right now, bro."

[6:10–6:11] **Cup Foods Employee:** "I just saw that man."

[6:11–6:13] **Donald Williams:** "Bro, he was just moving when I walked up here."

[6:13–6:16] **Cup Foods Employee:** "I know, I know. They did that to him, they did that to him."

[6:16–6:20] **Donald Williams:** "You just got back out here, bro, you just got back out here."

[6:20–6:21] **Cup Foods Employee:** "I've been watching it the whole time."

[6:21–6:22] **Donald Williams:** "Bro, you just got back out here."

[6:22] **Thao:** "Why is he trying to talk to you guys right now?"

[6:22–6:25] **Donald Williams:** "He does—Bro, he's not fucking moving!"

[6:25–6:27] **Bystander 6:** "Yo, did they fucking kill him, bro?"

[6:27–6:40] **Donald Williams:** "Bro, bro, what is you, 1087, bro? You're a bum, bro. 987, bro, you're a bum bro. First thing you want to grab is your mace because you're scared, bro. Scared of fucking minorities. You're a fucking bum, bro."

[6:40–6:42] **Multiple Bystanders:** "Get the fuck off of him! What are you doing?"

[6:42–6:43] **Donald Williams:** "Like three minutes, bro, he's not fucking moving."

[6:43–6:48] **Multiple Bystanders:** "He's dying! Why are you still on him? Oh my god!"

[6:48] [Medics arrive on scene.]

[6:48–6:55] **Donald Williams:** "Bro, he's not even moving, get off of his fucking neck, bro! Get off of his neck!"

[6:55–6:57] **Multiple Bystanders:** "Why are you still on him. You're still on him, for what!"

[6:57–7:00] **Thao:** "Get back on the street."

[7:01–7:12] **Donald Williams:** "Bro, bro, are you serious? And you, you, you're gonna keep your thing on his neck. Yeah, I bet. Bro, bro, I [inaudible] touch me like that. I swear. I swear I slap the fuck outta both y'all."

[7:12] [Ambulance takes stretcher out of back.]

[7:12–7:13] **Darnella Frazier:** "Now they want to call the ambulance."

[7:15–7:50] **Donald Williams:** "Bro, you're just going to let him keep his hand on his neck, bro. You're a bitch, bro. Thao, you're going to let him keep that like that? You're going to let him kill that man in front of you, bro. Huh? Huh! Bro, he's not even fucking moving right now, bro! 987, you're a bum, bro. You're just going to sit there with your knee on his neck, bro. You a, you a grow—you a real man for that, bro. He in handcuffs. I trained with these bum ass [inaudible]."

[7:52–7:55] **Genevieve Hansen:** "The fact you guys aren't checking his pulse and doing compressions if—"

[7:53] [Chauvin gets up, and medic and Chauvin drag a handcuffed Floyd onto stretcher.]

[7:57–8:00] **Alyssa Funari:** "Oh my god. They just dragged him like that."

[8:00–8:02] **Genevieve Hansen:** "And I have your name tag, bitch."

[8:04–8:05] **Thao:** "That's not very professional."

[8:05–8:07] **Alyssa Funari:** "It don't matter. So, what. Freedom of speech."

[8:07–8:12] [Floyd is on the stretcher.]

[8:09–8:16] **Thao:** [to Donald Williams] "Back on the street! Back on the street! You do not touch me again!"

[8:16–8:22] **Alyssa Funari:** "You touched him, you went to him, so shut up. You went to him, always trying to start something."

[8:29–8:38] [Floyd is loaded into the ambulance.]

[8:38] [Floyd is in the ambulance.]

The outraged bystanders weren't the only people horrified by the officers' treatment of Floyd. A 911 dispatcher, Jena Scurry, was watching the scene on a remote CCTV camera and became so alarmed by what she saw that she called her supervisor.

When she testified at trial, she said she thought the screen might have been frozen, but then realized, to her shock, that the officers had the man pinned to the ground for nearly ten minutes. Scurry called the sergeant in charge of the officer, saying, "You can call me a snitch if you want to," and told the sergeant about the long period of time the man had been pinned down.

Back at the scene, when the paramedics arrived, they had to tap Chauvin on the shoulder to get him to get off the motionless Floyd. Chauvin and company still had Floyd facedown on the pavement. Once the officers finally got off of him, paramedics rolled Floyd's lifeless body onto a stretcher before they could lift him onto the gurney. Floyd's hands were still cuffed behind his back.

Once inside the ambulance, an EMT unlocked the cuffs on Floyd.

I remember so vividly his body flopping onto the stretcher. Chauvin had very likely been kneeling on top of a corpse moments before he got off Floyd's body.

Even though Floyd was pronounced dead at the hospital, he was already dead at the scene. That's what the paramedics testified at the trial. He had no pulse. The paramedics later testified that when they arrived Floyd was "asystole," meaning that his heart's electrical system had failed, causing his heart to stop pumping. Most folks understand asystole as "flat-lining" because the absence of electrical activity on the electrocardiogram appears as a flat line.

During the first four minutes of the video, Floyd said "I can't breathe" at least twenty-eight times. He complained about pain a dozen times, begged for water, and said, "Everything hurts."

Minneapolis firefighter Genevieve Hansen and professional mixed martial artist Donald Williams demanded that the officers check Floyd's pulse at least fifteen times. Floyd predicted that the officers were going to kill him, and Williams and other bystanders told the officers the same thing several times.

The transcript of the video doesn't show the contempt Officer Thao displayed after Floyd's body was taken away. "That guy allegedly went to the police academy," said Thao about Williams.

Actually, Williams never said that. He merely said, "the academy," referring to the mixed martial arts academy.

Thao added, "Allegedly, she's a Minneapolis firefighter. Allegedly."

Both Williams and Hansen were correctly identifying their credentials, but as Kueng said, "We're not going to listen to nothing you saying."

Floyd lost consciousness at 4:06 in the video, and from that point until 7:53, a full *three minutes and forty-seven seconds*, Chauvin and company just sat on top of Floyd, with Thao stopping anyone else from assisting him. Floyd went silent, but despite their training—duty to intervene, give medical assistance, and CPR training—they did nothing. Chauvin, Kueng, Lane—none of them moved off Floyd. No one said it was time to stop. None of them offered chest compressions for CPR. Thao never allowed anyone to offer medical assistance. They simply failed their training, profession, and community.

After Floyd was taken away in the ambulance, Chauvin gave his only known explanation for his behavior when Charles McMillan confronted him. Chauvin told McMillan that Floyd was "a sizable guy," and "probably on something," and "we had to control him."

The transcript reveals that Thao's claims of being a "human traffic cone" are not credible. In fact, Thao taunted and mocked the gathering bystanders with "That's why you don't do drugs, kids," even after Floyd stopped moving at minute 5:15 in the video. The transcript does not show Chauvin at 4:30 (twenty-four seconds after Mr. Floyd has stopped moving) pulling out his mace from his tactical belt to menace the bystanders, all while his knee is still on Mr. Floyd's motionless body.

I wondered why. Why didn't the minimum educational requirement of at least an associate's degree or five years of continuous law enforcement or military experience matter? Why didn't the sixteen-week Minneapolis Police Academy training course make a difference? Why didn't the course work in patrol operations, procedural justice, and medical responses, including CPR training and certification, kick in? What overrode their training in managing mental disorders like claustrophobia, anxiety, and chemical dependency, which Floyd clearly suffered from? I saw no evidence that any of the officers had received training in crisis intervention, how to interact with the public, community relations, or ethics—even though I knew in fact that they'd all received ample training in each of these areas.

None of the officers showed any regard for the policies former mayor Betsy Hodges put in place. Mayor Hodges and former Minneapolis chief of police Janeé Harteau mandated a duty for all officers who see another officer using excessive force to intervene, to render first aid quickly to suspects, and to report possible misconduct.

Only one possible explanation came to my mind: the field training J. Alexander Kueng had with Derek Chauvin. I wonder what Kueng had picked up through that experience.

Minneapolis firefighter and trained emergency medical technician Genevieve Hansen, who was off duty when she came upon the scene that day, testified that officers ignored her requests to render medical aid to Floyd. Clearly, the duty to render medical aid was ignored. Perhaps it was because of what Thao said about the neighborhood being "Bloods territory," or, in other words, a type of war zone where no normal codes of conduct apply. Or maybe it was what Kueng said: "We're not listening to nothing you say."

Reasonable people can speculate about the "why," but one thing is for sure: The motivation—whatever it was—was derived from something stronger and more deeply rooted than training. It had to be something deeper, like culture.

Peter Drucker, the famous management consultant, said that "culture eats strategy for breakfast." Something buried inside the culture of the MPD determined the behavior Chauvin displayed and the other three mirrored, regardless of training, policy, or strategy. Drucker pointed out the importance of the human factor in any organization. If the people executing it protect, defend, and reinforce the wrong culture, your best plans and training programs are going to fail.

That culture creates behaviors that take over in critical situations, like when you have a six-foot-four-inch person whose anxiety, claustrophobia, and perhaps intoxication make him behave outside the expected norms. The officers were not under any duress. No one was threatening them, but they clearly felt pressure, and when they did, they managed it with one tool: brute force.

From the moment I saw the Floyd video, and months later when I saw the whole case file, I was struck by how unnecessary the use of force was, especially before Chauvin sank his knee onto Floyd's neck.

What about the behavior of the officers leading up to that moment? It's what some people describe as "lawful but awful" and it, too, while legal, is a problem. The gun in the face, the insulting tone, the cuffing, and the unnecessary confinement all set the tone.

The murder of George Floyd was, for many reasons, extraordinary. However, the treatment George Floyd endured at the hands of Lane and Kueng, and then Chauvin and Thao—before Chauvin kneeled on his neck, Kueng pressed his back into the ground, Lane held his legs, and Thao stood guard allowing them to do all of that—was tragically routine.

If Chauvin had stopped short of the knee on the neck, tried to justify the arrest with a charge like public intoxication or failure to comply, then the world would never have known about it. In that hypothetical situation, Floyd, though he might have survived, would have walked away very likely feeling angry and disrespected. The encounter would have compounded distrust or mutual disrespect, and it would have engendered contempt. It would have soured already strained bonds of trust between police and community.

None of the four officers seemed to have any awareness about the extent of damage they inflicted on the community's trust, even before Chauvin sank his knee on Floyd's neck.

The whole episode struck me as arbitrary, gratuitous, and, of course, unconstitutional. But the beginning of the incident, though perhaps legal, was also an unjustified use of force. Maybe not a crime, but certainly a cause for discipline and retraining.

As I approached the prosecution of this case, it was clear to me that there were two different cultures at work in the Minneapolis Police Department. There was the official culture of honor, service, and respect; and the unofficial culture of "get them before they get you," "all they understand is force," and "survive at any cost."

But, again, why? One answer is in the unique culture of the Third Precinct of the Minneapolis Police Department. This is the precinct that would be burned to the ground by arsonists and vandals in reaction to the murder of George Floyd. Those arsonists are criminals who deserve aggressive prosecution, but it would be unwise to ignore the fact that even among the law abiding, not many tears were shed for the Third Precinct.

Chauvin, Thao, Lane, and Kueng were from the Third Precinct, a police station with a reputation. In fact, only days after Floyd's murder, June 7, 2020, the *Minneapolis Star Tribune* (*Strib*) published an article titled "Minneapolis' Third Precinct Served as 'Playground' for Renegade Cops." The article noted that "between 2007 and 2017, the city paid out $2.1 million to settle misconduct lawsuits involving Third Precinct officers. Judges have thrown out cases for 'outrageous' conduct of the officers, and prosecutors have been forced to drop charges for searches found to be illegal, according to court records."

Abigail Cerra, a former Hennepin County public defender, observed, "My clients were constantly getting anal searches—not at the hospital—at the Third Precinct."

Before she went to law school, Cerra was the Latinx community outreach worker at the Legal Rights Center (LRC). Both jobs brought her in close contact with the neighbors living near and served by the Third Precinct.

She also raises her family in the neighborhood. She became a commissioner for Minneapolis's Police Conduct Oversight Commission but quit as a form of protest in 2022 after she realized that nothing was changing due to bureaucratic roadblocks. (Incidentally, I was the executive director of the LRC for about six years from 1993 to 1999. I talked with Abi Cerra, and she told me that she stands by her quote.)

The June 7, 2020, *Strib* article also quoted Greg Hestness, a retired Minneapolis deputy chief, about the "precinct's cocky, swaggering culture." According to Hestness, "The Third Precinct was kind of sleepy" until the 1980s, when "a flood of transfers from downtown's First Precinct and the then-recently shuttered Sixth Precinct brought a combustible mix of 'old timers' and 'young Vietnam vets.'"

The Third Precinct covers the largest amount of real estate in the city. It goes from I-35W to the Mississippi River and I-94 to Highway 62. It includes some of the most racially diverse neighborhoods in Minneapolis such as Little Earth, Prospect Park, Powderhorn Park, and many more. Little Earth is home to about 1,500 people, mostly Native American. It's a federally subsidized housing project and the site of tremendous culture and vibrancy, but also poverty, isolation, and violent crime. Little Earth was founded in 1973 and remains the only indigenous preference-based Section 8 rental-assistance community in the United States. It stands across the street from the headquarters of the famed American Indian Movement (AIM), founded in Minneapolis in 1968 for the purpose of advocating for the rights and dignity of indigenous communities, and specifically to confront police brutality and injustice in the criminal justice system.

MPD data shows that while the downtown precinct (the First) and North Minneapolis precinct (the Fourth) have more reported use-of-force incidents, officers in the Third Precinct are more likely to use force when responding to a call. According to many residents, a pattern of aggressive policing has strained relationships between the precinct and surrounding communities, especially with people of color.

I practiced law for thirty-two years in and around Minneapolis, and I have received mixed reports from neighbors about the Third Precinct. However, there's no denying that many neighbors strongly believe the Third Precinct has more than its fair share of "thumpers," or officers who routinely use unnecessary force. To be sure, many neighbors have expressed gratitude and appreciation for the police. Many have noted that violence among private citizens occurs more often than between law enforcement and private citizens. These folks have spoken up for the view that the community needs professional and effective law enforcement services, as well as more respect and better treatment from police.

Folks are, by and large, fair, and they will point out that it's not *all* officers, but it's a lot. Sadly, no one ever seems to do anything about those officers who use excessive force. Folks are also quick to point out officers who have helped them. Abi Cerra told me that the arbitrary force is usually not fatal, nor does it always cause injury. It's usually in the form of insults, slaps, shoves, or a harsh tone—similar to what Floyd experienced before Chauvin's knee came down. All of those who helped kill George Perry Floyd hailed from the Third Precinct, located on Lake Street, a few blocks north of Cup Foods.

But these officers are not just Third Precinct thumpers. They are individuals with their own stories. Some of the stories are made from dreams, and some of the stories are heartbreaking.

J. Alexander Kueng, twenty-six, always wanted to become a police officer. As a mixed-race kid who identifies as Black, he said on the witness stand—at his federal criminal civil rights trial—that he went into law enforcement because he wanted to bridge the gap between police and the Black community. He is the son of a white mother and a Nigerian father.

He grew up in North Minneapolis, the city's historically Black area. As a Northsider, Kueng joined the force to help rebuild trust. Perhaps Kueng is an example of how even well-intentioned people can get swept up into a culture that distorts their better judgment and instincts.

Kueng was impressionable because he is relatively young. He had his law enforcement license for less than a year and had only been cleared to work on his own shortly before George Floyd was murdered.

Kueng was a 2018 graduate of the University of Minnesota, where he worked part-time in campus security. He was a community service officer, an MPD program meant to foster diversity by grooming potential cops. He also worked nearly three years as a theft-prevention officer at the former Macy's in downtown Minneapolis. He did short stints as a stocker at the downtown Target store, and as a youth baseball and soccer coach in Brooklyn Center, a suburb of Minneapolis.

Kueng and family members knew what it meant to serve poor people. He joined family members to travel to Haiti to volunteer after the 2010 earthquake, according to relatives and his attorney.

Kueng has two sisters, and his involvement in the murder has strained things with them. They have spoken out critically about his role in Floyd's killing. The media reported that Kueng's mother was shocked that her son could be involved in Floyd's murder.

———————

Tou Thao's story at the federal criminal civil rights trial, and in his statements shortly after his arrest, was simple: He didn't touch Floyd and failed to realize Floyd's medical condition was worsening as Chauvin kneeled on Floyd's neck for so long. He declared that he was just a "human traffic cone." The first claim is irrelevant, and the second claim is not true.

Thao's defense story might be simple, but his life story is complicated, and parts of it are sad. At the federal trial, Thao talked about growing up with an abusive father. As a child, he let Minneapolis police into his house to arrest his father for threatening him and his mom with a gun. This led him to think later in life about a career as a police officer.

Born in St. Paul, Thao is a second-generation Hmong American. The Hmong are a mountain-dwelling people with a distinct language and culture. Originally from China, many Hmong people immigrated into the United Sates as refugees following the fall of Saigon in 1975.

Minnesota is home to a Hmong community of nearly 100,000 people. Numerous famous and notable people are from this community, including Olympic gymnastics champion Suni Lee, who won gold in the women's individual all-around at the 2020 Games and became the first Hmong American Olympian. Minnesota's Hmong community boasts numerous professionals, businesspeople, and other accomplished individuals, including Minnesota state senators Mee Moua and Foung Hawj, and state representatives Cy Thao and Fue Lee. Hmong farmers are well represented at nearly every farmers' market in the Twin Cities, and their presence among Minnesota's small farmers is growing rapidly.

But the Hmong community has had its challenges, too, and Thao's story of poverty, combined with urban struggles, is not uncommon. According to recent data, about 28 percent of Hmong families in Minnesota live below the poverty line, though only about 1.25 percent of Minnesotans are Hmong. Nearly everyone in the Hmong community shares a similar experience of either immigrating or coming from an immigrant family. Many Hmong people, as well as others with ties to southeast Asia, share the story of growing up in a poor refugee household in Minnesota after fleeing Laos, Thailand, or Cambodia. Not too different from Minnesota's east African communities or west African Liberians.

Thao is married, with two young daughters and an infant son. Like Kueng, Thao served as a community service officer. He had been a full-fledged police officer for more than eight years. He joined the force part-time in 2008 while attending North Hennepin Community College. He was laid off temporarily for a couple of years due to budgetary issues in the City of Minneapolis. Thao also had his fair share of odd jobs as a security guard, a supermarket stocker, and a trainer at McDonald's.

Thao's service record was not good, but it was nowhere near the worst. Disciplinary records show six complaints, including a federal lawsuit accusing him and now-retired Officer Robert Thunder, a well-known Native American officer, of excessive force. In the lawsuit, Lamar Ferguson claimed that in 2014, Thao and Thunder stopped him for no apparent reason while he was on his way to his girlfriend's house. During the traffic stop the officers beat him.

As is common, Ferguson's assault charges were dismissed, and he filed a civil rights lawsuit. The suit was settled for $25,000.

As Ferguson described it, his case was ugly. Ferguson said the beating he suffered left him with many injuries, including busted teeth, and damage to his face and torso. He also described emotional injuries: "I was terrified of being around police officers. I had to speak to a therapist. I didn't like the sound of handcuffs or the sound of keys. I had night sweats for a long time."

———

Thomas Lane was hardly a kid when he joined the Minneapolis Police Department. He was thirty-five, and was thirty-seven when he encountered Floyd. But, in a way, he was likely always headed to the MPD: He followed three generations of men from his mother's family into the force, including a great-grandfather who was once the police chief, according to Lane's attorney, Earl Gray.

Lane was a rookie and had no complaints against him when he encountered Floyd. He wasn't new to the criminal justice system. He did a stint as a corrections officer at Hennepin County's juvenile jail and as an assistant probation officer with a Ramsey County residential program for juvenile offenders.

Lane is a college graduate, which exceeds the minimum requirement to be a police officer. The University of Minnesota graduate earned his bachelor's degree in the sociology of law, criminology, and deviance in 2016. As I write this, his wife is expecting their first child.

———

And finally, Derek Chauvin. When I first watched Chauvin kill Floyd on May 25, 2020, I thought that I was watching a thoroughly cruel man. In 2021, when I saw him in court day after day during his second-degree murder trial, I thought, *Is that the same guy?!* Chauvin is a man of average height, about five-foot-nine or -ten, but he's thin, maybe 140 pounds. He seems fairly quiet. He's never said much about Floyd other than his words to Charles McMillan ("he's a sizable guy"; "we had to control him"), which has always struck me as more clueless than malicious.

Chauvin was on the police force for nineteen years, but he was not yet a sergeant. He was a patrolman, just like Thao, Kueng, and Lane. He served as a field training officer, but he never achieved higher rank than patrolman.

Chauvin was an enlisted soldier in the Army Reserve from 1996 to 2004. He made the rank of specialist but left the army at the same rank. His service in the Minneapolis Police Department and army were both unremarkable. Even his use of force, though prolific, wasn't the worst. Chauvin had seventeen complaints filed against him with Minneapolis police, six times in which he used force against arrestees.

Minnesota's commissioner of human rights, Rebecca Lucero, led a twenty-three-month investigation of the Minneapolis Police Department. Her office found probable cause that the MPD had a pattern and practice of racial discrimination against Black people.

One case she cited, without using Chauvin's name, involved a fourteen-year-old named John Pope.

In 2017, officers were called to Pope's home for a domestic disturbance. Chauvin entered Pope's bedroom, where Pope was on his cell phone and lying facedown on the floor. Chauvin hit the fourteen-year-old boy in the head with a flashlight twice before kneeling on his back for seventeen minutes. The boy said he couldn't breathe.

Even though there was bodycam video of the incident, we would never have known about it if Floyd hadn't died under Chauvin's knee, prompting a review of his previous conduct.

Chauvin wasn't disciplined by the Minneapolis Police Department for the Pope incident, but he was indicted for this conduct and took responsibility for it in federal district court. Pope received stitches on his ear at the hospital. According to Pope's lawyer, Bob Bennett, the incident involving his client "shows that Derek Chauvin is a serial predator, and that a fourteen-year-old John Pope and George Floyd were merely prey to him."

Also, just like in Floyd's case, Chauvin's excuse, as written in his police report, was that Pope was "approximately 6'2" and at least 240 pounds," and the officer "believed he would escalate his efforts to not be arrested."

Rebecca Lucero saw the incident as bigger than just Chauvin. She noted that the case might be even more damning for Chauvin's supervisor. "The supervisor reviewed the file and approved the use of force, reporting there was no violation of policy or law." She explained, "By deeming the officer's use of force appropriate, the supervisor effectively authorized the officer to continue using such egregious force in the future."

Another Minneapolis resident, Zoya Code, also claimed racism and civil rights violations in her lawsuit stemming from a 2017 incident. She claims that while handcuffed, Chauvin put his knee on her neck and ignored her pleas for him to get off.

Since October 2001, Chauvin had been disciplined by MPD for only one incident. It occurred in August 2007 in the Longfellow neighborhood. The Longfellow neighborhood is walking distance from ground zero of the protest movement, and on the same street as the MPD's Third Precinct.

Here are the facts of Chauvin's single, sustained infraction: He was accused of pulling a woman out of her car after stopping her for going ten miles over the speed limit. The woman filed the complaint the next day. Investigators found that Chauvin unnecessarily "removed the complainant from the car" and that he "could've conducted an interview from outside the vehicle."

Apparently, Chauvin's squad car video camera was turned off during the course of the stop. He received a letter of reprimand for the incident, the details of which were redacted.

Derek Chauvin had repeatedly gotten away with this egregious conduct, and these four officers were all part of the wheel that ground down on George Floyd that day. They got caught up in a system that had repeatedly beaten down Black and brown people.

But this system couldn't outrun Darnella Frazier, a seventeen-year-old with a cell phone and the courage to use it.

Chapter 3

THE PROSECUTION

It had been almost a week since George Floyd's horrific death under the knee of Derek Chauvin. But after months of COVID restrictions and days of peaceful protest, civil unrest, and even rioting by some, it felt so much longer.

It was Sunday night, May 31, 2020, and I was heading to downtown St. Paul. I had just gotten off the telephone with Minnesota governor Tim Walz, and we had an announcement to make. I grabbed my keys and walked out into the warm evening air.

I was off to a conference room in the Minnesota Department of Public Safety at 445 Minnesota Street. As I pulled the door closed on my old Pontiac G6, I sat in the driveway and stared out the front windshield. In a few minutes, I would be standing with the governor to announce that I was accepting his call to lead the investigation and prosecution for the death of George Floyd.

I turned the ignition key and buckled my seat belt. My mom, Clida, was on my mind. She would have been outraged by what these officers did to George Floyd. Her dad, Frank Martinez, my grandfather, was also in my thoughts. When he helped to organize Black voters in rural Louisiana in the 1950s, he was answering a call. When my mom served juvenile offenders as a social worker in Wayne County, Michigan, she was answering a call. Mom always made sure my brothers and I knew that she expected us to stand up and be counted. She probably had moments like this in mind. When Mom talked about how her dad had organized rural Black voters, how racist gas station owners boycotted him, how the Klan burned a cross in front of his home and terrorized his family, he was answering a call. Could Frank Martinez's grandson refuse to answer the call?

I turned onto West Broadway Avenue. This stretch of road was usually bustling and full of people. It was now eerily empty because of the curfew.

Still, the signs of people's outrage were all around. Boarded buildings lined the street and smashed glass was still on the ground, despite neighborhood efforts at cleanup. In fact, buildings were boarded up all over Minneapolis due to the unrest.

In contrast to the destruction, many of the boards covering windows and doors now had beautiful paintings of George Floyd. Boarded buildings also displayed slogans signaling sympathy with Big Floyd and the cause that sought justice for him.

As I merged onto I-94, I thought about what certain friends had just told me. One mentor of mine said, "If you take this case, you're probably going to lose, because Black victims of police brutality usually do, and people will blame you. This is not your problem. It's Freeman's problem; let him deal with it."

Another mentor said, "Keith, we have high hopes for you. You could be Minnesota's first Black senator one day, but if you take this case and win, then the cops will be pissed. If you take the case and lose, then people will be pissed. It's a lose-lose situation for you. You shouldn't do this."

I listened carefully to these friends and mentors, as I always do, but I had made up my mind by then. Though I never vocalized it to my friends, I thought, *Wouldn't I be deciding based on how the outcome affects me personally? Isn't that wrong?*

I was taking the case.

While the governor formally appointed me to prosecute the offenders in Floyd's murder, it was the people who put me in the position to do it. People were sick of the injustice they had seen so often. They had experienced the wheel of injustice so often that they'd simply had enough.

A friend who works for a local civil rights organization had called me that Saturday, the day before, and said, "Look, man, we are about to ask the governor to appoint you to take the case. You down? I mean, what you gonna say?" This guy was one of the brightest stars on the political landscape, and he was telling me that legislators of color had organized a letter to the governor insisting on my appointment as well.

I told him that I would do whatever I could to help, but it wasn't for me to assert myself here. I told him that I wouldn't say no, but it was up to them to make any requests. I would not do that. I learned later on that Floyd's family had separately and independently asked the governor to appoint me to take over the case.

People were expressing mass dissatisfaction with business as usual, and the investigation and prosecution could *not* be business as usual. There had already been five consecutive days of massive protests in Minneapolis, including one night when the Third Precinct police station, a Tires Plus, a Target store, and many other buildings were destroyed. A curfew was in place. The Minnesota National Guard had been called up, and multiple police departments were called in to try to restore order. This was just in Minneapolis.

Of course, the Floyd killing was on every news broadcast and all over social media. Protests were taking place in every major American city and many smaller towns. The world had taken to the streets in protest, including in Madrid, Spain; Paris, France; Lisbon, Portugal; Lagos, Nigeria; Nairobi, Kenya; Medellín, Colombia; Rio de Janeiro, Brazil; Buenos Aires, Argentina; and many more. Protests had already happened in more than 2,000 cities and towns in all fifty states and all five permanently inhabited U.S. territories, as well as in more than sixty other countries.

As I pulled into the parking garage of Bremer Tower, where the Minnesota attorney general's downtown offices are located, I knew the people had been speaking loudly. The governor and I were listening.

I met my colleagues John Keller, Donna Cassutt, and John Stiles at the press conference site, which was the conference room of the Minnesota Department of Public Safety. The governor and the commissioner had been working from there to coordinate everything from the COVID-19 response to the civil unrest taking place across the Twin Cities.

Keller, Cassutt, and Stiles are not just colleagues for me. They're friends. I needed them then. We were all new to the AG's office, and I was going to need their help to pull this massive task off successfully.

John Keller is the chief deputy in the office, and he manages the law firm side of the AG's office. He ran the Immigrant Law Center of Minnesota (ILCM) before he joined the Minnesota AG's office, and I knew he would do a wonderful job because he had built ILCM into a powerhouse. I knew I could count on him to lean into his role as chief deputy as I led the prosecution team.

Donna Cassutt, my former congressional chief of staff, former associate chair of the Democratic-Farmer-Labor (DFL) party of Minnesota, and director of Minnesotans for a Fair Economy, manages the political, legislative, communications, outreach, and public relationships of the AG's office. While I was focused on the Floyd cases, she would have to keep her part of the ship sailing smoothly. No doubt she was up to it.

Donna's right hand is John Stiles. He is the deputy chief of staff and head of communications and a veteran political hand. He was also a top aide to former Minneapolis mayors Betsy Hodges and R. T. Rybak, Ramsey County commissioner Toni Carter, and many others. Crisis communications was his forte, and this skill was going to be extremely important as we assumed control of the Floyd murder cases.

We all met up outside the conference room, and they started briefing me. They suggested keeping the announcement short, asking for the public's patience, and lowering the public's sky-high expectations.

Keller, ever the lawyer, reminded me that if anyone asked, the governor was appointing me pursuant to his authority under Minnesota statute 8.01 to assign any case to the attorney general. Keller tends to make sure our legal authority is covered. I asked Donna if there were any relationship calls that I needed to make right away. These are calls to allies with whom I usually check in when big stuff comes down. She offered a few names—some Black preachers and a few supporters who've backed me since I started in politics.

Then I walked into the room where the governor was preparing. It struck me that we were gathering in the same conference room where, only three months before, Commissioner John Harrington and I had announced the findings of our Working Group on Reducing Deadly Force Encounters with the Police. The attorney general and commissioner of public safety, two Black men, thought that if any two state officials could deliver change in this area, then maybe it was us.

Harrington and I were an interesting complement to each other. He was raised in Chicago and made his career as a police officer and, ultimately, police chief in St. Paul, before serving a term in the Minnesota Senate. I was raised in Detroit and made my career as a criminal defense attorney, human rights and police reform advocate in Minneapolis, before serving two terms in the Minnesota House of Representatives and six terms in the U.S. House of Representatives. John took office as Minnesota's second Black commissioner of public safety the same time that I became Minnesota's first Black attorney general.

Harrington and I had thought it would be good to convene this group of law enforcement leaders, civil rights leaders, academics, and philanthropists to study and make recommendations on how to reduce deadly force encounters with police. Our eighteen-member working group was composed of law enforcement officials, prosecutors, judges, subject-matter experts, mental-health advocates, philanthropists, and reformers—including victims of police violence. We released twenty-eight recommendations and thirty-three action steps for reducing police-involved deadly-force encounters on February 24, 2020—three months and one day before Big Floyd was murdered.

Despite our efforts, it looked like one of the worst incidents of police brutality had unfolded right in our state.

The governor and I made some small talk before we walked out in front of the cameras. Governor Walz is a friend and someone I have worked with for over a decade. We went into Congress together in 2006 and left at the same time in 2018, when he was first elected governor, and I was first elected attorney general. Now our offices are across the hall from each other in the state capitol. Tim felt the pain of the community and the Floyd family. He listened to them carefully, and it wasn't a matter of politics. It wasn't just for optics.

I remember when Tim and his wife, Gwen, joined a delegation led by Rep. John Lewis to go to Alabama to visit civil rights sites in Birmingham, Selma, and Montgomery. I was impressed by Walz, this northern white guy, a congressional representative from rural southern Minnesota, who was so intensely curious about the American civil rights movement. I could tell this trip was important to Walz, both as a former history teacher and as a human being. He was attentive, asked questions, and showed sincere concern. He continued to do the same with the Floyd family. He took time with them and heeded their call to appoint a special prosecutor: the attorney general's office.

On May 26, 2020, the day after the murder of Floyd, Walz and Lieutenant Governor Peggy Flanagan demanded justice. Walz said, "The lack of humanity in this disturbing video is sickening. We will get answers and seek justice."

We walked out into the conference room to face the cameras. The governor went to the podium first. He's a tall, solidly built farm boy originally from small-town Nebraska. You'd expect a former command sergeant major in the National Guard to be a strict disciplinarian, but you'd be wrong. Walz is pleasant, with a ready smile. A career teacher, he has a talent for explaining things. He walked to the podium and said, "Keith Ellison, our attorney general of Minnesota, needs to lead this case." Walz added that he had made this decision after talking to the Floyd family. "They wanted the system to work for them. They wanted to believe that there was trust, and chose to believe that the facts would be heard, and justice would be served.

"We have to make that process work for people. We have to start making sure trust is restored," Walz said. "This decision is one that I feel takes us in that direction and a step to start getting justice for George Floyd."

Then it was my turn. As I moved in front of that podium, I was trying to contain powerful emotions. I felt a deep sense of humility, but I also felt confident. It may sound immodest, but I was sure that I was up to this task. I didn't know if we were going to win, but I knew we were going to put on the best case possible. I felt that my whole life had prepared me for this moment. I was determined to be more than just a speed bump for the wheel of injustice. My goal was to break that wheel.

"Prosecuting police officers for misconduct, including homicide and murder, is very difficult," I said. "And if you look at the cases that have been in front of the public in the last many years, it's easy to see that is true." I continued, "Every single link in the prosecutorial chain will come under attack as we present this case to a jury or a fact finder."

When Governor Walz and I finished our remarks, we shook hands and went our separate ways. I am sure he was as tired as I was, after several nights of protest, civil unrest, and riot and mayhem. On top of the Floyd protest, COVID was still raging and claiming lives, as it had my mother's. The governor had a full plate, and I was hoping to take a few worries away.

I said goodbye to the team and walked out into the night to my car. I had a lot on my mind.

Prosecuting a police officer is not easy, even with the bystander video. In the brutal beating of Rodney King in Los Angeles in 1991, there was video, yet the state's case ended in acquittals for all the officers involved, although the federal government did get convictions for civil rights violations.

In the more recent Walter Scott case, in which an officer shot an unarmed fleeing suspect in the back, there was video. The state's case in Scott's death—which looked like an execution to me—ended in a hung jury. There was a video of Eric Garner's choking on Staten Island, but no true bill of indictment, even though Officer Daniel Pantaleo employed a banned chokehold. Pantaleo was fired, but not until more than five years after Garner's death.

So I knew the video was no magic wand. I knew from the start that we had to prepare the case as if we had no video. We would only add it to enhance the witness testimony, not substitute for it.

It's hard to prosecute police for a number of reasons, but one of the more notable is that police and prosecutors enjoy a close professional relationship, which prosecutors often use to protect their police officer allies. While probably an oversimplification, it is nevertheless true in some cases that human beings tend to see in a sympathetic light those whom they like, admire, and have connections with. Therefore, a prosecutor who fails to hold a police officer accountable for wrongdoing is not necessarily corrupt. He or she is simply inclined to believe their friend's version of events. (With the advent of cameras in cell phones, giving that friend or colleague the benefit of the doubt may be on its way to becoming a thing of the past because so often nowadays we have direct evidence via video.) Essentially, this is why some members of the public wanted me involved. In a letter to Walz, Freeman, and me, the Minnesota chapter of the American Civil Liberties Union wrote that having Freeman investigate the police, whom his office works with daily, "fosters distrust and suspicion in the community." The letter urged that the case be transferred to my office.

Another reason involves the courts, because the law itself grants police officers great deference regarding the use-of-force decisions. Minnesota Statute section 609.066, which is based on the U.S. Supreme Court decision *Graham v. Connor*, is an affirmative defense of an officer's use of force. This means the state carries the burden of proving, beyond a reasonable doubt, that the officer's actions were objectively "unreasonable" from the perspective of the average police officer without the benefit of hindsight.

And then, of course, there is the brotherhood of policing. Some call it the "blue wall of silence," but it's well known that police officers don't snitch on one another. They are expected to either refuse to testify against one another or align stories in a way to avoid criminal liability. Former Minneapolis chief Tony Bouza—the former Bronx borough commander—once compared the police code of silence with the Mafia's omertà.

I assumed—wrongly, as it turned out—that I would not be getting any cooperation from other officers. As it happened, we were eventually able to convict Chauvin because the blue wall finally broke.

As I walked back to my car, my mind was racing. *What experts will we need? Do we have enough lawyers? Have I gotten in over my head? What about the Floyd family?* I knew that I needed to comfort them. *How will the state prosecution relate to the federal case?*

I was glad I had a positive working relationship with the United States attorney for Minnesota, Erica McDonald. She was a Trump appointee, and so—this being the age of hyperpolitical polarization—I was surprised to learn that she was helpful and cooperative. Our offices worked well together as we navigated the COVID-19 pandemic. She was going to be an important ally, and I made a note to call her in the morning.

As I drove back on I-94 toward my home, I knew the fight would not be limited to the courtroom. Floyd's girlfriend, Courteney Ross, had given me a warning just days before. She'd said that Floyd's credibility and life would be on trial. It was true. Floyd's life would not only be on trial by the defense counsel, who would likely be formidable and very experienced, but also by the press.

Like Trayvon Martin, Mike Brown, and so many other African Americans before, Floyd's entire record would get ripped apart. The reputation of his family members would be scrutinized, too. That Sunday night, I was already making plans to head down to Houston to talk with the Floyd family to try to prepare them for what was coming.

When I arrived home, Moni was still up. She was in her "queendom," a guest room in our home that she had converted into her home office during the COVID-19 quarantine. It's her exclusive domain. She works in there, takes Zoom calls from her office, talks to her mom on the phone, and whatever else she pleases in her "queendom." I knock before I walk in.

When I walked through the door into the house, I think she was talking to someone, probably her mother, Theresita, or her niece, Maria-Jose, but she jumped off the call quickly. "How did it go?!"

"Whew! Fine. I don't know," which is what I usually say when I am thinking of a million things at once. Then she hugged me—for a long time. She ominously said, "We have to talk about security."

I had been the target of unwarranted threats and attacks before, including multiple death threats. I got them from Al-Qaeda, racist idiots, and other assorted bullies. I was used to it. I have weathered untrue allegations from political opponents and threats from run-of-the-mill racists. My skin had thickened through sixteen years in legal practice and sixteen years in political service. I was the first Muslim elected to the United States Congress, and that was only six years after 9/11, America's most horrific terrorist attack. I was also the first Black person to hold statewide office in Minnesota. I had become used to nasty people saying nasty things. So maybe I needed someone else to be more mindful of security measures than I was.

Oh boy, I thought, when I heard Moni's words. I responded, "Can we talk about this in the morning?" We went to bed, anticipating the days ahead.

Within a few weeks, Moni would upgrade our camera network,

meet with a security specialist, and convene my office staff. She played a critical role. She also forbade me from jogging or biking along the same route every day. There were other steps taken to ensure my security as well, which I am not allowed to share here. Anyway, she said, "You're going to need some rest." We went to bed to prepare for what was going to be a remarkable year.

———

The next morning, I got up early and called David Voigt, the deputy attorney general, and Matt Frank, who leads our criminal prosecution division. We had a case to plan.

It was Monday, June 1, 2020, and I had a mountain of press inquiries that had to be carefully managed. As the lead prosecutor I had an obligation to ensure the defendant received a fair trial. This meant avoiding statements in the press that could lead a potential juror to presume guilt. Any defendant, including Chauvin, is presumed innocent, and the state bears the entire burden of proof. Even—or especially—with the compelling video evidence the whole world had already seen, Derek Chauvin was entitled to the same presumption of innocence.

At the same time, this case was dominating the headlines of every newspaper and broadcast. I had a duty to dispel rumors with solid information. I accepted interviews with a great variety of local, national, and international media outlets, such as with ESPN's Stephen A. Smith, CBS, MSNBC, and the Minneapolis *Star Tribune*. I hoped—and, quite honestly, prayed—that my introduction into the case would calm the outrage that was still omnipresent. People were still protesting and the world wanted to know what was going to be done, as one of the biggest shifts was the prosecution now landing in my hands.

I took these interviews via Zoom in my office. I drove to the capitol early, around seven-thirty a.m., because I knew it was going to be a long day. When I got to room 102 in the capitol building, I was not surprised to see two of the most wonderful public servants anybody could have.

June and Colleen, both long-serving staffers at the Minnesota attorney general's office, were already brewing coffee, handing me a paper copy of my schedule, and briefing me on what was coming up. Things were crazy for these two dedicated public servants.

The week prior, legendary civil rights leader Rev. Jesse Jackson had visited our offices to meet with Mike Freeman and me. Though Reverend Jackson was managing the challenges of Parkinson's disease, he was upbeat and charismatic. June and Colleen took pictures with him. Here we were in the second week of the Floyd crisis, and they were eager to be helpful.

I sat at my desk, coffee in hand, and called David Voigt and Matt Frank. We arranged for a meet-up at the Minnesota Bureau of Criminal Apprehension (BCA) at four-thirty p.m. There, we would meet with the case agent, go over preliminary evidence, make arrangements to receive the case file, and discuss charges.

We planned to make our first phone contact with the Floyd family, which was a top priority. Although it was already Monday, I was determined to announce any additional changes to the charges or the language of the complaint by Wednesday, June 3. We had a big agenda. So I cranked through my day.

As attorney general, I had to take time away from the Floyd cases to appear at a virtual meeting with the state's Executive Council, which includes the governor, lieutenant governor, secretary of state, state auditor, and attorney general. During "peacetime emergencies," the Executive Council is required to approve or reject decisions of the governor after he has taken executive action to protect the public. The state was still under quarantine and still showing high numbers of cases of COVID infection and death. Before heading to the offices of the BCA, a few miles away from the capitol, I voted in favor of the governor's peacetime emergency measures.

I arrived at the BCA around 3:45 p.m. It was a really hot day and I was wearing a suit, which I hadn't worn since the pandemic had been declared a couple of months before. Then, despite the heat, I put on my mask and walked into the building to find David Voigt and Matt Frank.

Before I had told the governor yes to taking on this monumental task, I had checked in with Voigt and Frank. "We can do this, right? You guys are game for this, right?"

David Voigt, deputy AG for many years, seemed almost eager. Frank was a little more reticent, but that's just his personality. He's careful and meticulous, and I have grown to really appreciate that about him.

David Voigt has a ready smile and is always willing to help. Along with our chief deputy John Keller, Voigt was going to help manage the budgetary impact of the case.

Prosecutions are not free. On top of salaries, we would have some serious expenses, especially if all four officers demanded a trial. We would need to pay for experts' fees, transcripts, graphics, computer storage, and transportation expenses and lodging for expert witnesses. Other expenses included services for the victims' family and courthouse security. Mike Freeman and I worked out an arrangement to split the costs with Hennepin County.

Matt Frank, who stands about six foot one, has a deep voice and an exceedingly professional manner. He's a career prosecutor and a serious guy. He has been traveling the state of Minnesota for years helping rural communities and small towns prosecute murders, manslaughter cases, and rape cases. He's a Sergeant Joe Friday "just the facts, ma'am" kind of fellow, but his seriousness belies his compassion.

He insisted from the beginning that we prioritize the Floyd family, the victims in this case. He was adamant about wanting to make sure we listened to them, kept them informed, and consulted with them on every big decision. He cares about crime victims.

I was proud that my office had prosecuted thirty-eight homicides and countless criminal sexual assaults and white-collar crimes in the time since I had become Minnesota attorney general. We also conducted 167 criminal appeals for the prosecution in many involuntary commitment proceedings to protect the public from sexually dangerous predators. Our criminal team knew what we were doing, but we still had some gaps that I knew needed to be filled.

David, Matt, and I started identifying tasks before us. We were meeting with the BCA case agent to go over preliminary evidence, make arrangements to receive the case file, and discuss charges.

The case agent knew we needed to see everything and agreed to sending everything electronically. Eric Miller of the AG's office, who was a law student at the time, helped us get the voluminous file on the Floyd case transferred, stored, and made easily accessible to those of us working on it. Of course, this included the fake twenty-dollar bill, all witness statements including those from the officers, photographs, and all medical documents including the medical examiner's report. There was a ton of material to review, and we needed to have it accessible electronically.

Then there were other practical matters. The Minnesota attorney general's office only has three full-time prosecutors, who already had a full complement of cases. County attorneys—called district attorneys in other states—have original jurisdiction over almost all felonies in Minnesota. Rural counties across Minnesota counted on us to be available for their cases, but more than half of all Minnesota's eighty-seven counties have three or fewer prosecutors. Essentially, when a murder or another serious violent crime case occurs in their rural counties, they turn to us for help in prosecution and need us to be available. How could I justify assigning several of our best lawyers to just one case in Minnesota's largest county, when the needs of all the smaller counties were also our priority? Yet I knew we had to do it.

David, Matt, and I began to think about who we might tap from our staff internally. In addition to the folks from the Hennepin County attorney's office, I knew I could assign Matt as the team leader, Erin Eldridge, who is a seasoned criminal prosecutor, and Dionne Dodd as our paralegal. I felt like the team was starting to take shape, but we would need more help beyond these folks.

Although the governor assigned me as the lead prosecutor, Mike Freeman was an invaluable ally. He agreed to lend staff to the prosecution. I needed to become familiar with the legal talent Mike was providing. I didn't know Josh Larson and Jean Burdorf very well, but I would get to know them both as excellent lawyers who proved indispensable during the investigation and trial.

Freeman provided space for the entire prosecution team to work together, as well as parking during the trial. Freeman agreed to meet with me every Wednesday morning via telephone. For a year, we met faithfully and talked over every aspect of the case. Sometimes the calls were short, but other times they went on for quite a while. The topics varied, depending on how close we were to the trial date, but Freeman was always attentive and helpful.

From the beginning, I knew the case involved some complicated medical issues and would require use-of-force experts. We needed lawyers who had some experience prosecuting police officers. None of our staff had this experience. I also knew we needed the best lawyers who could sort through complicated medical testimony. Medical causation was going to be an issue. This was when I began to wonder whether my old friend Jerry Blackwell might be willing to consult with us.

Jerry had an encyclopedic knowledge of the human body, and he had a lot of experience representing people and companies who might not be viewed sympathetically by the public. By this point, smears against Floyd were coming. In fact, they had already started. Jerry knew how to humanize giant multinational corporations, and he could help us humanize George Perry Floyd, no matter what the defense counsel and Fox News pundits had to say. I made a mental note to call him.

The medical case against the typical murder defendant is generally straightforward. The medical examiner performs the autopsy and testifies to the obvious (e.g., the victim was shot, stabbed, drowned, or whatever). Usually, the medical examiner carries most of the weight. This case would be different.

Despite the video the world had seen, I knew Floyd's cause of death would certainly be contested. Defense counsel wasted no time trying to shape the public and media narrative around George Floyd. We needed some support navigating the media environment.

John Stiles and Keaon Dousti of my staff would be a great help in this area. I assigned them to the prosecution team. We would not be making public statements about the defendants' guilt, but we would monitor what the defense was putting out there. And of course, everything we put in our filings would be available to the press and the public. The prosecutor should not make public comments about the guilt or innocence of the defendant in any criminal case outside of what is written in the initial court filings. In the beginning of the case, it's permissible to make clarifying comments for the public record about what is happening and why, but after that initial stage the prosecutor should confine his or her talking to the courtroom. The defendant has a right to a fair trial and an unbiased jury. The risk of tainting the jury pool, with comments from the state about the defendant's guilt, is too great to continuously make comments after the initial stage of the case. It's simply unethical for the prosecutor—who represents the state and, by extension, the people—to do so.

Renowned defense attorney Earl Gray, who was representing Thomas Lane, was on multiple networks from the start. He argued in the press that Chauvin's knee-on-the-neck arrest of George Floyd had nothing to do with his death. According to Gray—a folksy, regular-type-guy trial lawyer with many wins under his belt—Floyd had "killed himself." Gray employed the common defense tactic of blaming the victim and trying the victim in the court of public opinion, when in fact it is the defendant who should be tried in a court of law.

Gray said that the real cause of Floyd's death was an overdose of fentanyl. "None of these guys—even Chauvin—actually killed him," Gray told the *Los Angeles Times*. Gray could be found on MSNBC, CNN, CBS, and many other outlets. It was important for us to track his efforts at seasoning the potential jurors. Plus, he was telegraphing what his argument to the jury would be.

The Floyd Family

As we finished our meeting at the BCA, we had one more critical task that evening: a telephone meeting with the Floyd family. The famous civil rights lawyer Ben Crump was the family's counsel, and he began the call with a round of introductions. I introduced our prosecution team and then we talked. I shared a few things. And they did the same.

As I listened to their voices, I heard Southern drawls, accents, and manners of speech that were familiar to me. In their voices, I heard dignity and pain. Some of them sounded pure Texas, and others' accents were more neutral, but all were serious and earnest. Philonise Floyd emerged as the family spokesperson. He was a professional over-the-road truck driver, married for many years to his lovely wife, Charlie, who was always with him. Philonise, along with Rodney, were George's younger brothers.

They asked many questions, including whether we were going to charge Chauvin with first-degree murder. Someone on the call asked about whether the death penalty was on the table. This was a logical question for a Texan to ask, since that state leads the nation in capital punishment, but I informed them that Minnesota did not sanction death for any crime.

I told them we were looking at all the possible charges, and nothing was off the table as long as we had evidence to support it. I tried to signal, however, that we did not have evidence of premeditation and deliberation yet, which would be necessary to charge first-degree murder.

During the call, Matt Frank took notes as he listened carefully. This family had suffered an incalculable loss. We were determined to lighten their burden by keeping them informed and treating them with kindness.

I told them that I planned on coming to Houston to meet them in person, and, as Matt Frank insisted, I promised to keep them informed.

Reflecting on the Governor's Appointment

Perhaps no aspect of the Floyd cases is more out of the ordinary than the governor's decision to appoint the attorney general for the prosecution. This break from conventionality may have been the most important decision in the entire case. Tragically, a person like George Floyd being killed in police custody is not unusual. Even videos like Darnella Frazier's are not unusual.

Criminal prosecutions of police officers are rare. According to Philip M. Stinson, former police officer and current professor of criminal justice at Bowling Green State University, about 1,000 people a year die at the hands of law enforcement officers across the United States. Since the beginning of 2005, 121 officers have been arrested on charges of murder or manslaughter in on-duty killings. Stinson noted that of the ninety-five officers whose cases have concluded, forty-four were convicted, but often of a lesser charge. However, the number of police officers prosecuted "seems extremely low to me," Stinson told me. "In my opinion, it's got to be that more of the fatal shootings are unjustified."

These rare convictions include cases that almost were never prosecuted. One example is the on-camera shooting of seventeen-year-old Laquan McDonald in Chicago in 2014. The squad dashcam video, not released until thirteen months after the shooting, is nothing short of horrific.

In the video, McDonald is obviously walking away from the officers as Officer Jason Van Dyke shoots him sixteen times, including while he was lying limp on the ground. In his statement, Van Dyke claimed that McDonald had lunged at him with a knife. An independent police review authority concluded the shooting was justified.

The video was revealed only when a journalist sued to force its release. That was the exact moment when the district attorney filed charges against Van Dyke. As bad as the video was, the McDonald case almost never saw the light of day.

Prosecutions of police officers for outrageous and illegal conduct are rare, and convictions are rarer still. Declinations—prosecutors' decisions not to prosecute—are the norm. Why?

There is an embedded conflict of interest that is present every time a local prosecutor is confronted with prosecuting a member of the local police department. By appointing the attorney general to lead the case, Governor Walz helped us overcome this conflict of interest.

As I mentioned earlier, there are so few police prosecutions because cops and prosecutors rely on each other to do their jobs. Therefore, prosecuting a police officer means exposing a friend, associate, or someone you may have to rely on someday. The opening line of the series *Law & Order* is accurate: "In the criminal justice system, the people are represented by two separate yet equally important groups: the police, who investigate crime, and the district attorneys, who prosecute the offenders. These are their stories." Cha-chunk!

That's how the public perceives the relationship between the prosecutors and the police—inextricably linked together, inseparable.

Public perception is often better served by removing the complication of having a local prosecutor choose between competing loyalties when the potential defendant is a police officer. It's better to allow the local prosecutor to maintain a working relationship with a colleague rather than force them to choose between that relationship and equal justice. I am sure there are many prosecutors who might disagree: I have heard from them in the past. They would argue that they are sufficiently professional to prosecute everyone who breaks the law equally. Of course, many are right about that, but not always.

Even among prosecutors who say they can and do prosecute crimes committed by police officers equally, there is still the perception problem. The public perception that criminal conduct by police officers is not prosecuted is something prosecutors must take seriously. The Standards for Criminal Justice Prosecution Function §3-1.2(c) state, "The prosecutor should avoid an appearance of impropriety in performing the prosecution function." If only for public perception that justice is being equally applied, prosecutors should consider assigning the state attorney general to prosecute cases involving police misconduct.

Chapter 1 on George Floyd and chapter 2 on the cops describe a tragic pattern that has been plaguing Minnesota, the United States, and Black communities for more than 100 years. But the prosecution, the subject of this chapter, has broken the pattern.

If the wheel of inaction is ever going to break, if there is ever an inflection point regarding police violence, it must begin with how officer-involved cases are prosecuted.

HCA's Complaint

By the time Governor Walz had assigned the case to me, Derek Chauvin was already facing two charges: third-degree murder and second-degree manslaughter. Our first job was to figure out whether the charges against Derek Chauvin—and potentially Lane, Kueng, and Thao—were appropriate. The county attorney's charges against Chauvin of third-degree murder and second-degree manslaughter were a place to start. Freeman agreed with me that the AG office's staff should take a fresh look at the charges and the language of the complaint.

The charging decision is a consequential decision in every case. The charges determine, to a large degree, the ultimate sentence. Of course, judges have a lot of discretion about sentencing, but the recommended sentence in the sentencing guidelines is based on the charge, which is decided by the prosecutor. So the charging decision must be driven by a sincere and reasonable belief that the evidence is sufficient to persuade a jury unanimously that the defendant is guilty beyond a reasonable doubt, and that any reasonable defenses are not true beyond a reasonable doubt.

Though I knew them well, I looked over the American Bar Association (ABA) standards for prosecutor conduct before sitting down with Voigt and Frank. I was a trial lawyer for a solid sixteen years before going into politics. I have dealt with all kinds of prosecutors: state prosecutors, federal prosecutors, district court prosecutors, and appellate prosecutors. But I dealt with those prosecutors as a criminal defense lawyer. My primary duty as a criminal defense lawyer was to be a zealous advocate for my client, to raise every legitimate issue on my client's behalf, and to test every link in the prosecutorial chain. In the criminal justice system, guilty defendants—and even pretrial detainees—can get their liberty taken away. In America, liberty is the priority.

The primary duty of the prosecutor is to seek justice within the bounds of the law, not merely to convict. It is to be a minister of justice. The prosecutor serves the public interest and should act with integrity and judgment to increase public safety. This involves a balance between pursuing criminal charges of appropriate severity and exercising discretion to not pursue such charges as are unwarranted. The prosecutor should seek to protect the innocent and convict the guilty, consider the interests of victims and witnesses, and respect the constitutional and legal rights of all persons, including suspects and defendants.

In Minnesota, the prosecutor has two options for accusing a defendant of a crime, by grand jury or complaint. A complaint is a court document that states the accusations or charges, or "counts." The list of counts is accompanied by a probable-cause statement, which is a written presentation of the relevant facts supporting the counts in the complaint. In the Floyd murder, the defendants were charged via complaint. Only first-degree murder requires a grand jury indictment.

When Dave, Matt, and I sat down to review the Hennepin County attorney's complaint, dated May 29, 2020, I noticed several concerning factors. For the most part, the probable-cause statement in the Hennepin County complaint read like a normal statement; however, certain sentences seemed to be unnecessarily helpful to Derek Chauvin.

Additionally, the overall tone of the Hennepin County complaint struck me as biased against Floyd. Normally, the probable-cause statement offers facts designed to support the counts in the complaint and the defendant's guilt. Complaints don't normally paint the victim in an unsympathetic and unfavorable light, but this complaint did.

For example, in the third paragraph of the Hennepin County complaint it stated, "Mr. Floyd actively resisted being handcuffed." That's not an accurate description of what happened. In the bodycam video, Lane shoved a Glock 9mm handgun in Floyd's face and was yelling curses at him. Floyd was noticeably afraid and said so. Kueng yelled, "Stop resisting," but that doesn't mean Floyd was resisting.

The fourth paragraph stated, "Once cuffed Mr. Floyd became compliant," but he had been compliant all along. Floyd repeatedly addressed Lane and Kueng as "Officer," and said "please" multiple times. It appeared that he might not have understood all of Lane's and Kueng's commands, but the Hennepin County complaint attributed resistance to what really appeared to be confusion.

In the seventh paragraph, the Hennepin County complaint stated: "Mr. Floyd did not voluntarily get in the car and struggled with the officers by intentionally falling, saying he was not going into the car, and refusing to stand still. Mr. Floyd is over 6 feet tall and weighs more than 200 pounds. While standing outside the car, Mr. Floyd began saying and repeating that he could not breathe."

This is simply inaccurate. More bodycam footage showed that Floyd never refused to do anything, including getting into squad 320 or standing still. In fact, he said he would get in the car, but he had anxiety and claustrophobia. He offered to sit on the ground. He was cooperating.

The whole mess was about his using a fake twenty-dollar bill, a misdemeanor. It doesn't seem unreasonable for Floyd to ask for an accommodation before getting into the squad. The complaint writer also offered Floyd's size as an explanation for the officers' use of force against him. Further, the complaint highlighted Floyd's declaration that he couldn't breathe before Chauvin put his knee on Floyd's neck, thereby suggesting that the knee on the neck wasn't the cause of death.

In the thirteenth paragraph, the Hennepin County complaint cast doubt on whether the actions of the officers caused Floyd's death at all. "The full report of the ME [medical examiner] is pending but the ME has made the following preliminary findings. The autopsy revealed no physical findings that support a diagnosis of traumatic asphyxia or strangulation. Mr. Floyd had underlying health conditions including coronary artery disease and hypertensive heart disease. The combined effects of Mr. Floyd being restrained by the police, his underlying health conditions and any potential intoxicants in his system likely contributed to his death."

When I read this paragraph, red flags shot up for me. This summary of the ME's preliminary findings in Hennepin County's complaint seemed to be handing "reasonable doubt" to the defense. The complaint highlighted that the "autopsy revealed no physical findings that support a diagnosis of traumatic asphyxia or strangulation," but this doesn't preclude asphyxia (low oxygen). It's quite common for people who die of asphyxia not to have injuries to their throat and neck area. A person who is smothered dies of asphyxia but may not have bruising, hemorrhage, or physical signs of trauma.

Then the Hennepin County complaint went right into Floyd's "underlying health conditions, including coronary artery disease and hypertensive heart disease." How could a forty-six-year-old man go from walking around and acting normally to dying of coronary artery disease within nine minutes and twenty-nine seconds? It seems like the complaint writer never even asked Dr. Andrew Baker, the medical examiner, whether that was a sound medical statement to make.

The author put it in the complaint for the world to see, and speculation began about what really killed George Floyd. But the witnesses that day who had called for Chauvin, Lane, Thao, and Kueng to "get off of him" had no doubt.

The final sentence of paragraph thirteen stated, "The combined effects of Mr. Floyd being restrained by the police, his underlying health conditions and any potential intoxicants in his system likely contributed to his death." This sentence really struck me as ridiculous, but also legally irrelevant. It seemed like the complaint writer was trying to minimize Chauvin's culpability by blaming Floyd for having imperfect health.

Under Minnesota law, and the general criminal law anywhere, the defendant can't escape liability because the victim is frail. Defendants must "take their victims as they find them." There was no evidence that "intoxicants" played a role in Floyd's death. It simply was not an overdose. How this suggestion or intimation made it into the county's complaint, I am not sure, but it was not helpful to the prosecution. We would take it out.

We had to review the charges, but we also had to redraft the county's complaint, as I viewed the county complaint's language as unhelpful. Dave and Matt agreed, and Matt took on the assignment of redrafting the criminal complaint to reflect the undated medical examiner's report. He would also remove the victim-blaming language and use clearer, better wording more suited to a criminal prosecution.

For example, the county's complaint described George Floyd as suddenly becoming unresponsive: "BWC video shows Mr. Floyd continue to move and breathe" until 8:24:24, when he "stops moving." It just didn't happen like that. Multiple videos showed visible signs of increasing medical distress over the duration of the encounter. Floyd's breathing was clearly growing labored and heavy. He had foam at the edges of his mouth. He said, "I'm about to die." Floyd continued to make slight movements while officers held him prone on the pavement. His movements, however, slowed, and his utterances and groans decreased and became gradually weaker, until 8:24:24, when he stopped moving.

Matt Frank updated the complaint based on what we had learned from the video and the medical examiner's report. He explained that the officers played a key role in Floyd's death, not coronary artery disease. We used the medical examiner's language—that is, that Floyd "died from cardiopulmonary arrest while being restrained by law enforcement officers" and that the cause of death was "cardiopulmonary arrest complicating law enforcement's subdual restraint and neck compression."

The medical examiner had concluded the manner of death was homicide and that Officer Chauvin's restraint of Floyd in this manner for such a prolonged period was a substantial causal factor in his death, constituting substantial bodily harm and causing Floyd's death as well.

The Counts

After we had amended that probable-cause statement, we needed to review the charges. I started with the facts we could prove, then what we could not prove. For example, we had no facts to prove that Chauvin knew Floyd and deliberately killed him. Then we asked ourselves, based on what we knew, what really happened?

It seemed to me that rookie cops were bumbling through a nothing case about a fake twenty-dollar bill. Instead of protecting the public, they were trying to prove to themselves and the community at 38th and Chicago that they were in charge and not to be messed with.

Along came Chauvin and Thao. Chauvin's only tactic appeared to be force. Thao voiced the general attitude of all the officers: They were in gang territory, and therefore entitled to be harsher, less respectful, and more suspicious of everyone—suspected gang member or not. Chauvin got on top of Floyd's neck, without even really figuring out what was going on. When the people in the neighborhood objected, Chauvin got more focused. He stayed on Floyd to prove a point: He's in charge, and they, including Floyd, are powerless. None of this was about his actual duty as a police officer. None of this was about protecting and serving. He had forgotten about any of that. Now, it was about who was boss—the sin of pride. Pride over policing.

It seemed to me that Chauvin didn't intend to kill Floyd, but he applied force long after it was justifiable, with no law enforcement purpose. That's assault. Because the assault caused Floyd to lose consciousness, that's assault with substantial bodily injury, which is assault in the third degree. Because Floyd died as a result, that becomes second-degree unintentional murder. We had our top count. Matt Frank had all that he needed to draft the complaint.

Now, what about Lane, Kueng, and Thao? In my mind, they were certainly morally responsible. Chief Medaria Arradondo had already fired them because of their failure to live up to departmental rules and expectations. But were they criminally negligent? Did their conduct help Chauvin commit the crimes we were charging him with?

We looked at Minnesota Statute 609.05, the aiding and abetting statute. In Minnesota, anyone who "intentionally aids" is liable, even if another person did the actual crime. You can't hold a person down while another assaults that person. You can't be the lookout for someone committing a crime. If you intentionally help the crime happen, you're liable.

Certainly, Lane, Thao, and Kueng knew that. In this case, Kueng pressed down on Floyd's back while Chauvin had his knee on his neck, and Kueng twisted his hand in a pain-compliance move while it was already in handcuffs. Kueng took Floyd's pulse and didn't find one. Despite not finding a pulse, he went right on pressing on Floyd's back and did not render any medical aid even though he was trained in CPR and first aid. One video shows him being so nonchalant about everything that he is picking rocks out of the tires on squad 320.

Meanwhile, Lane held Floyd's legs so he could not turn his body to get a breath. The autopsy said there were bruises on Floyd's face, and this was a result of his pushing his face against the asphalt street to get more room for his lungs to expand. Lane was so aware Floyd was in serious medical distress that he suggested turning him over. Lane suggested this, but he didn't do anything to make this happen.

Thao did not physically touch Floyd, but the crime could not have been completed without his help. He kept anyone from intervening to assist Floyd. He specifically kept Genevieve Hansen, a trained Minneapolis firefighter and paramedic, from rendering aid. And he did so much more than that. He told the other officers to lay Floyd prone on the ground. The bodycam shows him rejecting use of the hobble because "if we hobble him, the sergeant is going to have to come out." Yet the hobble would have allowed Floyd to be in the side recovery position as opposed to prone on the ground. It might have saved him.

Thao also taunted the people who assembled to help Floyd: "This is why you don't do drugs, kids." He also said, "If he's talking, he's breathing." (To which Alyssa Funari responded, "He's not talking now.")

Despite his CPR and first aid training, Thao also did nothing as Floyd lost consciousness, lost his pulse, and stopped breathing.

Under Statute 609.05, a person is not liable for aiding and abetting if he abandons the criminal purpose and makes a reasonable effort to prevent the commission of the crime prior to its commission. Therein lies the problem: None of them stood up. None of them said, "Enough! He's unconscious." None of them took any action to abandon the assault on Floyd that they were part of.

We asked ourselves the question of whether the status of Lane and Kueng as rookies mattered. I believed that Chauvin had, indeed, failed them, but they had failed George Floyd. A whole group of people assembled to plead for them to stop killing Floyd, and none of them had police officer training. The police academy is supposed to make you smarter about helping people, not dumber. Somehow, three seventeen-year-olds and a nine-year-old could plainly see what Thao, Lane, and Kueng were indifferent to.

We agreed. We would announce that the new charges would include second-degree unintentional murder, third-degree murder, and second-degree manslaughter. The attorney general's office's (AGO's) complaint would include three counts as opposed to the county's two counts.

The highest AGO count of second-degree unintentional murder

carries a statutory maximum of forty years, as opposed to the county's top count of third-degree murder, which carries a statutory maximum of twenty-five years. The AGO complaint would charge all four officers with all three crimes. Also, we planned to file a redrafted probable-cause section of the complaint. This would reflect Floyd's obvious medical distress and his general compliance. It would also reflect the medical examiner's opinion that Floyd's cause of death was "cardiopulmonary arrest complicating law enforcement subdual, restraint, and neck compression" and concluding that the manner of death was homicide, meaning death by another.

We picked June 3, 2020, a Wednesday, as the date for the announcement. This was exactly nine days after the killing of George Floyd.

I called Mike Freeman and shared that we had an amended complaint for his review. Mike welcomed our position and never showed any resistance to our approach. Both Mike and I would sign the amended complaint. When I asked him to join me at the podium for the announcement, he enthusiastically agreed.

The venue for the press conference was the Minnesota Department of Revenue. I stood at the microphone and read my statement. I knew that everything I planned to say would be scrutinized, so I had carefully considered every word I chose in my statement, and why. I started by thanking everyone for granting me the time we needed to carefully review the facts and the applicable law, and then I announced the increased charge of second-degree murder. I also announced the arrests of Lane, Thao, and Kueng, and their charges.

I thanked United States Attorney Erica McDonald and FBI Special Agent-in-Charge Rainer S. Drolshagen, who were conducting a parallel federal investigation.

On June 2, 2020, the day before our announcement, we gathered in McDonald's office for a meeting with state AG and federal teams for a private conversation. It was important for Erica and me to build strong lines of communication. She had a saying I admired: "One team, one goal, one mission."

Erica, born and raised in Texas, had a lot of empathy for the Floyds. She and I had decided to travel to Houston to visit the family. Erica had also set up a phone call with U.S. Attorney General William Barr and me. We only talked for a moment, but Barr assured me that the federal government was taking the Floyd case very seriously. I was pleased to hear it. I am sure that many of my progressive friends would be shocked to know that I had a pleasant and fruitful conversation with Bill Barr, but I didn't care. I was "eyes on the prize" and willing to work with anyone to succeed with these prosecutions.

During the presser, I concluded my remarks by reminding everyone that I would not be making many public statements in the future. I said that we would be doing our talking in the courthouse. I thanked the protesters. They made this moment happen. Without them raising their voices, I probably would not have had this case. I wasn't about to let them down.

Finally, I looked past the Floyd case and pointed people to the undone work of justice. "What I do not believe is that one successful prosecution can rectify the hurt and loss that so many people feel. The solution to that pain will be the slow and difficult work of constructing justice and fairness in our society. That work is the work of all of us."

I ended my prepared remarks that day by saying, "A protest can shake a tree, and make the fruit fall, but after the fruit is in reach, collecting it, making the jam, must follow. The demonstrations are dramatic and necessary; building justice institutions is more of a slow grind, but equally important."

Ben Crump, counsel for the Floyd family, held his own press conference in support of my office's work. "We are deeply gratified that Attorney General Keith Ellison took decisive action in this case," Crump said in a statement. "This is a significant step forward on the road to justice, and we are gratified that this important action was brought before George Floyd's body was laid to rest."

Crump also mentioned that the family had conducted its own autopsy. They retained Dr. Michael Baden of New York and Dr. Allecia

Wilson, University of Michigan, Pathology and Forensic Science. They concluded that George Floyd died as a result of mechanical asphyxia due to the knee on his neck and the other two on his back that were pressing down on his lungs, not allowing them to expand and contract.

Crump added, "These officers knew they could act with impunity, given the Minneapolis Police Department's widespread and prolonged pattern and practice of violating people's constitutional rights. Therefore, we also always demand permanent transparent police accountability at all levels."

Rev. Al Sharpton joined Ben Crump and the family at the press conference to announce that he would be delivering the eulogy for George Floyd the following day at North Central University in Minneapolis.

I declined my invitation to attend the funeral because I didn't want to give ammunition to anyone who might claim I was swayed by sympathy, or biased in favor of the George Floyd family. I was motivated by the pursuit of justice alone, and it had to appear that way, as well as be that way.

The case was too important, and I didn't want to give anyone reason to think my motivations were about vengeance. But I asked my wife, Moni, to go to the funeral, along with my kids Amirah, Elijah, and Jeremiah, a Minneapolis council member. Governor Walz, his wife Gwen, Lieutenant Governor Peggy Flanagan, as well as many others, were present as well.

After I left the Minnesota Department of Revenue building, I had a few press hits to do. I was about to stop talking to the press altogether, and I wanted to get these remaining few out of the way.

We had a ton of work ahead of us, not to mention sky-high expectations.

Assembling a Prosecution Team

The day before George Floyd's Minneapolis funeral, I was hard at work and feeling the pressure. It was Wednesday, June 3, and buildings in

Minneapolis were still smoldering, windows were still boarded up, and the city was on edge.

At this point, I had some recruiting to do, but there were also people who were stepping up to help.

Fellow staff members Natasha Robinson and Zuri Balmakund Santiago called and wanted to get involved. These talented young lawyers were a team, and they were ready to dig into research and document review. Natasha and Zuri became invaluable members of the prosecution. They took notes at every meeting and drafted our first timeline.

I needed someone with experience prosecuting police officers, as well as someone who could really deal with the complex medical causation issues.

I asked Voigt and Frank for recommendations of people who had experience prosecuting police officers. The name of Steve Schleicher came up. I had heard of him and seen him on TV offering legal commentary. According to Voigt and Frank, he used to work for the AG's office, and he was an assistant U.S. attorney. He had helped solve the tragic case of the murder of eleven-year-old Jacob Wetterling. I made a note to give him a call.

There were several friends and mentors guiding me through this entire process. The legendary Barry Scheck was generous with his time. The world knows about his historic win in the O. J. Simpson case as he displayed his mastery over DNA evidence, but Barry has also led the nation in securing the release of innocent people who have been wrongly convicted. Barry can tell you that one of the main reasons innocent people get convicted is due to unconstitutional policing.

Barry made several recommendations, but two ideas proved critical. The first was about the controversial medical theory of excited delirium. Barry noted that Thomas Lane had referred to it on the body-worn camera video, and that it was a major medical-legal theory that had been used successfully in the past to justify excessive force from police. Barry gave me several resource leads and warned me to have someone who could really handle the medical causation case.

Barry also told me to get the appellate lawyers involved right up front. He said this case was the biggest one in recent memory, and that everything we did was going to be scrutinized. He warned, "You do not want to create appeal issues." Barry was a great source of moral support. Along the way, he jumped on our Zoom calls to pump up the team.

I was also in touch with my friend Tom Perez, who was the former chair of the Democratic National Committee (DNC), where he served during the Trump era. Tom had also been the assistant attorney general for the civil rights division of the DOJ under President Obama. He had a lot of experience with police issues.

To name just a few, Tom led the DOJ investigation into the death of Trayvon Martin by George Zimmerman in Sanford, Florida, in 2012. He also led an eight-month investigation into the use of excessive force by the Seattle Police Department, sparked by the death of a Native American man, John T. Williams. In the Seattle case, Perez's office issued a report citing "unconstitutional violations in the use of force resulting in structural problems as well as serious concerns about biased policing." Under Tom, the DOJ and the city of Seattle reached a settlement that resulted in the Seattle Police Department being placed under the supervision of an independent court-appointed monitor.

Tom also sued the infamous Maricopa County sheriff Joe Arpaio, who refused to cooperate with a DOJ investigation. The suit was brought under the 1964 Civil Rights Act, the first such action since the 1970s.

Tom's advice to me was to set up a Garrity committee. Under the U.S. Supreme Court's 1967 decision in *Garrity v. New Jersey*, public employees like police are compelled to give statements as a condition of their employment; however, these statements are inadmissible against the public employee in a court of law. Further, any information obtained as a result of the Garrity statement is deemed to be "tainted" and inadmissible. Any lawyer who saw the Garrity statement might be disqualified from participating in the investigation and prosecution because they might use the information flowing from it. A Garrity committee would first go over the officers' statements to ensure nothing the officers were compelled to give as part of their employment was seen by the prosecution.

This was great advice; only someone who had experience in police cases would be aware of how important this can be. Tom also arranged for me to speak with former U.S. Attorney General Eric Holder.

I knew Holder, and I appreciated the chance to speak with him. He advised me to call Neal Katyal, the former acting solicitor general in the Obama administration and a renowned appellate lawyer. Neal, born in Chicago to immigrant parents from India, has argued more cases in front of the U.S. Supreme Court than any attorney of color since the legendary Thurgood Marshall. I had seen him on television on numerous occasions—he's a regular legal commentator on MSNBC and has a huge following on Twitter. I was eager to speak with him. If I could convince him to help us, for free, which I did, I could engage that appellate counsel at the trial court level to prevent the creation of any appellate issues, as Barry Scheck had advised me.

On the complex medical front, I gave Jerry Blackwell a call to get some advice. I had known Jerry for years, but I didn't expect the call ending with Jerry agreeing to be a special assistant attorney general.

In the days ahead I discovered how important it would be to hear from diverse voices.

A fellow staffer who had never even worked on the case helped me understand this need. Carly Melin, the AGO's legislative director, was on the regular Zoom staff meeting call when she shared a new perspective: "He called for his mother."

I am embarrassed to admit that I had heard Floyd say everything in those videos, but his calls for his mother didn't really stick. I don't know how I managed to gloss over it. Carly helped me understand how significant it was for Floyd's final thoughts to be about his mother. Carly said, "As a mother, I just felt it when he called for her like that." We needed diverse perspectives like Carly's to draw out all the critical angles in the case.

The last call I made that evening was to an amazing lawyer named Lola Velazquez Aguilu, chair of the governor's judicial selection committee. Lola's day job was in the corporate counsel division at the pharmaceutical giant Medtronic, based in the Minneapolis suburbs. Lola and I had become friends over the years, and she had served on my transition committee after I was elected attorney general. We had talked at length about getting more judges of color on the bench in Minnesota. As the chair of the governor's judicial selection committee, Lola was in a perfect position to ensure that Minnesota judges were a highly qualified and diverse group.

I remember a specific case involving a Black female judicial candidate. I thought this candidate was receiving unfair criticism from some lawyers while her candidacy for a judgeship was under consideration. The rap was that she was too "stern" or "tough," which is usually a compliment for a man—but for a Black woman, suddenly it was a disqualifying blemish. I told Lola about my concerns; she asked the right questions and therefore got the right answers. Today, that former judicial candidate presides in Dakota County District Court with distinction. Her name is the Honorable Dannia Edwards.

Lola poured out a list of things that I needed to be doing—right away. Lola had been an assistant United States attorney for the district of Minnesota. Though she had never prosecuted a police officer, she knew how to prosecute criminal cases, and she had a very firm grasp of the complex medical issues at play, probably because of her work at Medtronic.

I asked her to consider advising our team. I had hopes that perhaps Lola could be one of our in-court trial lawyers because of her persuasive ability and her command of the medical issues. Also, Lola had a unique perspective. She was born of Puerto Rican parents in Madison, Wisconsin. Her father was a member of the Black Panthers, while her mother was a police officer who became the first woman detective in the Madison Police Department. Lola disclosed that her Afro-Latino brother had unpleasant encounters with police in the past. Also, like Carly, Lola mentioned the significance of Floyd calling for his mother, saying that "when George Floyd called for his mother, he engaged all moms."

I thought she could see the case from all sides and help us make a compelling presentation to a jury. When I asked her if she could join the team, she told me she would like to, but she would have to think about it. Medtronic would have to approve. Her family would also have to approve because she would certainly be taking time away from her two grade-school kids and her husband. Ultimately, she agreed to be appointed as a special assistant attorney general, and she played an indispensable role.

Friendly Critics

Before the night was over, I got one more call. An old friend, a mentor, called me weeks after my press conference and gave me a piece of her mind. She did not appreciate me saying positive things about Mike Freeman. She blamed him for police brutality. "If he would hold some of them cops accountable, they wouldn't always be killing us," she lectured.

She told me that he had failed to protect Black victims of police violence. This friend of mine was not a young person. She reminded me often that she had "been around," was proud to have been born a Southerner, and was now "north of seventy." She reminded me about how she grew up in the segregated South and how she had survived racist sheriffs and complicit district attorneys.

She thought of me as a good person, but maybe a little naive. She was "pretty sure" I was being used, and that Freeman and "the system" were exploiting my credibility in the community. She knew they planned to deliver the usual bad outcome.

I said, "Mike is the only one who actually convicted a police officer of murder." She shot back, as if she anticipated me making this point: "Sure. When a white woman gets killed by a Black Somali officer, they are always going to do something about that. Of course he was prosecuted. That's nothing but the system working as designed."

Sometimes you just had to disagree, I said.

I explained to her that the governor assigned this case to me and that I was in charge of everything, assuring her that the buck stopped with me and nowhere else. I told her Freeman would be an important partner. I realized there was a lot of public anger because of his statements several days before, when he said, "There is other evidence that does not support a criminal charge." I assured my friend that I would handle communication with the public and the press from now on. Finally, I informed her the case would be infinitely harder without his help.

Freeman had agreed to share the considerable financial load. Hennepin County paid for 50 percent of all costs in connection with the prosecution, and Freeman had assigned some of his best staff, including Josh Larson, Jean Burdorf, and especially victim-witness advocate Vernona Boswell, who is simply an awesome human being.

When the call came to its end, all I could say to my mentor friend was, "I need you to trust me."

She uttered skeptically, "Mmmm-hmmm."

Chapter 4

COURTS AND THE LAW

What is the difference between a federal district court judge
and God? God does not think he's a federal district court judge.
—Unknown

We were lucky to get Peter Cahill as the Hennepin County district court judge to preside over the Derek Chauvin trial. I had known Pete Cahill for years, but I didn't expect any favors: I knew better. I had met him when he was a criminal defense lawyer at Colich & Cahill. He was good at that and at being a prosecutor. That was before he became a judge.

As a criminal defense counsel, he gave clever arguments and had much success in the court. As a prosecutor, he took to the job quickly.

I remember representing a young fellow who was facing deportation because of a prior drug case. I was asking the court to resentence him to something less than 365 days, because that is what the immigration courts define as a felony, a deportable offense. It didn't matter that the kid had never spent a day in jail because the 365 days were all stayed; I just needed the judge to give the guy 360 days or 364 days to avoid removal proceedings. I knew it was a long shot, because my client had a few blemishes other than this felony.

Prosecutor Cahill opposed my motion, and we lost. As I said, I knew it was a long shot before I filed the motion, but I was somewhat hopeful because Pete had been a criminal defender. I thought he'd sympathize, give the guy a break. Nope. I was wrong, but he was not one to take personal umbrage that a lawyer would dare disagree with him.

I knew Judge Cahill wasn't about to grant any favors in the Floyd murder trials, either, but I knew he'd try to be fair and even-tempered— for the most part. I knew he would read the briefs, do his research, and then decide. We couldn't ask for more than that.

Judge Cahill had risen to be the chief deputy to former Hennepin County attorney and current U.S. senator Amy Klobuchar. I didn't talk to him much during those days, but I considered it a good sign that my friend and political ally Amy Klobuchar had faith in him.

Upon meeting Judge Cahill, the first thing anyone notices is his great smile. It's a smile that might make one think he is always an easygoing guy, slow to anger. They'd be wrong. Judge Cahill can go from zero to sixty in no time flat if you cross him, and you don't want to be the target of his wrath.

At a preliminary hearing on September 11, 2021, Judge Cahill disqualified four members of our prosecution team because they had had a meeting with the medical examiner to discuss Floyd's autopsy results. They were all from the Hennepin County attorney's office, including Mike Freeman. This meeting with the medical examiner happened before Governor Walz had appointed me to lead the prosecution.

Judge Cahill, in my view, misconstrued an ethical rule that discourages lawyers from interviewing witnesses. If a witness were to give testimony contrary to their original statement, the lawyer could be called to testify. This ethical rule is in place to avoid the need for lawyers to testify. There were several other people in the room who could have testified if the medical examiner said something different from his original statement. On the record, Judge Cahill called the decision for those Hennepin County lawyers to meet with the medical examiner "sloppy." It seemed like overkill to me.

Judge Cahill had the opportunity to reconsider. In a letter, Freeman and I pointed out that the lawyers had acted within Minnesota Supreme Court rules and that the medical examiner meeting was routine.

As a practical matter, Judge Cahill's disqualification order had no impact, but it was still a blow to our morale. Two of those attorneys, Amy Sweasy and Pat Lofton, had already bowed out of any role in the prosecution and the other two, Mike Freeman and Andy Lefevre, weren't going to make any court appearances anyway—though they were very helpful behind the scenes. I shrugged my shoulders and carried on, but I noted the signal: Don't mess with Cahill.

Under Minnesota law, each party is entitled to strike the first judge assigned without offering any reason, like a peremptory, no-cause-needed strike for jury selection. There was no way we were going to strike Cahill because, even if he made some rulings we didn't like, there were other judges who were a lot less experienced and less prepared for this sort of case.

If we filed to remove him, hoping for a judge more to our liking, then defense counsel would likely have exercised their right to remove, or "strike," that judge, leaving us with Lord knew what. The defense and state have the right to strike the first judge, not the second. Cahill was acceptable to both sides.

Prosecutors are one reason it's difficult to hold police officers accountable, but judges, both appellate and trial court, are another. They are the rule setters, the law interpreters, the gatekeepers, and the deciders. They are much more than mere referees.

Long ago, appellate judges gave police officers a wide degree of discretionary latitude regarding use-of-force decisions. Every day, trial court judges make critical decisions that determine the outcomes of cases, and it was no different for the Floyd case.

The social phenomenon of police brutality cannot be understood without having an understanding of the role that judges play. As much as anyone in the system, judges determine how society handles arbitrary force against civilians by agents of the state. By choosing when and how to dismiss cases, grant or deny motions, exclude evidence, admit evidence, and the manner and demeanor in which they conduct the rare jury trials, judges decide how much police brutality will be tolerated.

In a trial, the judge physically sits higher than anyone else in the courtroom, and everyone—including the jurors—must stand when the judge enters the courtroom. "All rise" and we all get up, signaling who the real VIP is.

When a judge loses patience with a lawyer or a witness, juries generally assume that the target of the court's wrath is in the wrong, and the judge is right—even if they have no idea why. Yet judges are people, no better or worse than any other group of people. No matter how much schooling a judge may have, they cannot escape the fact that they have emotions, prejudices, loyalties, and biases. Everyone knows to tread lightly around them because they have the power to facilitate justice or destroy a righteous case.

I have had the pleasure of knowing some great judges, like Pam Alexander, Kevin Burke, Michael J. Davis, James Rosenbaum, John Tunheim, Mark Kappelhoff, Lyonel Norris, and more. All of them are extraordinary people. Of course there are others who have somehow finagled themselves onto the bench due to cronyism, family connections, or political partisanship.

Judges, generally speaking, are not really neutral. Far more than the average juror, they reflect the sensibilities of people with power. They mirror what local elites deem important—not necessarily what is true or right or just, but what people in power want and expect.

Judges are lawyers, and they tend to be from families with enough economic and social power to get them into law school. Law school is not a cross section of America. It's an elite slice of America. I finished University of Minnesota Law School in 1990, and I found that it was the kind of place where kids use "summer" as a verb. A typical conversation went something like this:

"Are you summering in the Hamptons again?"

"No, we have a cabin on the North Shore. I'll be summering there."

Of course, more and more poor kids, working-class kids, kids of color, LGBTQ folks, and women are making it into America's law schools, but the profession is still very much an old-boys network. Judges are the oldest old boys in that network. Their choices and rulings are acceptable to the folks at the local chamber of commerce, or the local yacht, tennis, or golf clubs. Judging is not known to attract renegades, but rather it attracts conformists who want to perpetuate power in the hands of those who already have it. It's why the nonconformists, like Ruth Bader Ginsburg and Thurgood Marshall, and my own personal hero, Pam Alexander, stick out so much.

Judges have biases, and often they rule in favor of people they know and trust: the police. On many occasions, when police officer defendants have waived their right to a jury trial and allowed the judge to decide, they have demonstrated a stunning lack of objectivity.

For example, a police officer named Alan Buford was charged with misdemeanor negligent homicide for the death of eighteen-year-old Brandon Jones on March 19, 2015. Jones was unarmed when he was fatally shot. Cleveland Municipal Court judge Michael Sliwinski found Buford not guilty after a three-day trial that July. Buford was acquitted despite testimony from his partner, Gregory King, who said during trial that he thought the shooting was unnecessary.

Here's another example of what many deemed to be judicial bias in favor of the police: Cleveland officer Michael Brelo was found not guilty of voluntary manslaughter and felonious assault in connection with the deaths of Timothy Russell and Malissa Williams in 2012. Brelo had stood on the hood of a car and shot downward at close range through the windshield, killing the unarmed couple inside. This verdict was not by a jury, but by Cuyahoga County Judge John P. O'Donnell alone.

There's also the example of the Cook County, Illinois, judge who acquitted officers David March, Joseph Walsh, and Thomas Gaffney for falsifying police reports in connection with the 2014 shooting death of Laquan McDonald. If you recall, McDonald was shot sixteen times as he was walking away from Officer Jason Van Dyke. The officers were acquitted of conspiracy charges and official misconduct and obstruction of justice for falsifying details to cover up the shooting death.

The judge assignment in the Floyd case was critical to any hope of obtaining a conviction, and we knew it.

Cahill was not the only judge directing events in the cases concerning the death of George Floyd. Both state and federal trial judges were involved, as well as trial court and appellate court judges. Judges of the Minnesota Court of Appeals, the Minnesota Supreme Court, and federal district court judges Paul Magnuson and Patrick J. Schiltz all put their stamp on the Floyd cases.

Judge Schiltz, who was supervising the secret federal grand jury proceedings in 2020–21, ordered the FBI to investigate the Minnesota attorney general's office when newspapers published leaked information about the grand jury's work regarding Chauvin, Lane, Kueng, and Thao.

Of course, my office had nothing to do with the leak. We cooperated fully to prove our innocence, but nonetheless we had to endure an FBI investigation on a judge's orders.

A court reporter captured Judge Schiltz's words: "I think [there is] reason to believe a federal crime has been committed here, and it could have been committed by somebody working for the State." Judge Schiltz continued, "I'm concerned generally about the State leaking. I was really struck by how many different people were involved in the State side. This was really a very big Goliath versus a very small David case."

Nothing ever came of the judge's investigation, but a few things were made clear. He could make us jump on a whim. He suspected us of committing a federal crime (leaking grand jury testimony). He admitted this on the record. He ordered an FBI investigation against us with no evidence. He demanded that we supply affidavits swearing we didn't leak, which we provided. He expressed his disapproval with the state's Chauvin prosecution on the record in front of a court reporter. He considered the attorney general's office to be a "Goliath" and Chauvin, Thao, Kueng, and Lane to be "Davids." He never acknowledged that it was George Floyd who was the outnumbered, overmatched victim, who died under the knee of an armed government agent who had sworn to serve and protect him.

Meanwhile, in the February 2022 federal civil rights prosecution of Thao, Lane, and Kueng, Judge Magnuson made his objections to their prosecution very clear in his order denying a defense motion for judgment notwithstanding the verdict.

He wrote, "This is not to say that the Court countenances the Government's trial strategy in this case, which often seemed vindictive and overbearing. This Court has had the privilege of working in dozens of emerging democracies around the world to ensure that judicial independence is preserved as the fundamental building block of the rule of law. In many former totalitarian states, the rule of law suffers because of the disproportionate power of the prosecutor vis-a-vis the accused and the judiciary. The Court views the Government's conduct in this case—not the least of which was assigning no fewer than seven prosecutors to try the case—as frighteningly close to that line of overzealous prosecution."

Judge Magnuson did not mention the problem of armed agents of the state, targeting arbitrary force at members of national minority groups in the emerging democracies around the world. In fact, I have never heard of him objecting on moral grounds to anyone being prosecuted for killing someone else, except for the case in which four police officers literally squeezed the life out of an unarmed man.

The judges of the Minnesota Court of Appeals and Supreme Court also played critical roles in the George Floyd cases. None of them expressed their disapproval of prosecution of the officers who killed Floyd, but their decisions had a massive impact on the outcome of the case. Specifically, the state appellate courts' decision on how to handle the charge of third-degree murder, depraved indifference, had a huge impact on the outcome.

So, yeah, the power of the judge was apparent to us.

Orange Juice and Policing in America

How is it that incidents of police brutality occur, many involving unarmed people, yet it seems the officers are rarely held accountable? American police officers kill more people per capita than many other police forces around the world. U.S. police kill more people in days than other countries kill in years, and yet all we see are the headlines. People want to know why. What's the back story?

The answer lies in large part with the wide discretionary latitude that the U.S. Supreme Court granted police officers in a case titled *Graham v. Connor*. Long before any Minnesota judges put their stamp on the George Floyd case, another set of judges set the frame for a police officer's use of force for the entire country.

It all started over orange juice.

It was November 12, 1984, in the city of Charlotte, North Carolina. A Black man walked into a convenience store, Pilot's Service Station on West Boulevard, and exited quickly. The man got into the passenger seat of a waiting vehicle, which pulled away but was not speeding. A police officer, who was also Black, saw the man leave the scene in an apparent hurry, and he suspected that this was maybe a case of shoplifting or a robbery.

The officer didn't report hearing any store alarm, and he didn't receive any report over the radio of shoplifting or robbery. No clerk ran out after the man yelling for police help. The officer didn't report seeing the man carrying a weapon or items that appeared to be stolen. Neither of the men in the car appeared to be trying to hide their identity with masks. The officer just saw a guy leaving the store with another guy and driving away.

Following this, the officer, M. S. Connor, activated the lights and sirens, and the driver pulled over. Officer Connor approached the driver's side. The driver identified himself as William Berry, a friend of the man who exited the store and who was now sitting in the passenger seat.

Berry explained that the man was Dethorne Graham, a diabetic in the throes of an insulin reaction.

Graham had gone into the store to get a sugary drink, like orange juice, to counteract the insulin reaction, but he saw the checkout line was too long. So Graham put the OJ on the counter and left the store in search of another place to get something to drink.

The officer figured Berry and Graham were lying. So as Graham's health was deteriorating from his untreated insulin reaction, Connor demanded that Graham just sit and wait, at a time when every second counted. Connor asked his partner to question the shop clerk as to whether there was any evidence of theft while he called for backup.

When a diabetic's blood sugar is too low, a condition known as hypoglycemia, the person can exhibit symptoms like slurred speech, walking oddly, or seeming incoherence. Though Connor was a trained police academy graduate, none of this occurred to him, nor apparently to the United States Supreme Court.

Graham got out of the vehicle and ran around it twice. He sat on the curb and passed out. By this time, backup officers arrived and handcuffed him even though he was passed out.

When Graham revived and woke up, he was lying facedown on his stomach, on the sidewalk, hands cuffed behind his back, just like George Floyd. Police officers then picked him up by pulling his arms backward. Graham groaned in obvious pain, and he asked the officers to look in his wallet to find the diabetic decal card, which would have explained the situation. They ignored him.

One officer told him to "shut up" and then slammed his face into the hood of the squad car. Another officer said, "Ain't nothing wrong with that motherfucker but he's drunk." Meanwhile, a crowd had gathered around the scene, similar to the Floyd murder. One officer testified that it appeared things were getting out of hand.

Then officers threw Graham, headfirst, into the back of the squad. The officers handled Graham so roughly that they broke his foot, injured his shoulder, and caused him to suffer multiple cuts, bruises, and lacerations on his head, wrists, and other parts of his body.

A friend of Graham's, Ben Alderman, arrived with orange juice and tried to get it to Graham.

Graham explained at trial that he had asked the officer: "Please give me the orange juice." The officer's exact words: "I ain't giving you shit."

Finally, another officer had talked to the store clerk, who assured the officers that nothing was taken from the store. The officers drove Graham home, which was a few blocks away, and they dropped him off on his front lawn.

According to William Berry, "The officer took the handcuffs off of him, and Mr. Graham fell immediately to the floor—I mean to the ground. I had his left shoe in my hand, and then he went to put his shoe on, and he couldn't get it on because it was hurting."

X-rays showed fractures in Graham's foot in two places.

The officers didn't bother taking the cuffs off Graham until they dropped him off at home. Then they just drove away, without an apology or explanation.

Not that it matters, but Dethorne Graham was an upstanding citizen. He worked at the North Carolina Department of Transportation in maintenance as a patch foreman, leading crews fixing cracks and potholes on the highway. He was proud to serve North Carolinians by repairing potholes on their roads.

Graham was a churchgoer, a family man, and a college graduate. Of course, no one has to be a model citizen to receive basic civil rights and human decency.

Graham grew up on a tobacco farm in North Carolina, facing racism and discrimination. According to his son, Dethorne Graham Jr., his father was the first Black person admitted to Duke University, but his grandmother persuaded him not to enroll because she feared he would face racial discrimination, including violence. Instead, he went to Fayetteville State University, a historically Black college, located in the same city where George Floyd was born. Graham Jr. described his dad as a man of courage who would not accept abuse from anyone. According to his son, Graham would assert his rights in court.

Long before the horrible day with the Charlotte police department, Graham had sued his employer, Precision Spring, for racial discrimination. He won that case. Graham Jr. also described his father's challenges with diabetic seizures. He described how on occasion his father would stare blankly into space, bite his tongue, develop beads of sweat on his forehead, slur his speech, and be unsteady on his feet. The family knew that orange juice would help every time, and then they would do what they could to make him comfortable as he recovered. Of course, he was dependent on his insulin injections.

Graham knew what had happened to him that day wasn't right. He went to see a lawyer, a young fellow, only thirty-two years old at the time, named Woody Connette. Graham learned from Woody that the unfair treatment might have also been a violation of his civil rights. With Connette's help, Graham sued the five officers and the City of Charlotte under Section 1983 of the Civil Rights Act.

Unfortunately, the case hit a roadblock before the jury had a chance to weigh in, and that roadblock was known as "Maximum Bob," the Honorable Robert D. Potter, chief judge of the U.S. District Court for the Western Division of North Carolina. Judge Potter had been a distinguished lawyer before taking the bench. He was born in Wilmington, North Carolina, in 1923, received an undergraduate degree from Duke University in 1947, the height of Jim Crow segregation, and earned his law degree from Duke three years later. He practiced law in Charlotte for thirty years and served as a county commissioner in Mecklenburg. Potter was also a Jesse Helms staffer.

Helms is famous and infamous for many reasons, all leading back to his support for racism, racial segregation, and authoritarian governance. As a campaign strategist supporting U.S. Senate candidate Willis Smith against Frank Graham (no relation) in 1950, Helms published a campaign ad saying, "White people, wake up before it is too late. Do you want Negroes working beside you, your wife, and your daughters, in your mills and factories? Frank Graham favors mingling of the races."

The blatantly racist ad worked. Smith prevailed over Frank Graham in that 1950 senate race, but this type of stuff was typical of Helms, Potter's candidate. Helms led the opposition to the federal Martin Luther King Jr. holiday, supported South African apartheid, opposed civil rights bills, and waged his own racist senate campaign against Black senate candidate Harvey Gantt. Helms thought so highly of Robert Potter that he recommended Potter to President Ronald Reagan in 1981 for a federal judgeship.

Judge Potter was a firm defender of the status quo, tough on crime and a harsh sentencer—hence the nickname "Maximum Bob." Potter's benefactor, Senator Helms, said in 1981, "Crime rates and irresponsibility among Negroes are facts of life which must be faced."

Before he was a judge, Potter could be found demonstrating against school integration, or school busing, as he did in 1969. As a judge, Potter ordered the school system of Charlotte-Mecklenburg to end desegregation efforts through busing to remedy the damage of generations of Jim Crow schools.

When Judge Potter was assigned his case, Dethorne Graham had what lawyers call a "bad draw" for the vindication of his civil rights, but Potter wasn't Graham's only problem. It was the law itself. Judge Potter, despite his personal background, gave Graham his day in court. Witnesses showed up and gave their sincere testimony, including Graham himself. Nevertheless, before the case went to the jury, defendants moved for something called a directed verdict at the close of the plaintiff's evidence.

Basically, a directed verdict is when one side, in this case the defendants, say to the judge, "Judge, this case is so open and shut, it doesn't need to go to a jury. Even if you assume every single word of the plaintiff's case is true, I still win because the plaintiff has not stated facts that amount to a claim."

In legal talk, the court must consider the evidence in the light most favorable to the plaintiff, and if there is no genuine issue of material fact, then the judge decides the case based on the law. Judge Potter ruled in favor of the defendants. He applied the leading precedent in the area of police brutality cases, called *Johnson v. Glick*, which required that the plaintiff prove the excessive force was tied to malicious intent, which he concluded Graham had not done.

The *Glick* factors considered by Judge Potter included the following: whether or not there was a need for the application of force; the relationship between the need and the amount of force that was used; the extent of the injury inflicted; and, most important, whether the force was applied in good faith, or whether the force was applied maliciously and sadistically.

Based on the *Glick* factors, Judge Potter found that Graham's erratic behavior justified the use of force and that the amount exerted wasn't excessive. Potter concluded the force used was just handcuffing. Potter found that Graham had no injuries, despite the testimony about multiple injuries. Potter acknowledged Graham's broken foot but concluded that he failed to prove it was caused by the officers. (Graham's foot was fine before he encountered Officer Connor and company.) Finally, Potter determined that the force was applied in a good faith effort to maintain or restore order in the face of a potentially explosive crowd situation, not maliciously or sadistically.

Judge Potter then undermined the force against Graham, stating, "This Court does not deem every push or shove under the circumstances of this case to rise to the level of a violation of constitutional rights." And that was almost it.

Graham's lawyer, Woody Connette, filed an appeal to the Fourth Circuit Court of Appeals, and it rubber-stamped Judge Potter's order granting the motion for a directed verdict. At that moment, all seemed lost for Dethorne Graham. The police had denied him medical treatment, beat him up, broken his foot, caused other injuries, and refused to provide a simple drink of orange juice when his life could have been hanging in the balance. According to Judge Potter's application of the *Glick* factors, there was nothing that could be done about it.

It would have been over except that legendary lawyer H. Gerald (Jerry) Beaver stepped in. Beaver is not only a legend in his home state of North Carolina but is well known across the United States. He lectures and occasionally writes interesting articles about criminal defense issues and civil rights.

Beaver reached out to Woody Connette and offered to file a petition for review to the United States Supreme Court on Graham's behalf. Beaver had an interesting idea. What if police brutality cases were evaluated not based on good faith or bad faith, but on objective reasonableness under the Fourth Amendment to the United States Constitution? The Fourth Amendment protects citizens from unreasonable search and seizure.

Graham's problem, as Beaver saw it, was this *Glick* requirement to prove bad faith or that the officer had used force maliciously or sadistically. It was an impossibly high standard.

Unless the plaintiff could look inside an officer's mind, or unless the officer says, "Hey, I'm using this force just to inflict pain on you, I have no legitimate law enforcement purpose," then the officer escapes accountability. Under *Glick*, a claim of good faith, supported by any post-hoc rationale, would end the plaintiff's civil rights case. Potter ruled that the officers did not use excessive force.

Beaver favored the application of the Fourth Amendment, and he wanted to make his argument to the highest court in the land. He applied to the Supreme Court to hear the case, but he knew it was a long shot. Writs of certiorari to the Supreme Court are always challenging.

According to the U.S. Supreme Court website, the court receives approximately 10,000 petitions each year requesting a writ of certiorari. Only about 100 receive the writ (i.e., they get permission) and present oral arguments before the court. Graham's case was one of those 100 in 1989. The case came before the court for argument on February 21, 1989, with learned counsel Jerry Beaver representing Graham and Mark I. Levy representing the City of Charlotte and the officers.

It was a "hot bench," which means the justices were active during the oral argument and engaged in lively dialogue with the lawyers. Justices were pressing both sides with questions and hypotheticals. Much of the parley focused on whether the right standard was subjective intent of the officers, the requirement of proof of maliciousness or sadism by the officer, or the Fourth Amendment standard of objective reasonableness.

Justice Thurgood Marshall was in rare form. He asked Levy the simplest of questions, which Levy had a tough time answering.

Justice Marshall: "What reason was there for handcuffing a diabetic in a coma?"

Levy: "At the time, the officers didn't know that he was a diabetic in a coma."

Justice Marshall: "What was he doing that was so violent that he had to be handcuffed?"

Levy: "You have to go back one step even before that. Officer Connor saw Petitioner act in a very suspicious and unusual manner. He saw Connor hurrying from the convenience store."

Justice Marshall: "Violent?"

Levy: "It wasn't clear. He saw him hurry into a convenience store. He was hurrying out."

Justice Marshall: "Well, what did he do that was violent?"

Levy: "Petitioner's own witness said that Petitioner was throwing his hands around; that he was resisting putting the handcuffs on that Berry had asked for Officer Connor's help in catching—"

Justice Marshall: "But what was he doing? I'm talking about before they put the handcuffs on him. What was he doing before they tried to put the handcuffs on?"

Levy: "He was acting in a very bizarre manner…"

There was some more back-and-forth, and it was clear that Levy did not want to answer Justice Marshall directly.

Justice Marshall: "Was that threatening anybody? Did he strike anybody?"

Levy: "Well, the officers didn't have to wait until he was—"

Justice Marshall: "Did he strike anybody?"

Levy: "I don't believe the record indicates that he struck anybody."

Justice Marshall: "Did he threaten to strike anybody?"

Levy: "He was acting in an unpredictable and potentially dangerous manner."

Justice Marshall: "Can you answer? Did he threaten to strike anybody?"

Levy: "He did not overtly threaten to strike anyone."

Justice Marshall: "Did he have a weapon of any kind?"

Levy: "The record doesn't indicate, I don't believe so."

Justice Marshall: "The record didn't show he had a weapon of any kind?"

Levy: "That's correct."

Justice Marshall: "Well, why was he handcuffed?"

Levy couldn't come up with anything better than Graham was acting "suspiciously" or "bizarrely," neither of which is a crime. His behavior was not a justification for the use of coercive power of the state, without any recourse for the damage that coercion may have caused.

Justice Marshall was asking practical questions, and counsel for the respondents were giving answers that people who have an investment in the status quo come up with. Justice Marshall engaged the advocates in a simple but profound way. Marshall clearly brought a level of concern for the civil rights of regular people that Judge Potter just could never fathom.

Through his simple questions, Thurgood Marshall showed that it was just plain ridiculous and wrong for a police officer to handcuff a diabetic in a coma, who wasn't violent, had no weapon, and was clearly in need of help, not rough treatment and handcuffs.

Graham won (sort of). Beaver's position, that objective reasonableness under the Fourth Amendment was the proper constitutional standard, prevailed in a unanimous decision. The Court overruled *Johnson v. Glick*, and thereby overruled the near impossible standard of the plaintiff having to prove malicious intent tied to excessive force. Dethorne Graham had another bite at the apple, this time under a new, and hopefully fairer, standard of proof.

After he won at the U.S. Supreme Court, Dethorne Graham's case went to trial in Mecklenburg County under the new objective reasonableness standard, but the jury still decided in favor of the police.

The police officer's lawyer convinced the jury to focus on his client's perspective, per the language of the *Graham* opinion. Here's this guy acting weird, out of control, and they don't know why. Maybe he could have stolen something, and the stuff about the insulin reaction is just a story. Defendant's counsel persuaded the jury that it might have been reasonable for the officer to subdue this person. Graham lost, again.

According to his son, Graham didn't want to talk about it. He ended up suffering with substance abuse issues. His son speculated that he might have been trying to soothe the pain of being treated so unjustly without any redress. "I don't know if this was his way of trying to deal with dehumanization. It strikes at your core. Strikes at your very being," said Dethorne Graham Jr. in an interview on *Radio Lab*.

Dethorne Graham Sr. died at the age of fifty-four.

At the time, the ruling was considered a breakthrough. But was it? The U.S. Court invented the idea of a reasonable police officer, and police brutality cases would now be required to be evaluated from the perspective of a reasonable officer on the scene, not 20/20 hindsight.

The Supreme Court just made up this law, by the way. The *Graham* standard of "objective reasonableness" is loosely connected to the Fourth Amendment, but the Fourth Amendment doesn't say anything about the perspective of a reasonable officer on the scene, nor 20/20 hindsight. Despite Marshall's brilliance, *Graham v. Connor* has become something very different.

The *Graham* standard was applied and used to exonerate the officers who killed Mike Brown, Tamir Rice, Eric Garner, John Crawford, Freddy Centeno, Samuel DuBose, Jonathan Ferrell, Tycel Nelson, Lillian Weiss and Lloyd Smalley, Sal Saran Scott, Alton Sterling, James Crutcher, Keith Lamont Clark, Terrance Franklin, Freddie Gray, Jamar Clark, Philando Castile, and many more. In all these cases, the standard established in *Graham v. Connor* was the thing that prevented the victim from getting relief. Instead, it protected the police.

Graham v. Connor is enshrined in Minnesota law under statute section 609.066: "The use of deadly force by a peace officer in the line of duty is justified only if an objectively reasonable officer would believe, based on the totality of the circumstances known to the officer at the time and without the benefit of hindsight, that such force is necessary to protect the peace officer or another from death or great bodily harm." That's *Graham*.

The Minnesota statute refines the circumstances when force can be used a little more narrowly than *Graham*. Paraphrasing: Minnesota requires the threat to the officer to be specific, immediate, and urgent to justify use of deadly force. The Minnesota language is an attempt to address uses of deadly force when the only justification is along the lines of a vague statement like, "I was in fear of my life." This is also true for a type of situation where the suspect may have a weapon but he's across the street and not an immediate threat.

We were confident early on that we could prove the elements of second-degree unintentional murder including the following: Floyd ultimately died, the defendants intentionally inflicted substantial bodily injury on him causing his heart to stop due to "subdual, restraint, and neck compression," and that the act took place on May 25, 2020.

What worried me was whether Eric Nelson—Chauvin's defense counsel—could convince the jury that, while maybe Chauvin carried things too far in hindsight, it was reasonable for him to kneel on George Floyd in the moment.

It was, arguably, understandable from the perspective of a police officer because the events were escalating quickly, it was a gang area, he had seen knee restraints in training, Floyd was a large man, the drugs, excited delirium, and the crowd was unpredictable. Who on the jury could judge him? They weren't there. They don't know how hard policing can be.

I was well aware that *Graham v. Connor* would be the prevailing law to be applied in the murder of George Floyd. Could the state, represented by the Minnesota attorney general's office, prove beyond a reasonable doubt to each and every one of the twelve jurors that Chauvin, Thao, Kueng, and Lane acted in an objectively unreasonable way? We would see.

Chapter 5

ROLLING UP OUR SLEEVES

Earl Gray and the other defense counsel took their role as "zealous advocates" seriously. They seemed to be pursuing a two-pronged strategy: Season the jury pool with a drug-equals-thug narrative and prosecute the prosecution.

Throughout this entire trial, defense counsel would try to make his client's conduct look objectively reasonable. On CNN's *Prime Time*, Gray said, "If the public is there and they're so in an uproar about this, they didn't intercede either." Gray's comments were designed to make the behavior of his client seem reasonable.

The host, Chris Cuomo, didn't cooperate. He said to Gray, "The idea that the civilians should have rushed into a policing situation in the inner city of Minneapolis against four police officers that have weapons and are kneeling on the neck of a man—don't you think that's asking a little too much of civilians and a little too little of your client?" For the first time that I've known him, Earl Gray had no quick retort.

Meanwhile, other demonstrations and protests continued in the Twin Cities and around the country. By June 11, fourteen Minneapolis police officers signed an open letter publicly condemning the actions of Derek Chauvin and company. The letter not only condemned the killing of George Floyd but also embraced Chief Arradondo's decision to fire the four officers.

The letter began, "Dear Everyone—but especially Minneapolis citizens…" The letter went on to pledge constructive action to rebuild trust.

By this time, I had cut my public comments, but plenty of verbiage was out there on the most pressing issue of the day: police brutality.

On June 29, Judge Cahill held a preliminary hearing centered on public comments. This time Robert Paule, a lawyer I've known and admired for many years, started his public effort to prosecute the prosecution. Paule, lawyer for Tou Thao, took aim not only at me, but at President Donald Trump, Governor Tim Walz, and numerous Minneapolis officials, claiming that pretrial publicity was prejudicing the jury against his client.

I saw this as an attempt to set up a motion for a change of venue. The fact was, people all over the world were making public comments about the nine-minute-and-twenty-nine-second video in which George Floyd was murdered. Discussions about this situation were ubiquitous and unescapable no matter where anyone went. It was on every channel, top of the fold of every newspaper, and all over social media. I couldn't blame Paule for trying.

Paule even made unsubstantiated allegations against Ben Crump, the Floyd family's lawyer. He claimed that Crump's team had leaked information to the press that had been privately shared with them by my office. Of course, this was ridiculous, and I assumed it was simply part of Paule's strategy to prosecute the prosecutors. Ben Crump went on Erin Burnett's *OutFront* on CNN and flatly denied his claims.

———

By July, the dual defense strategy of prosecuting the prosecutors and portraying Floyd as a dangerous drug-addicted Black felon had shifted from the airwaves to the court filings. Gray filed motions to dismiss on July 8 and was squeezing Lane's conduct into the *Graham* factors of objective reasonableness. Contained within his motion to dismiss, Gray argued that Lane's "decision to restrain Floyd was *reasonable* because Floyd was 'uncooperative,' 'actively resisting,' and 'acting erratic.'" Gray also introduced another old excuse: *I was just doing my job.* Gray wrote that "Lane trusted Chauvin's judgment as a twenty-year veteran and waited for the ambulance to arrive. His trust was *reasonable* and not criminal."

We were well aware of these defense narratives, and we were making plans to destroy them. I saw Gray's verbosity as a prosecution gift, but I also saw some risks.

Talking in the press had multiple benefits for the defense. The defense might exert undue influence on the jury pool, and they could argue pretrial publicity tainted the fairness of the trial if their client was convicted. It was a little like the defendant who killed his parents and then argued for leniency as an orphan.

The chatter got so bad that Judge Cahill issued a gag order on July 9, 2020, banning public discussion of the facts of the Floyd cases by the legal teams. I was comfortable with this. We didn't want to allow any appealable issues to crop up. Plus, we weren't saying anything publicly about the facts. Our team was planning to say a lot at trial.

Judge Cahill also announced the dates we had been anxiously waiting for: September 11 for a preliminary hearing on defense motions to dismiss for a lack of probable cause, a state motion to join all four cases into one trial against all officers at the same time (motion for joinder), and other motions as well. And March 8, 2021, for the trial to begin.

Cahill set bail for Chauvin at $1.25 million or $1 million under certain conditions. Cahill set bail for Kueng, Thao, and Lane at $1 million each or $750,000 under certain conditions. All four bailed out eventually.

By this time, it was mid-July, and I already felt like we were running out of time. Nothing could be done fast enough for me, and I—with love and kindness—tried to subtly convey urgency in every single meeting with our prosecution team.

———

We had bodycam video, at least three witness videos, CATV footage from the city cams, video from a local restaurant, witnesses on the scene, medical experts, use-of-force experts, the medical examiner, and Minneapolis police officers. Oh yes, and a fake twenty-dollar bill. All this evidence, all these witnesses, and all this video footage had to be examined thoroughly.

We set up several subcommittees to manage the immense amount of work that had to be done.

I figured the best way to get these very smart and accomplished lawyers to work together cooperatively was to give them their own spheres of influence. We grouped ourselves into each of the following areas: administrative matters, narratives and themes, use of force and experts, fact witnesses, motions, notices, and legal research, technology and discovery, jury research, medical experts, and, finally, media. I led all weekly general meetings and was active on many subcommittee meetings throughout the week, being careful to never micromanage.

I showed up for meetings with critical experts like Dr. Jonathan Rich, a cardiologist; Seth Stoughton, a law professor specializing in use of force; and Dr. Andrew Baker, Hennepin County medical examiner.

For months leading up to the trial we did practice runs of arguments, openings, closings, and more. We drafted and redrafted direct examinations and cross-examinations. We drafted motions, memoranda of law, pretrial motions to ask that some things be found inadmissible, and more. We were grinding and getting ready for the trial, a beehive of activity. The sheer number of hours these gifted lawyers, paralegals, and investigators put in was staggering.

We organized agendas for each meeting. My assistant, Jillian Sully, was super helpful with this. When we got within two months of our March 8, 2021, trial date, we knew we had a potentially huge list of witnesses. We assigned two lawyers to each witness: one in-court lawyer to examine the witness, and the other a drafting lawyer, who scripted the examination of the witness. This way, we minimized mistakes by getting everyone involved and benefited from each other's brilliance. I was known around the staff for saying, "Teamwork makes the dream work."

Matt and I led the administrative subcommittee, and it addressed matters like scheduling court appearances, the COVID challenges, the courtroom logistics of in-person trials, updates from the judge, security, parking, and a dozen other details.

The narratives and themes subcommittee led by Jerry Blackwell would develop our authentic and true story about how and why Derek Chauvin and company were guilty of murdering George Floyd. Jerry has an uncanny grasp of how a story impacts human understanding. The only way to create an idea that persists in the minds of people, jurors in our case, was to tell a story. Jerry understood this on an intuitive level.

Jerry also knew how to conduct mock trials. He had a long-standing relationship with Litigation Insights, a consultative trial and expert services firm. Litigation Insights was eager to help us conduct mock trials and help with jury selection.

Jerry wanted to test some themes on potential jury pools from around the state, like St. Cloud in Stearns County, Duluth in St. Louis County, and Rochester in Olmsted County. At this point, we didn't know what was going to happen with the defense's motion for a change of venue. We needed to be ready for anything.

In the Rodney King case, Los Angeles judge Stanley Weisberg had ordered a change of venue to Simi Valley, in Ventura County, a predominantly white and conservative community. By doing so, he tilted the outcome of the case in the defendants' favor. The state court acquittal of the officers who brutalized King led to mass civil unrest, and many believe Weisberg's fateful decision to change the venue was the reason.

We were not going to let this happen to the Floyd family.

If we lost a change of venue motion, it could have changed everything, and this was exactly why I asked Neal Katyal to lead our motions, notices, and legal research subcommittee. Neal was the best person to lead the effort to defeat the defense motion for a change of venue, and any other motions. He was the former acting solicitor general of the United States, and he is among the best appellate lawyers in the United States.

Neal teaches criminal law at Georgetown Law School. He has argued forty-four cases in front of the U.S. Supreme Court, including opposing Donald Trump's Muslim ban executive order in 2018. Neal also brought with him an amazing team from his firm, Hogan Lovells.

I knew that Judge Peter Cahill was no Judge Stanley Weisberg, but I couldn't afford to leave anything to chance.

————

Jerry led the effort for medical experts, and his colleagues at Blackwell Burke, Corey Gordon and Mary Young, helped to indentify medical experts, prep them for testimony, and even drafts parts of Jerry's direct examinations. Assistant AGs Erin Eldridge and Matt Frank also played key roles here. They had to anticipate the defense's attack, find a medical witness to rebut it, and prepare that witness to testify.

Along the way, we were aided by Keystone Strategy, who helped us find the right experts, like our star witness, pulmonologist Dr. Martin Tobin. The medical subcommittee had to identify experts to address every crack of doubt the defense would try to create in our medical causation case. The medical subcommittee also needed to figure out how to manage the Hennepin County medical examiner's report, which was less than ideal, because it did not identify asphyxia as a cause of death.

Steve Schleicher oversaw the use-of-force subcommittee. Steve's assignment was at the very center of our case. Given the video and the on-scene witnesses, the defense's best shot was to throw up *Graham v. Connor* as a shield. They would try to convince the jury that maybe Chauvin and company were wrong to hold Floyd down so long in the prone position, but their actions were reasonable based on what they knew at the time. Defense counsel would hammer on Floyd's size, the drugs in his system, and the gathering crowd.

This use-of-force subcommittee would have to destroy that

argument. They would have to identify use-of-force experts who were well informed, had practical experience, and knew how to testify in front of a jury. Steve also had to be prepared to cross-examine the defense's experts and the defendants: Chauvin, Thao, Kueng, and Lane.

This was a tall order, but Steve was perfect for the job. He had to know *Graham v. Connor* inside and out. The defendants' team would test every angle to argue that their clients' conduct was objectively reasonable under the circumstances.

Steve had double duty because I asked him to lead our jury research effort. He got help from Merrie Jo Pitera and Christina Marinakis, who strategized, planned, read through and graded every questionnaire, and then rated every juror. Social media research was done on every juror, which turned out to be very helpful. The insights this team came up with helped us seat a jury that would prove to be the right one to hear our case.

––––––––––

The fact witnesses subcommittee, led by Josh Larson and Vernona Boswell, would handle our "Good Samaritans"—those people who had stopped and pleaded for the life of George Floyd. This subcommittee was charged with not only identifying all these people, but subpoenaing them, preparing them to testify, and securing their presence at trial. Several of these folks, like Charles McMillan, Darnella Frazier, Alyssa Funari, and Judeah Reynolds, were fragile. They had never chosen to have a public profile. They didn't volunteer for fame, death threats, or even admiration. Ultimately, the case was about people who had stopped to try to help another person.

The fact witnesses subcommittee also had to work with reluctant, demoralized, and annoyed MPD officers. These folks were feeling pretty beat up, too. Their Third Precinct had been burned to the ground. They had been subjected to widespread criticism, and they were not exactly thrilled to testify, especially against one of their own. For the most part, these officers were experienced with court, but that didn't mean they felt good about it. A number had already retired, and others said department morale was lower than they had ever experienced. It would take real work to secure some of them at trial.

Eric Miller, a tech whiz, led the effort on our technology and discovery subcommittee. We needed Eric to set up the right software program to organize and access all the discovery materials, which were voluminous. He trained us, held our hands, and troubleshooted for us. The management of exhibits at the trial, such as video, photo, and numerous documents, was also part of this committee; that was all handled by Brad Eltiste.

Finally, the media subcommittee was critical to our success. John Stiles led this subcommittee, with help from Keaon Dousti, the AG outreach director. Neal Katyal connected us with a wonderful group of communicators known as the Glover Park Group (GPG). They helped us monitor what the defense counsel were saying, and what social and mainstream media were saying. Our team simply would have been flying blind without this media awareness, and working with this group gave us a vision of what was out there, whether our narratives were working, how we were doing overall, and how the defense was doing.

We had our team. We were all feeling pretty energized. The fight was on.

———

By August, I could feel the September 11 hearing date drawing near. It was time for the state to answer the defendants' motions and submit them to the court.

Lane's counsel had put forth a motion to dismiss for lack of probable cause. We argued that each defendant absolutely had to face accountability. In our opinion, there was ample probable cause for Thomas Lane to stand trial as an accomplice to the murder of George Floyd because his actions fit the legal requirements for the charges against him.

Despite the fact that Lane had mentioned turning Floyd on his side, which was Earl Gray's argument, Lane still didn't do anything to help.

In fact, the suggestion to turn Floyd was evidence of conscious awareness: Lane knew Floyd was in a serious medical crisis as he, Chauvin, and Kueng pressed Floyd's body into the concrete in a prone position. By asking if Floyd should be turned on his side, Lane indicated he recognized the officers were inflicting harm and that Chauvin was violating police training and policies.

Lane continued to participate in this dangerous restraint even after Floyd complained the police were killing him.

We also debunked the "I'm just a rookie" defense. We argued that there was no free pass for rookies who chose to disregard their training. Nine-year-old Judeah Reynolds knew enough to call a stop to the attack on George Floyd. Thirty-seven-year-old police academy graduate Thomas Lane had extensive police training as a juvenile officer and a correctional officer before he had even started the job. There was simply no excuse.

The state filed its own motion for joinder. This would have combined all four trials into one. I really wanted Judge Cahill to grant this motion because I believed the city of Minneapolis, the state of Minnesota, and the world should only hold this trial for the state one time. I saw absolutely no point in trying this case four times—although I was committed to doing it if need be.

We argued to Judge Cahill that joinder was the right decision because all four were charged with the same counts and faced the same evidence. I was also concerned about the victim and witness impact. Why should the Floyd family and all the witnesses have to relive the sight of George Floyd dying over and over again on video? The whole bloody nine minutes and twenty-nine seconds was traumatizing. Why traumatize these people multiple times?

Finally, joinder made sense because the defendants committed the crime together. The best way to help the jury understand the crime would be to show it was a joint enterprise and that each of them played an important role in accomplishing the crime.

As the September 11 hearing date drew closer, some of the same old themes began to spike as well. On August 19, defendants filed for Floyd's records concerning his criminal background in Texas and in Minnesota. None of the officers knew anything about Floyd when they met him on May 25, but they wanted to justify their use of force on him as "reasonable" because of his record.

I saw it as a naked attempt to convince the public that Floyd deserved what he got because he had been in trouble before. I knew we would see a lot more of this. Trashing the victim is one of the reasons there is so little accountability when police officers commit acts of violence against Black victims. The defendants argued that Floyd's "persistent" use of illegal drugs left him in the position with police that caused his death.

The defendants' case was coming into focus: smearing the reputation of George Floyd, making jurors have contempt for him, and presenting the officers' conduct as reasonable, reasonable, reasonable under the circumstances.

This was about the time Jerry Blackwell began to counsel our team that we could not naively approach the case as if race were not a factor. Our little team could not escape the emotions that were driving the national conversation around race. In one meeting, I pointed out that defendants' lawyers were talking about race all the time but they just weren't saying it explicitly. They were using coded language in order to have plausible deniability about employing racism in their defense. Every time they brought up Floyd's criminal record, his physical size, drugs in the system, and the utter reasonableness of their extreme force, they were talking about race.

I noted that defense counsel were not racists; they were zealous advocates employing whatever means, perhaps immoral but not illegal means, to free their clients. We had to rebut the racist underlying assumption that they were trying to appeal to if we planned on winning the case.

How could we do that unless we came to some common understanding among ourselves? I knew we had to escape the cycle of blame and shame that so often marks conversations about race.

I'm generalizing, but many white people feel like they are being blamed. They often note they weren't even around when slavery, America's original racial sin, was being committed.

At the same time, America's racial sins are not a thing of the past for Black and other people of color. Many of them feel like these same white-led institutions are simply avoiding the issue. They want to address perceived and real slights, snubs, and injustices occurring in the present, which they feel are connected to centuries of injustice.

So often, the way Black people are feeling in moments like this has to do with something said, or done, or not done in the present that triggers feelings connected to history, generational trauma, and being discounted and undervalued.

In order for our group to function at a high level, we had to gel as a team, have frank conversations, and focus on winning. Nevertheless, coming together as a team is a process. It takes time and cultivation. We had a bigger mission, and we needed to keep that in mind, but we couldn't gloss over it. We had to talk, and we did.

Our meetings got a little more tense as we grappled with all kinds of things: who was doing what, the racial dynamics in the case, how to approach a given witness, and of course all the same stuff the country was grappling with, including COVID-19. We talked about all these things. I focused on the mission, the common purpose, and then I talked one-on-one with teammates.

In due time, everyone agreed that what happened to George Floyd would likely not happen to a white doctor or executive in a well-to-do suburb. We agreed, though many kept their individual views, that some combination of race and class and the officers' individual choices were the reasons why George Floyd was dead. Although Chauvin never used a racial insult and might not even have held conscious racial bias in his mind, the circumstances under which Chauvin and Floyd met on May 25 were highly racialized. Everybody knew it.

We needed empathy and understanding in our team. Quite frankly, by dealing with the issues head-on, we all bonded through the process. Everyone's social worker–psychologist skills really came in handy at this moment. Our team was dealing with the racial reckoning—just like the rest of the country.

Some team members were having difficult feelings about the brutality Floyd suffered. The emotional impact of Floyd's demise was not the same for each individual. For some, it was deeply personal and deeply emotional. Some imagined Floyd's tragedy as if it might one day happen to them, or one of their dearest loved ones.

Some team members, no matter what background, were noticeably crying on some of our one-on-one calls. One individual had reviewed a lot of video of Floyd getting killed. The emotion of having to watch these videos over and over inevitably took a toll. This person cried and then immediately apologized. "No apologies needed," I said. "You're not a robot. This stuff is tough."

Another person said working on the case was hard but also therapeutic for her. She told me working on the case made her feel less powerless because she was doing something affirmative, and that made her feel like she was taking back some control. I told several of our teammates that if they needed to step away, to let the emotional pain subside, they should feel free. No shame. No judgment. None of them took me up on that, but they knew they could.

As the September 11 hearing approached, I felt we were finally beginning to gel as a team. We had respect and empathy for one another, and that made for greater comfort and collaboration. I welcomed it all.

Chapter 6

THE PRELIMINARY
HEARING

The day of the big preliminary hearing arrived: September 11, 2020. It was nineteen years after America's worst terrorist attack, which took the lives of 2,977 people, injured more than 6,000, and traumatized a whole country.

The night before, we were working hard to make sure we had everything we needed and that we were ready to go. Neal Katyal had flown in from D.C. to make arguments directly to Judge Cahill. We were primarily concerned about making solid legal arguments, but other issues, like security and COVID-19 precautions, were on our minds as well.

Chief Judge Todd Barnette, who oversaw the administration of the trial, had decided that the Family Justice Center, about three blocks away from the Hennepin County Government Center, was a better place to hold the September 11 hearing. I hoped that someone would rethink this experiment.

We had tried to arrange with the Hennepin County sheriff's office to enter the courthouse through the back so we could avoid the gauntlet of protesters who would be assembling outside the Family Justice Center. The deputies were professional and accommodating, but they couldn't approve that request. Deputies had no prior experience with providing courthouse security in the middle of a pandemic.

So we would have to walk through a channel of fencing to the courthouse. I doubted anyone in charge had walked the route that lawyers had to walk that next morning. And, well, things were a bit chaotic.

Protesters and press began assembling early in the morning, well before the nine a.m. start time. They were in a pen of sorts, but quite visible and vocal. From what I could see, a ton of press was present, and there was an even bigger group of protesters. They were peaceful for the most part, but they were still outraged by what the officers had done to George Floyd.

Even the defendants and their attorneys had to walk the gauntlet. Defendants had it much worse than us, which I was sorry to see. They had to withstand all the jeers, taunts, and insults of the protesters, both coming in and going out of the courthouse. As they left the court building after the hearing, they were surrounded by angry protesters. Thank God no one was hurt.

In the course of the case, I know the attorney general's office got a lot of hate calls and hate mail, but the defense lawyers also got hate phone calls and messages, nearly all threatening. I felt for Eric Nelson, Derek Chauvin's lawyer, who reported that he received over 1,000 threats directed to him and his coworkers.

I was used to that kind of hostility. I had been receiving threatening phone calls and emails for years. When I became the first Muslim elected to the United States Congress in 2006, the hate poured out from diverse sources. Extremists, right-wingers, and even some claiming to represent Islam, like Al-Qaeda, hurled ugly threats in my direction. By the time I was assigned to the Floyd cases, I had a rhino hide for hate.

I wanted to hold the defendants accountable according to law, not see them or their lawyers mistreated, harassed, or insulted. The Sixth Amendment guarantees everyone the right to a lawyer. A criminal defense lawyer is a pillar of American democracy. You can't logically or constitutionally blame a lawyer for representing his or her client. Now, you can find fault with the manner in which a lawyer defends his or her client, but everyone—even Chauvin, Thao, Kueng, and Lane—has a right to a good defense.

I'm not saying some of these dog-whistle, racist arguments we were hearing about Floyd were okay. No, they were disgusting, but I am absolutely certain that criminal defense lawyers play an essential role in our democracy. If the government can accuse you of a crime and throw you away based on the law (without the assistance of someone who knows the law), then you just don't have democracy. It no longer matters if you have elections or not at that point.

The lawyers and clients all made it into the Family Justice Center. Chief Judge Barnette was hovering around, checking on logistics, security, and anything else. Judge Cahill was running the trial, but Barnette was running the show outside the courtroom with the heavy input of the sheriff's deputy.

The January 6, 2021, insurrection had not yet happened, but a summer of unrest had occurred, and I believe Judge Barnette was especially concerned about order and security at his court facility. He was also quite concerned about the spread of COVID-19.

Todd Barnette is an easygoing, hard-to-rile person, firm and resolute, but very calm. We used to play intramural basketball as law students. Todd was quick as a whip back then, and he could hit the jumper or drive to the basket. What we were dealing with now was no game.

I decided to be in the courtroom for this hearing along with Neal, Matt Frank, and Sundeep Iyer. Sundeep was a lawyer who worked with Neal Katyal, and he was a sharp researcher. I loved the scholarly aspect of practicing law, and he was good at it.

We set up the Floyd family in the Hennepin County attorney's office. Josh Larson and Vernona Boswell made things comfortable for the family, and much of the credit for that goes to Mike Freeman. For all the flack he took, he really went out of his way to help the effort.

The moment came for the hearing to start, and we all took our seats. The judge's door opened, and the bailiff barked out, "All rise." Everyone stood as Judge Cahill walked in. He situated himself in his seat and looked around. "You may be seated."

In addition to the four motions to dismiss for lack of probable cause, the defense had thirty-seven additional motions, and the state had fourteen motions. Some of the motions went to the core of the case while additional critical actions included the defense motion for change of venue, and state's motion for joinder for all four cases.

Other motions were simply housekeeping matters, referred to as motions *in limine*. It's common for judges to hold preliminary hearings to sort out issues before the case goes to a jury trial. This way when trial day arrives, we can just start picking a jury.

It was during this September 11 hearing that Judge Cahill disqualified four members of the Hennepin County attorney's office, including Mike Freeman (the Hennepin County attorney himself). I thought Judge Cahill was wrong, but the decision didn't matter much.

Judge Cahill told us that he had read all the material connected to the defense motion to dismiss for lack of probable cause. He asked us to focus on new or essential arguments, and not restate everything contained in our briefs. He would try to respond to the defense motions to dismiss before October 15.

The ruling on the motions put forth could determine the outcome of a case. If Judge Cahill granted these defense motions, then he would be saying that even if the state's allegations were true, the law doesn't prohibit the alleged conduct.

I wasn't worried about any of the motions succeeding, except one. The third-degree murder charge was always on shaky ground. Usually, third-degree murder is reserved for drug traffickers who kill their customers through drug overdoses. Obviously, these dealers aren't intentionally killing their buyers because their buyers are putting money in their pockets. They're putting this poison into the stream of illegal commerce without any regard to who dies as a result of using their inherently dangerous product. They're not singling out a particular victim.

In *State v. Chauvin, et al.,* the defendants did, in fact, single out George Floyd. When I took over the case, I certainly believed third-degree murder fit the crime because Chauvin's actions were "eminently dangerous to others and evincing a depraved mind, without regard for human life," but I was aware of the controversy. In fact, we added a count of second-degree murder, in part for insurance purposes.

Judge Cahill heard arguments from all parties on the issue of joinder of the defendants. Neal made solid legal arguments. He was logical and eloquent.

Technically speaking, the law regarding joinder is different under Minnesota state law than under federal law. The federal law favors joinder because it's more efficient. Defendants who commit crimes together are presumed joined.

However, the state doesn't favor joinder or severance of parties. When two or more people commit a crime together, the judge asks several questions. Would it be fair to make these defendants stand trial together? What's the risk of guilt by association? What's the risk that the defendants might blame one another?

Courts want to avoid a situation where a defendant is facing two prosecutors: the prosecutor and the co-defendant. If the defendants' defenses are actually helping the state prosecute each of them, then it can be argued that it deprives each defendant of a fair trial. If the defendants did the crime together, then the court looks for inconsistent defenses. In other words, are they basically pointing the finger at each other?

For the state, Neal argued that the charges and evidence against all four defendants were similar. He pointed out that the eyewitnesses and Floyd family members were likely to be traumatized by multiple trials. Most important, Neal pointed out that any defendant who goes to trial second, third, or fourth, is going to face a jury who almost certainly has heard that the others were found guilty, which will make it very tough to impanel an impartial jury. One big trial was the best way to go. Neal also pointed out that the defendants didn't appear to have inconsistent defenses.

They all blamed Floyd for his own death. In court filings, Earl Gray, Lane's lawyer, wrote that Floyd's arrest was the latest chapter in his "ongoing cycle of chemical dysfunction, violence, theft," and that "he was an addict, a distributor of drugs, and evident danger to the community." Attorney Eric Nelson, Chauvin's lawyer, wrote that Floyd had "been addicted to opiates for years." Robert Paule, Tou Thao's attorney, called Floyd's death a tragedy. "However, a tragedy is not a crime," he said. Blaming the victim is a common defense strategy; it's used to show officers acted reasonably.

The defendants' lawyers, of course, wanted it both ways. As they were arguing Floyd contributed to his own death, they also threw dirt in Chauvin's direction in order to help defeat the state's joinder motion. Judge Cahill took the matter under advisement.

The state stated for the record it had served notice on the defendants' lawyers and that it would be seeking a sentence above the recommended range in the Minnesota Sentencing Guidelines, known in legal lingo as an "upward departure."

In 2004, the U.S. Supreme Court decided that a judge couldn't just give a convicted defendant more prison time on the judge's whim. Under the right to a jury trial, as mentioned in the Sixth Amendment in the U.S. Constitution, the Supreme Court found in *Blakely v. Washington* that trial court judges, like Judge Cahill, are prohibited from increasing criminal sentences unless a jury decides, based on the facts in the case, that the punishment was justified because the defendant had acted with exceptional cruelty.

The reason for the upward departure must be given in advance. Then, the facts have to be proven beyond a reasonable doubt to a jury, unless the defendant either admits it or agrees to waive a jury trial and let the judge decide.

Matt Frank spoke up for our side and pointed out to Judge Cahill that Minnesota courts have long recognized "particular cruelty" as a basis for upward departure. He noted that Floyd was particularly vulnerable because the defendants knew or should have known that Floyd's arms were handcuffed behind his back, he was in a prone position, and his body positioning was associated with mechanical asphyxia. Matt noted the officers were in a position of authority and abused that authority. All four were in full uniform and in a position to dominate and control him. Yet they used that authority to commit a crime against him. Holding Floyd down, refusing to render him any aid, and ignoring his pleas for help are all signs of being particularly cruel.

One factor would be controversial with Judge Cahill: our allegation that the defendants committed their crime in front of children. Judeah Reynolds was only nine years old when the crime occurred, and Darnella, Melissa, and Alyssa were minors as well, at seventeen. We thought this factor was well supported by the facts.

Judge Cahill had another point of view. He would not determine whether these factors applied at the September 11, 2020, hearing. These factors needed to be noted for the record.

One strange motion was for an "order compelling the prosecuting attorney to provide defense counsel with the substance of conversations between him and any and all persons in the attorney general or Hennepin County attorney's office having information on the case." No lawyer, including the prosecutor, is required to disclose work product, which includes opinions, theories, or conclusions of that prosecutor, staff, investigative staff, or others working for the prosecution. Judge Cahill denied this ridiculous request.

Some motions were more substantive. For example, the defense wanted to preclude Donald Williams, the eyewitness who is a mixed martial arts fighter, from offering opinions about mixed martial arts, boxing, and training. We objected to this because his training was part of the reason he stopped and objected to what the officers were doing to Floyd. His training and experience gave him insight into the dangerous position Floyd was in with Chauvin kneeling on his neck, Kueng pushing down on his back into the pavement, and Lane holding his legs.

Cahill allowed Williams to testify freely; I saw that as a victory for the state.

———

We moved for an order prohibiting the defense from introducing into evidence a series of slides entitled "excited delirium syndrome." Excited delirium is a highly controversial explanation for why a high number of Black men die in police custody. Some leading medical officials deny the existence of excited delirium, and others believe it exists. It didn't apply to George Floyd, who was not particularly excited or delirious.

Delirium is a legitimate medical term, referring to "an acute change in attention, awareness, and cognition caused by an underlying medical condition, substance, or exposure to a toxin or withdrawal from one," according to the *Diagnostic and Statistical Manual of Mental Disorders* (DSM). Delirium is not associated with sudden death. Excited delirium, however, is not listed in the DSM.

We wanted to preemptively stop the claim of excited delirium as a cause of death. We knew they couldn't prove it, but we were worried about any doubt the defense might want to raise regarding how George Floyd died. We argued to Judge Cahill that we would need a full-blown hearing on the legitimacy of excited delirium if they wanted to bring that up as a cause of death, outside the hearing of the jury. Judge Cahill granted that one, too.

We talked about the introduction of *Spreigl* evidence. *State v. Spreigl* is a 1965 case stating that usually the prosecutor can't bring evidence of other crimes or bad acts to prove the defendant has bad character and therefore likely committed the current offense. However, such evidence is admissible to prove things like motive, opportunity, intent, preparation, plan, knowledge, identity, or absence of mistake or accident.

For example, on July 22, 2020, Chauvin and his wife, Kelly, were charged with falsely claiming Florida residency to avoid paying Minnesota taxes, resulting in six charges for filing false or fraudulent returns and three counts of failing to file tax returns. The defense asked the court to prohibit the state from introducing evidence regarding the defendant's tax-related crimes.

Cahill ruled that the state could not introduce this evidence, but if Chauvin claimed he would not lie or that he has a reputation for honesty, then the court might allow the state to introduce evidence to rebut a claim of honesty with the tax cheating.

Chauvin also had received more than eighteen complaints of excessive force, including the one where he kneeled on the neck of fourteen-year-old John Pope for seventeen minutes. Thao had four prior complaints, including an excessive use lawsuit settled favorably for the plaintiff. These matters would be evaluated closer to trial. Internally, we weren't sure we wanted to use these matters in trial, but we wanted to preserve our ability to do so. We knew that the defendants were going to try to muddy George Floyd's reputation. However, neither one of these officers had pristine records themselves.

The defense asked Judge Cahill to consider two prior incidents for Floyd. One motion was for an order allowing them to introduce information regarding George Floyd's May 2019 arrest and hospitalization. Cahill properly stated that no statements indicating that the arresting police officer suspected George Floyd of dealing narcotics would be permitted. However, Cahill said the paramedic from the May 2019 incident could testify that he was called to the scene, treated Floyd, and Floyd had made statements for the purpose of medical diagnosis that he had ingested drugs.

Cahill also denied defense requests to introduce evidence about Floyd's involvement in a 2007 armed robbery in Texas. It was irrelevant, a smear. Good decision.

One very important motion the state brought was regarding Baltimore medical examiner David Fowler. The defense had identified him as a potential expert, and we were concerned. We asked Judge Cahill to prohibit Fowler from testifying regarding the opinions of any other nontestifying expert he consulted in preparing the report of the forensic panel or testifying that other experts agreed with his opinion, analysis, or conclusion.

The defense took a very unorthodox approach to expert testimony. They gathered a bunch of forensic professionals, had a general conversation, and issued a single report. Dr. Fowler did write his own report but relied on findings in the other report to reach his conclusions.

Cahill agreed that Fowler's testimony would be limited to opinions that can reasonably be developed pursuant to his own training and his own experience as a forensic pathologist.

Dr. Fowler became the subject of extensive conversation in our planning meetings. We needed to devastate his testimony. Jerry Blackwell was assigned the task.

A disappointing ruling from Cahill was regarding Dr. Sarah Vinson, an African American psychiatrist. She's an expert in trauma and anxiety. She evaluated Floyd's behavior in the videos from the moment he appeared in Cup Foods until he was carried away by paramedics.

She concluded that Floyd's behaviors were consistent with a person who has suffered trauma, stress, and anxiety. The defense argued that Floyd was simply resisting arrest, which justified the officers' use of force. We thought it would be helpful to the jury to understand why Floyd might be reluctant to get into squad 320.

Judge Cahill ruled that the state would not be able to present testimony from Dr. Vinson because she had never evaluated Floyd directly, and that made her potential testimony speculative. We fought to include Dr. Vinson's testimony until the end, but Cahill was not having it.

The decision on the all-important issue of change of venue was deferred until closer to trial. Judge Cahill concluded that he had an incomplete record. He decided that the court would issue a jury questionnaire to all the potential jurors and make a determination about the motion for a change of venue based on their responses.

This meant that before the trial in March, Judge Cahill would revisit the issue after taking arguments from both sides. I viewed this as a win. I was absolutely against the change of venue. It very well might have determined the outcome of the case. Thao's attorney, Robert Paule, said he was concerned Minneapolis residents would fear the impact their verdict would have on themselves and their communities, considering the recent "lawlessness." The judge countered that there wasn't a county or state in the country that hadn't heard about Floyd's killing.

Judge Cahill ruled that the jury would be partially sequestered. During the presentation of the evidence, they would be allowed to go back to their homes, but once deliberations started, they would have to stay overnight until they reached a verdict.

After the hearing, we let out a collective breath. A tense and unpredictable moment had come and gone more or less okay. I didn't think Judge Cahill handled the Hennepin County attorney issue properly, but otherwise he was turning out to be a reasonable and fair decision-maker. We sensed that Cahill wasn't going to let the defense smear George Floyd, and that it was possible he would not move the trial to another county. It made us feel like we really had a shot at this.

We went back to the Hennepin County Government Center to talk with the Floyd family. George's brother Philonise and his wife, George's sister Bridgett and nephew Brandon, and other family members were all patiently waiting for the trial team to come into the room. The family members were dressed like they were going to church because they understood how important this was. They appeared to be still grieving, and they didn't have a ton of questions.

I asked the family members to gather around and then explained what the pretrial hearing was all about. I told them the date the judge was scheduled to issue his order and answer all motions. They silently nodded their heads. Matt Frank, a true victims' advocate, added a few critical remarks and then shook hands with Philonise and other family members. Vernona Boswell was instrumental in providing emotional support for the family as they experienced this whole ordeal. I'm sure it couldn't have been easy for any of them.

We said our goodbyes, but every one of us knew the trial team and Floyd family would be spending much more time together.

———

About six weeks after the September 11 hearing, Judge Cahill issued an order memorializing his rulings, but one substantial event took place before that: Chauvin was bailed out.

Protesters, commentators, and politicians the world over condemned Chauvin, but he certainly had a cadre of people who supported him beyond his family. Apparently, some of them had substantial means.

On October 7, Chauvin was released from jail after posting bond, or rather 10 percent of the $1 million bail with conditions. The 10 percent of the bail amount, in this case $100,000, was paid to the bond company as their fee. Since Chauvin had posted bond, the bond company would be required to pay the bond amount if he failed to appear.

It is not clear how Chauvin obtained $100,000 to pay the bond company, but it is plausible to infer Chauvin did not pay this amount out of his own pocket. If he had $100,000 to pay a bond company, he likely would have done so much earlier.

Chauvin was one of the fortunate few. A very small number of people can afford to give $100,000 to a bail bondsman. According to a 2016 report by Harvard Law School, about 34 percent of Americans charged with crimes can't bail or bond out before trial simply because they don't have the money.

The Minnesota Freedom Fund is a bail reform organization that helps people who can't afford bail to get out. The organization also works on reforming the bail system. They "believe that wealth should never determine who is kept in jail. That's what the money bail system does. It puts a price on freedom that only a few can afford, and many cannot. This system is unjust." The Minnesota Freedom Fund experienced a deluge of money as people looked for ways to fund reform of the system in the wake of George Floyd's death. The organization is working to get rid of cash bail statewide.

––––––––––

When Judge Cahill finally issued an order memorializing his rulings, there was one big surprise to the prosecution team. Judge Cahill found no probable cause for the third-degree murder charge.

We had a decision to make about whether we would appeal or not. I thought we should take it to the Minnesota Court of Appeals. Neal and his team started working.

By November 5, 2020, the judge issued more rulings. Overall, I was happy with them. Cahill granted our motion for joinder, meaning that the defendants Chauvin, Lane, Kueng, and Thao would be tried together in the March 8, 2021, trial. Judge Cahill wrote, "While testifying at multiple trials is likely to be traumatic for many witnesses, this is especially true for Ms. Frazier and any other minors who were witnesses standing on the sidewalk mere feet from where Chauvin, Kueng, and Lane restrained Floyd face-down on Chicago Avenue."

It was a good ruling; we would see if he stuck to it. Judges do have the power to change their minds.

Judge Cahill also vacated his September 11 order kicking Mike Freeman and three staff members off the case. While they still would not be allowed to appear in court or sign court papers, they were permitted to assist in any other way with the prosecution.

Judge Cahill denied the defense attorneys' motion for changes of venue. This was huge. I would mark it as one of the most consequential decisions of the entire case. Often, we don't calculate the effect of what didn't happen. Avoiding a change of venue was crucial.

Cahill wrote, "No corner of the state of Minnesota has been shielded from pretrial publicity regarding the death of George Floyd. Because of that pervasive media coverage, a change of venue is unlikely to cure the taint of potential prejudicial pretrial publicity." I agreed completely. Social media had made the Floyd matter ubiquitous.

We were not exactly out of the woods. Cahill signaled that he might revisit the issue if circumstances warranted it.

What might those circumstances be?

If Judge Cahill could not identify an adequate number of jurors from Hennepin County who could take everything they'd seen and heard about the Floyd case, set those things aside, and then render a fair and impartial verdict of guilty or not guilty, then Cahill might move the case. I was confident that Hennepin County had more than an adequate number of people who could deliver a fair and impartial verdict. I believed in my neighbors.

———

One barometer of whether we could find a fair and impartial jury would be how the members of the jury pool, about 260 randomly selected people, might respond to the questions contained in the jury questionnaires that Judge Cahill would be sending out in advance of the March 8, 2021, trial.

The jury questionnaire is an important tool for building a fair and impartial jury. The survey contains questions designed to help the judge and lawyer learn about the jurors' knowledge of the case, media habits, and police contacts.

The questionnaire in *State v. Chauvin* was fourteen pages long. An example of a question is this: "Have you ever watched a video of George Floyd's death on the news or the Internet? If yes, how many times?" The questionnaire asked the juror whether they or someone close to them had participated in demonstrations or marches against police brutality, and/or whether they knew someone who had been injured or suffered property damage during the protests. The follow-up question on that topic: "Do you believe your community has been negatively or positively affected by any of the protests that have taken place in the Twin Cities area since George Floyd's death?"

Jury questionnaires are a great tool. For one thing, a juror will say more in a questionnaire than during the public court questioning jurors go through. Jurors get asked personal and potentially embarrassing things. When a juror is filling out a questionnaire at home or in the jurors' lounge, they might reveal more. Jurors are more likely to divulge their sincerely held beliefs, rather than share the "right" answers that we all know we are supposed to give. Jury questionnaires help jurors avoid having to censor their responses because of social acceptability, pressure from the judge to "be fair," and a desire to keep out of the spotlight.

A questionnaire can give early information about who is going to be a potential for-cause challenge. At trial we were able to work with defense counsel Eric Nelson to strike an agreed-upon list of jurors who were not right for this jury due to cause/hardship challenges. This process allows both parties, the state and the defense, to avoid wasting time questioning these potential jurors. Certainly, a good questionnaire is one that gives you valuable information about who is likely to be favorable or problematic for your case.

Cahill accepted input from both sides and then mailed out the questionnaire. It was one of the helpful steps Judge Cahill took to assure the defendants' Sixth Amendment right to an impartial jury.

In addition, Cahill decided to keep the names of jurors confidential. He decided to sequester jurors during deliberations and have them escorted by the sheriff's deputy in and out of the courthouse as a group.

In November 2020, Judge Cahill decided to allow cameras in the courtroom. I disagreed at the time. I was worried that it would be harder to get witnesses to show up if they knew they were about to become celebrities.

Judge Cahill, however, thought a televised trial would ensure the defendants' right to a public trial, and it would ensure the public's right to witness the trial. This decision was also made in deference to COVID-19, which was continuing to sicken and kill Minnesotans.

The judge allayed my concerns about how witnesses would be treated. He accommodated the vulnerable witnesses, which was the most important thing. Everyone who was a minor on the day George Floyd died would not appear on the court cameras. Only their voices would be heard.

It was Ben Crump who helped me see that televising the trial was the best outcome. He said, "Yeah, man, let the world see it, and everybody is going to be a witness if something unfair happens..."

I was reluctant, but I came around. Cameras in the courtroom bring transparency and accountability, and it turned out that fears about showboating lawyers and reluctant witnesses was somewhat overblown. Televising the trial was one of Cahill's best decisions.

Chapter 7

THE MOCK TRIAL

Winter was beginning to settle into the Twin Cities, and the holiday season was just weeks away, but there was little reprieve for our prosecution team. Our subcommittee structure was humming, and the agendas of our regular meetings were full. We had a mock trial to get ready for.

During a meeting, one of our career prosecutors said, "Criminal juries tend to be different from civil juries because—"

Jerry Blackwell interrupted, "There's no such thing as a civil jury or a criminal jury. There are just people—people who are called to jury service, as all of us are at one time or another. These people are just regular folks—like anybody. They have thoughts, dreams, fears, and if we can figure out how their feelings are going to interact with the facts in this case, then we can put forth a winning case."

Jerry continued, "Figuring out what people consider persuasive or ineffective is something we can learn through a mock trial. I do them all the time and wouldn't go to a real trial without doing one."

It sounded good to me, but I wanted to know how much this was going to cost us.

Merrie Jo Pitera of Litigation Insights said, "You've got to pay the mock juror stipends, and the rest we will do pro bono. We believe in the case. Plus, Jerry has built a lot of credit with us."

"Great. Let's go," I said. The case was too important to just roll the dice.

Jerry Blackwell and Steve Schleicher were well acquainted with using mocks to figure out the best way to present a case to a jury, and these guys were recommending it.

A mock trial was an opportunity to see what jurors found persuasive, which would give our trial lawyers real data provided by real people.

The folks at Litigation Insights were experts at developing themes that would work and discovering the ones to avoid. Jerry liked to say, "The trial theme is the hook on which the jury will hang its verdict." According to Jonathan Purver, author of *The Trial Lawyer's Book: Preparing and Winning Cases*, "the theme is the 'storyline' of the case."

We were going to take these themes and weave them into the opening statement, into every motion, into every question to a potential juror, every direct examination of a witness, every cross-examination, and of course, closing arguments. We would be pounding themes all trial long in subtle and overt ways.

Themes have to be repeated. For example, no matter what you think about Donald Trump, he communicates effectively because he employs themes. He's not eloquent, he's not sophisticated, and he's anything but poetic. Nevertheless, he is extremely thematic: "Build a wall"; "Mexico is going to pay for it"; "no collusion"; "witch hunt." Trump's followers understand him because he speaks to their visceral fears and anxieties. He goes straight for the amygdala—the center in the brain that detects threats. He says it simply and he says it a lot.

I think that nearly everything Trump says is BS, but no serious student of communication would dismiss him. Trump didn't invent this method of persuasion, but he uses it effectively. Democrats should try it.

Our team would not go straight for the amygdala. In fact, we would try to appeal to higher faculties. We knew the defense would be working fear-based themes all over the place. Our mock exercises helped us combat what we knew was coming.

A mock trial is conducted like a real trial. Mocks are an abbreviated form of an actual trial, with opening statements, testimony, presentation of documentary evidence, closing arguments, and jury deliberations. The idea is to give the mock jurors a real experience. I assigned different lawyers various roles in the mock trial, and the mock jurors rated all of them in terms of persuasiveness.

Litigation Insights recommended that we recruit three separate groups of people to hear the second-degree murder and manslaughter charges. We drew groups from different parts of the state, including Hennepin and Stearns counties, because we knew Judge Cahill might change his mind on the issue of venue.

We needed to prepare for a Stearns County jury. Stearns County is a beautiful part of Minnesota, a kind of natural wonder. It has institutions of higher learning, many small farms, businesses, and cities. It's also blood-red politically. The defendants in the Floyd cases would likely have many sympathetic ears in Stearns County. So we drew a contingent for our mock trial from Stearns to see how they reacted to some of the facts in our case, as well as themes we were developing.

I chose not to be visible at the mock trial. As an elected public official, there was a chance that I might be recognized. We didn't want a mock juror's views about me to influence how they viewed the evidence presented to them.

Jerry, Steve, Erin Eldridge, and Matt were our presenters. They each took a witness, an opening statement, a closing. We asked Steve to play defense counsel, and to not hold back. He didn't.

We tried several themes: "In your custody is in your care"; "Chauvin put his pride over policing"; and "You can believe your eyes."

"In your custody is in your care" is the idea that even if Floyd was high on drugs, or had comorbidities like heart disease, hypertension, and sickle cell trait, Chauvin had a duty to care for Floyd's medical needs. He couldn't pass Floyd's death off on something else.

We tested this theme at the mock, and it worked. We planned to argue to the jury that "in your custody is in your care" is a fundamental lesson taught to all MPD. It means officers are meant to keep someone safe. It's not just a moral responsibility; it's what the law requires under the United States Constitution.

The theme of "pride over policing" was an explanation of Chauvin's behavior. We couldn't figure out exactly why Chauvin and company didn't just get up. We had several sessions about "Why?" We knew that jurors might naturally want some explanation for Chauvin's decision to stay on top of George Floyd, especially in light of the alleged murder being unintentional.

Chauvin's facial expression and body language had signaled something. He was facing down that crowd, even though people assembled were pointing cameras at him, recording him, and telling him to stop. We concluded that he was operating out of arrogance. No one was going to tell him what to do or challenge his authority.

So we decided to test the narrative that Chauvin "chose pride over policing."

Finally, "believe your eyes" was one of our themes. Our argument to the jury here was this: Don't allow the defense to try to talk you out of what you see on the nine-minute video.

———————

We expected the defense counsel to have their own themes, too, and based on data our media team was picking up, the defense themes were likely to be: "Blame the army, not the soldier," "Big scary (Black) man," "Hostile crowd," "Something else (not the knee on the neck) caused Floyd's death," and "Lawful but awful." We knew we had our work cut out for us.

We tested these ideas. While the trial was not explicitly about race, we expected the defense to use all these themes and allow the assumed prejudices of the jury to do the rest. The unspoken subtext was "Look how big this Black man is. Drug-crazed. Dangerous. Of course Chauvin had to use force on him." So, while the trial wasn't about race, the whole subtext of the defense was that extraordinary force against a person like Floyd was understandable and justified.

The theme we were nervous about was "Blame the army, not the soldier." The idea here was that the Minneapolis Police Department implicitly condoned everything Chauvin did. Not only that, but they trained him to do it. Now, the argument would go, that same department was hanging him out to dry when things went bad. This was a powerful theme. It cast Chauvin as a sympathetic person who was "just following orders."

This "don't blame the soldier" theme was a variation on "lawful but awful." What soldiers do isn't pretty, but it's what they are trained to do. If you don't like it, blame the army brass, the chief, not the soldier. Of course, this theme would fit into "the force isn't pretty, but under *Graham*, it's reasonable given their training."

We knew we were going to call several MPD officials, including Chief Medaria Arradondo. We expected him to receive a brutal cross-examination.

We conducted our mock trial, and it was fascinating to watch. We learned that even our Stearns County mock jury would convict all the defendants for second-degree manslaughter, and almost all would convict for second-degree murder. Our Hennepin County mock juries came back guilty on all counts.

Our themes resonated. Several juries believed that the officers had a duty—moral or legal—to render aid to George Floyd. None were too concerned about the drugs. Even the Stearns County jury thought Floyd's drug history was irrelevant.

Up until this point, I had not assigned who would do what at the trial. I was waiting on the mock to figure it all out. Jerry Blackwell and Steve Schleicher tested the best with the mock juries. The mock jurors found both of them to be energetic and effective communicators. Matt and Erin did well also, but not as highly rated as Jerry and Steve.

I decided to ask Steve to do the jury selection, Jerry to do the opening statement, and requested both of them to close. At closing Steve would do the main closing, and Jerry would rebut.

We had our themes, their expected defense themes, and our assignments. It was about time to go to trial, but then we got some crappy news.

—————

The first COVID-19 vaccination in the United States took place in December 2020. We'd be lucky to get vaccinated by the time the trial started in March. In mid-January 2021, COVID was raging. As important as our trial was, we couldn't act like COVID wasn't a looming reality—it was, and we needed to adjust.

As the pandemic surged, the state asked Judge Cahill to postpone the March 8 trial to reduce public health risk. Our proposed date was June 7.

Judge Cahill had another idea. He was not so optimistic that June would be much better given news reports about problems with the vaccine rollout. He decided to reconsider his decision to join the cases. Instead of postponing, Chief Judge Barnette and Judge Cahill decided to make more room for social distancing in the courtroom, and that meant severing the four cases.

In his decision, Cahill wrote, it is "impossible to comply with COVID-19 physical restrictions" given how many lawyers and support personnel the four defendants say would be present.

Chauvin would be going to trial in March alone, while Lane, Kueng, and Thao would go to trial together the following August. I wasn't happy about it, but that was the judge's decision.

Cahill had taken the third-degree murder charge off the table, and we were trying to figure out if we should put it back on. Should we appeal, or should we proceed to trial with the two remaining charges, second-degree unintentional murder and second-degree manslaughter? It wasn't an easy question to answer.

We discussed it as a team, and it helped to have our appellate specialist, Neal Katyal, to lay out our options. Neal pointed out that Judge Cahill had found probable cause for the remaining charges; so we were on solid ground to proceed to trial. We were confident that we could prove every element of both offenses beyond a reasonable doubt. Maybe it would be simpler to just proceed with the two charges.

On the other hand, maybe we should appeal. The Court of Appeals could disagree with Judge Cahill on the third-degree murder count and overrule him. Losing the third-degree murder count deprived the jury of a compromise count if they could not agree on the top count of second-degree murder. We knew that convicting a police officer of second-degree murder had never been done in Minnesota.

Some team members feared that appealing Judge Cahill's decision might anger him. I didn't think so. Any judge who gets vengeful enough to retaliate because a lawyer appeals his or her decision has no business being a judge. I knew Cahill to be professional, and I doubted he would get vengeful simply because we asked the Court of Appeals to take a second look. I can't say that about every judge. I can't say that about every judge who touched the Floyd case, but it was true of Cahill. Even if he was wrong, he wasn't petty and vindictive.

But on February 1, 2021, something happened that the team did not expect. The Minnesota Court of Appeals affirmed the third-degree murder conviction of the former Minneapolis police officer Mohamed Noor, directly contradicting trial court judge Cahill's decision to dismiss the third-degree murder charge against Chauvin and company for a lack of probable cause. Basically, Cahill dismissed the charge because in his view it was appropriate only when the defendant was directing some criminal act toward the random public, not an individual. Because

Chauvin's conduct was directed specifically at George Floyd, Cahill believed it did not apply. The Minnesota Court of Appeals disagreed. (The Minnesota Supreme Court eventually agreed with Cahill, but not in time to affect our case.)

So our prosecution team asked Judge Cahill, based on the Court of Appeals decision, to allow us to amend our complaint to include the charge of third-degree murder against the officers who killed George Floyd. He said no.

I was surprised when Judge Cahill rejected our request on the grounds that he felt the Court of Appeals' decision was not yet binding.

We appealed that. The Court of Appeals ruled in our favor, and not a moment too soon. It was already March 2021, and the third-degree murder charge against Chauvin was reinstated.

————

As the mock trial experience ended, we were all feeling anxious. Day by day the calendar was inching toward the start of the trial. The tension was building, but that didn't take away from the useful information we got from the mock jurors. We learned that even though jurors still resolved doubts in favor of police officer witnesses, jurors also tended to frown on behavior that dishonored that badge.

With shattered glass from businesses still littering the battered streets, people were still out there sweeping up, helping the community.

Just like those people, the mock jurors felt they were helping to clean up a noble profession.

Chapter 8

JURY SELECTION

I had no trouble getting out of bed that morning. My pulse was racing about as fast as my mind. It was the day I had been waiting for since May 31, 2020, almost a year earlier. The trial was finally on.

Derek Chauvin was about to face the judgment of his peers. Our case was about to face judgment, too. With the trial being televised, the whole world was about to find out how much unjustified violence a jury would tolerate from a police officer.

When I stepped into the shower at five-thirty, Moni wasn't even awake yet. I picked out a blue blazer and black pants, a white shirt, and a blue-and-black tie with an argyle pattern. My pants felt a little snug in the waist. Sacrificing my workouts for this case was starting to catch up with me. I got dressed quickly and gave Moni a kiss without disturbing her sleep. I was out the door by 6:20 a.m.

Leading up to this morning, we had to go through a bunch of security precautions in preparation for the trial. Three different security badges: one for the eighteenth-floor courtroom where the trial was taking place, one for the underground parking garage, and one for the Hennepin County office suite the prosecution team was working in. In light of the security issues, it was all necessary.

Other members of our team had hired private security to accompany them back and forth from court. In the beginning, I didn't do that, even though I had already received numerous death threats, two protests from anti–police brutality groups at my home, along with a steady supply of threatening mail. By the end of the trial, I had arranged for a security team, too.

The courthouse looked like a fortress. I was startled by the presence of armored personnel carriers, razor wire, automatic weapons, and lots of uniformed folks. I appreciated the Minnesota National Guard members who halted their lives to provide security. Roughly 3,500 Guard members were brought in to protect the government at one time or another. By the time the trial was over, the price tag for all the security measures would amount to $25 million.

A few folks remarked that it felt like overkill, but maybe that was the point. Just a few months before the trial, the U.S. Capitol had been overrun by right-wing insurrectionists. I think the massive security apparatus was Judge Barnette's way of saying, "Not here."

Protesters had already begun to assemble by 6:50 a.m. I saw a person, whom I would see nearly every day for the next several weeks, peacefully expressing his outrage. As the day wore on, the demonstrators' ranks swelled, and as weeks wore on, the ranks of the demonstrators would rise and fall based on what was happening in the courtroom. Nonetheless, there was always a presence. From my office space on the twenty-first floor, I could hear the chants, songs, drums, and horns from outside. The First Amendment right to free speech was getting a workout.

On the southeast side of the Government Center, there was a fleet of news vehicles assembled: Court TV, ABC, NBC, CBS, CNN, and more. Huge satellite trucks posted up, catching and sending signals near and far. It was one of the most closely watched trials in recent U.S. history.

That morning, March 8, we were at the big moment. The jury—yet to be assembled—would determine whether Chauvin would be held accountable for Floyd's death or not. News media nationwide were covering the trial, and a few, like Court TV, were streaming it live online.

The whole scene was crazy—the National Guard, camera crews, and protesters—but I wasn't too focused on any of it. I was concentrated on presenting an undeniable case, and so was every member of our team.

Freeman reserved half a floor for the prosecution team. On that first day, Steve and I arrived at the same time, and we entered the office with a key card. Josh Larson, Hennepin County attorney staff, had already beaten us both there. Josh decorated the walls of his office with pictures of his beautiful family. There were also numerous comic books, all of which had a similar theme: fighting crime. Josh had vintage Batman, Superman, and all the regulars, like *True Crime, Crime-Fighting Detective, Crime, Crime Mysteries, Guilty*, and more. He had several that I had never heard of.

It was a wintery day, and I could see snow-covered Minneapolis skyscrapers from my high perch. I took a picture on my cell to remember the moment. I looked out over the city that I've called home for decades. I could feel that this moment was giving way to some new moment of mutual respect, a new chance to break the old patterns and build enduring cooperation and peace between police officers and the people they serve. We had momentum moving into this trial, and I wanted to capture this moment that could lead to real change.

The office began to fill up with our staff. Matt Frank, Jerry Blackwell, our paralegal Dionne Dodd, and everyone else. The space included four or five offices, along with workspaces in an open space. We had a conference room on the twenty-first floor where Josh posted a photograph and short bio of each of the thirty-eight witnesses on the wall, in order as we expected to call them. We planned to go through four to six witnesses per day. Josh would mark each photo after we completed the examination of the witness.

The Floyd family was stationed in the grand jury room, which was one floor below and across the building on the twentieth floor. Vernona Boswell, the county attorney's lead victim witness advocate, made sure the room was comfortable for these victims. Over the next four to five weeks, they would have to rewatch and relive the tragedy of their family member's death numerous times.

Some family members confided to me they never had the strength to watch the video all the way through until the trial. Now, they would be seeing it many times over the course of the next few weeks. Vernona would be with them through it all. She was trained to counsel victims when their grief got to be too much.

At nine a.m., the legal team and I went down to the eighteenth floor.

It was time to get started. Jury trials tend to run the same way everywhere. Jury selection. Openings. State's case. Defense case (if they have one). Closings. Judge's instructions. Verdict. And that's it. But yeah, right. Any real trial lawyer will tell you that jury trials are like chess: You can teach anyone how to move the pieces, but to become a master is a whole other matter.

I have done many jury trials and picked many juries in my sixteen years as a trial lawyer before I went into politics. I've done criminal, civil, state, and federal trials—from DUIs to first-degree murder. All trials are dramas. They all have serious consequences for the victims, the state, plaintiffs, and, of course, the defendant.

Trials are presentations, meaning that they can be conducted with flair, wit, and organization, or they can be bumbling, confused, and ineffective. Our goal was to put on a superb case. Trials often are dramatic and, therefore, theatrical, despite most judges hating that aspect of the trial. Most judges want to see a straightforward, sober presentation of the law and facts. Well, only trial lawyers who don't care about winning their cases do it that way.

If we were going to achieve justice for George Floyd, we were going to need to pour heart and soul into it, and selecting who would decide the case meant everything. We set out to "win" jury selection, meaning two things: One, the prosecution team, led by Steve Schleicher and Christina Marinakis, was going to find jurors who we believed would convict Chauvin; two, Steve and Christina were going to identify and eliminate anyone from the jury who held a prejudice against George Floyd. Steve's military mindset was helpful here.

Of course, Chauvin's lawyer, Eric Nelson, was trying to do the opposite, and he had fewer restraints and more peremptory strikes than we did. From the standpoint of the rules of professional responsibility, Eric Nelson was singularly focused on getting his client acquitted. Eric is a just person, but we didn't expect him to be fair. We expected him to fill the jury with people who were reluctant to second-guess a police officer, hyper-concerned about mass protests and civil unrest, and unconcerned about what had happened to George Floyd. Eric wasn't about to strike jurors who were regular Fox News watchers, or people who had no understanding of American racism.

The truth about prosecuting a police officer is that most people, of all colors, cultures, and faiths, tend to resolve doubts in the officer's favor. Juries are one of the reasons it is difficult to convict a police officer, even when there is video evidence.

"There is a tendency to believe an officer over a civilian, in terms of credibility," said David Rudovsky, a civil rights lawyer who co-wrote *Police Misconduct: Law and Litigation*. "And when an officer is on trial, reasonable doubt has a lot of bite. A prosecutor needs a very strong case before a jury will say that somebody we generally trust to protect us has so seriously crossed the line as to be subject to a conviction."

As Steve and Christina prepared for jury selection, our prosecution team knew what they were up against.

A lot of folks consider this part of the trial to be dull. You rarely see an episode of *Law & Order* where prosecutor Jack McCoy, played by Sam Waterston, spends a lot of time on jury selection. However, astute court observers know that it's where the whole case can be won or lost.

When the elevator doors opened to the eighteenth floor, there were already several deputies posted. Judge Cahill was allowing only court personnel, lawyers, defendants, the Floyd family, witnesses who were about to testify, and a couple of reporters to be on that floor. Cahill was going to be strict. He ordered no pictures, no unauthorized photography, and he meant that. Everyone had to have a security badge. Anyone without a badge would be escorted off the eighteenth floor. Security was tight.

That morning, we walked into the courtroom and noticed the COVID-19 accommodations immediately. Juror chairs were separated according to social distancing guidelines. The witness stand and lawyers' spaces were surrounded in plexiglass. The state and the defense each had two tables. Eric Nelson and Derek Chauvin sat at the defense's front table, next to the judge, and Eric's team sat at the other table. Judge Cahill assigned our team to the back of the courtroom, next to the Floyd family. I was happy with that. We rotated the seating arrangement depending on whose witness was on the stand. In the back of the room, sufficiently socially distanced, there were three or four chairs for family, and on the side of the courtroom, there were two seats available for press, and one seat for Court TV.

By nine a.m., Judge Cahill's permanent law clerk, Gary Schaefer, greeted us after everyone had arrived and invited the lawyers into the chambers to talk with Judge Cahill before the jury selection began. As is customary, Judge Cahill asked the parties if there was any potential for a resolution. Eric Nelson assured everyone that there was no plea deal possible.

This case was going to be tried, which is an increasingly rare event. Between March 2019 and March 2020, only about 2 percent of federal criminal cases went to jury trial across the United States. The state court numbers are comparable.

Everyone facing confinement has a right to a jury trial. Derek Chauvin was facing a statutory maximum sentence of forty years, so he had that right. Since the state was asking for an aggravated sentence, Chauvin could waive a jury trial on the aggravated factors with the approval of the court as long as he did so personally. A jury's verdict must be unanimous. Even if eleven jurors decided that a person was guilty beyond a reasonable doubt, one lone juror could hang the jury.

As we picked the Chauvin jury, we had in mind that one juror who could defy the other eleven. We might not be able to secure twelve super-awesome jurors, but we were on alert for the one who might revel in playing spoiler.

A lot of folks were disappointed that we ever entertained the possibility of a plea deal with Chauvin's lawyer. Truth is, if Chauvin had waived his right to trial and admitted his responsibility for the death of George Floyd, it might have eased the pain of Floyd's family. It would bring finality and foreclose the possibility of an appeal. It would save the state of Minnesota and Hennepin County all the money expended to secure the courthouse, and it might help the country heal to see a police officer take responsibility for unjustly killing a person.

As it happens, Chauvin was not of that mindset. The common practice of plea bargaining was out of the question. In a few minutes, the process of selecting the jury would begin. I had suspected from the beginning that we would be trying Derek Chauvin. I welcomed it. The world would be better off having witnessed the entire case, no matter the outcome. It was time for a reckoning.

––––––––

Before we started jury selection, a few good things happened that made a moral difference. These things didn't hurt Chauvin, but they comforted the Floyd family a little bit. Even though Philonise Floyd, who was the state's "spark of life" witness, would be part of the trial, Eric Nelson agreed to allow him to watch the trial. In Minnesota, and in many places, the judge may order a witness to be excluded from watching the trial so that he or she cannot hear the testimony of other witnesses. The idea is to prevent a later witness from tailoring his or her testimony to a prior witness's testimony, basically getting their stories together.

So either party can ask the judge to order witnesses excluded. Anyway, Philonise was not a fact witness; he would be testifying about who George Floyd was as a person—as a human being. In Minnesota, the state is entitled to show that the victim, who can't be present because he or she is dead, was "not just bones and sinews covered with flesh, but was imbued with the spark of life." The prosecution is not allowed to "invoke any undue sympathy or inflame the jury's passions." It would have been sad if Philonise couldn't watch the trial because Nelson objected.

———

All criminal trials are guided by the Sixth Amendment to the U.S. Constitution, which states: "In all criminal prosecutions, the accused shall enjoy the right to a speedy and public trial, by an impartial jury of the state and district wherein the crime shall have been committed…"

The right to an impartial jury starts with a representative initial pool of people called to jury service. We don't really pick a jury. Jury selection is a process of exclusion; each party excuses jurors until twelve jurors plus alternates remain.

The jury is composed of people whom neither side objected to. Jurors who express a bias are excused for cause, and for-cause challenges are unlimited. There are also challenges known as peremptory challenges. Each side has a limited number of peremptory challenges, which means the excusing party can use one to release a juror without giving a reason.

In first-degree murder cases in Minnesota, the defendant has fifteen peremptory strikes, and the state has nine peremptory strikes. For other cases, the defense has five strikes, and the state has three. Even though Chauvin was only facing second-degree murder unintentional, Judge Cahill assigned Chauvin and the state the same number of peremptory challenges as there would be in a first-degree murder case.

I was glad Cahill did this. The level of pretrial publicity was so great that jurors likely heard a lot about the case and had formed firm opinions.

One exception to the peremptory challenge is racial bias. In a 1986 case, *Kentucky v. Batson*, the U.S. Supreme Court found that the prosecutor's decision to use peremptory challenges to strike the Black jurors solely based on race was unconstitutional. James Kirkland Batson was a Black man, resident of Kentucky, who was accused of burglary and receipt of stolen goods and had been convicted on both charges by an all-white jury.

In Batson's case, the prosecutor had used his peremptory challenges to strike all four Black jurors from the jury pool, leaving only white jurors. Batson challenged the removal of the Black jurors, arguing that striking all of them violated his Sixth Amendment right to an impartial jury and violated his right to equal protection under the Fourteenth Amendment.

The Kentucky Court of Appeals affirmed Batson's convictions, and then Batson took his case to the U.S. Supreme Court. The court decided that while a defendant is not entitled to have members of his own race on the jury, the state is not permitted to use its peremptory challenges to exclude potential jurors because of their race. The *Batson* decision established a test, which created an exception to the use of peremptory challenges.

First, the party making a *Batson* challenge must make an argument showing that the peremptory strike was based on race. Second, the party exercising the strike must offer a race-neutral explanation. Finally, the challenging party can argue that the race-neutral reason is phony, or as they say in legalese, "a pretext." Then, based on everything, the judge decides.

Something that made *State v. Chauvin* unique was that the state was the party ready to make the *Batson* challenges, not the defense. When a police officer is on trial, everything is reversed. Several jurors would be showing up for duty, from diverse racial backgrounds, and the defense would try to seed the jury with people who identified with, sympathized with, and wanted to protect Derek Chauvin. We anticipated that Eric Nelson would do all he could to strike jurors who might identify with George Floyd, and we weren't going to let him do it. Steve Schleicher and Christina Marinakis were ready to defend the diversity of the jury.

Steve and Christina were a good team. Steve is an affable guy who laughs easily and looks like a linebacker. Christina is quiet and more reserved, focusing on her notes and charts. As a jury selection specialist, she reminded me of an oracle who could give prophetic answers by using a mysterious process.

We used the *Batson* challenge two times during jury selection. In both cases, the state lost the challenge.

Here's the breakdown of who Eric, representing the defense, pre-empted: Six of twelve were Black, Indigenous, and People of Color (three Hispanic, two Asian, one Black).

———

Jury selection is critical. I knew, based on my own experience and study of police-community relations, that juries have tended to give officers the benefit of the doubt and have viewed the credibility of Black victims skeptically. Many jurors have often associated Black victims with danger and criminality. Over the expanse of American history, juries have been part of the repeating pattern across the country of acquitting officers who shoot unarmed people, often Black men. The sheer number of officers who have been acquitted after killing unarmed citizens is impressive. Here are just a few recent examples.

In July 2016 a Minnesota jury acquitted police officer Jeronimo Yanez, who shot and killed Philando Castile. Yanez pulled Castile's vehicle over because days before another Black man allegedly robbed someone. According to Yanez, Castile fit the description. Yanez asked Castile for identification, and Castile informed Yanez that he was a licensed gun carrier.

A dashcam video showed Yanez telling Castile not to reach for the gun, and Castile said he was not reaching for it, which Castille's girlfriend (Diamond Reynolds) confirmed. Reynolds was livestreaming the event on Facebook.

Yanez yelled in a panicked voice: "Don't pull it out!" He then drew his gun and fired seven shots into Castile. Reynolds and their young daughter were within inches of the bullets that killed Castile. Officer Yanez testified that he feared Mr. Castile was grabbing for the gun, but he never claimed to have seen one.

In 2016, a Mesa, Arizona, police officer, Philip Brailsford, was found not guilty of murder in the shooting of Daniel Shaver, who was unarmed. Shaver, a white man, was visiting Mesa for a business trip when he was killed. He was entertaining friends and showed them an air rifle.

Someone outside saw it and called the police. Police arrived and ordered him to come out of the hotel room on all fours. Shaver said, "Please don't shoot me." Upon being instructed to crawl, Shaver put his hands down and crawled on all fours. While crawling toward the officers, Shaver moved his right hand toward his waistband. Brailsford, who later testified he believed that Shaver was reaching for a weapon, then opened fire with his AR-15 rifle, striking Shaver five times and killing him almost instantly. Shaver was unarmed.

In 2008, Lima, Ohio, police officer Sergeant Joseph Chavalia was acquitted by a jury after the killing of twenty-six-year-old Tarika Wilson. In the drug-raid shooting, Chavalia killed Wilson and shot her infant son while she was holding him. Bullets hit the boy in the shoulder and hand. One of the child's fingers had to be amputated. An all-white jury acquitted Chavalia of negligent homicide and negligent assault, misdemeanor charges.

In 2021, a Little Rock, Arkansas, officer, Dennis Hutchins, was acquitted for the shooting and killing of Roy Richards Jr., who was allegedly holding a pellet gun. Hutchins fired five shots at Richards, hitting him twice with fatal result.

In Duluth, Minnesota, in 2020, Officer Tyler Leibfried injured Jared Fyle when he shot through the door of an apartment. According to the complaint, Leibfried told investigators that shortly after the officers' arrival, he heard two gunshots from inside the apartment. He fired his gun into the closed door, striking and injuring Fyle in the shoulder, who was on the other side of the closed door. After searching the apartment, officers discovered that Fyle was not armed, and had no firearm or ammunition. The only bullet fragments discovered were those fired by Officer Leibfried. According to prosecutors, he made the decision to use deadly force through a closed door "at what he knew not." In 2022, a Duluth jury of seven men and five women found Leibfried not guilty.

Picking the jury in an officer-involved death or injury case is probably the most critical part of the case, according to Stew Mathews, an attorney who has represented officers in high-profile cases including the Samuel DuBose shooting in Cincinnati and Breonna Taylor's death in Louisville.

Juries commonly acquit police officers in circumstances where logic and evidence suggest a conviction would be the right outcome. We knew we had to stay focused and study each juror with a keen eye.

———————

Both Steve Schleicher and defense counsel Eric Nelson tried to build some rapport with the jurors before asking substantive questions. Eric appeared to be looking for jurors who understood that police officers sometimes use violence based on their training and that violence might be misunderstood by the public. In other words, he was looking for jurors who would be reluctant to judge an officer's conduct in hindsight.

The state was looking for jurors who understood medical causation, were unafraid to judge a police officer's conduct, and who did not demonstrate racial resentment.

The first potential juror was a Latina, Mexican immigrant, naturalized U.S. citizen. She was middle-aged, had a calm disposition, and seemed like a person who knew what a hard day's work looked like. She had a heavy accent, but her English was quite understandable. She struck me as a sincere, unpretentious person, who had ample common sense. When asked, she said she would decide the case based on the "evidence."

Eric Nelson tried to get her to express a bias but failed. So he asked Judge Cahill to excuse her for cause because he didn't think she would understand the proceedings. Eric Nelson used a peremptory challenge. We didn't make a *Batson* challenge, although we came close. There was at least some basis to believe she might need some assistance with her English-language skills, which technically was a nonracial explanation.

Next up was a white male chemist. He was thoughtful and introspective. He volunteered and was active in his community. He said he attended a synagogue in town, one that was known for its social justice activism. I doubt Eric knew that. Of course, we had no obligation to tell him, and we didn't. Juror Number 2 was acceptable to both sides.

After the questioning of two jurors, the styles of the lawyers began to emerge based on the manner and tone of the questions, the theme of the questions, and the choice about exercising peremptory challenges. For example, Juror Number 2 said he was an advocate for community policing. Nelson did not explore his motivation, or ask about any occasions when he acted on his belief. However, Juror Number 2 reported that a protester had blocked his car. Nelson asked him how he felt about this protester, and Juror Number 2 reported that it "had a souring effect." It appeared to me that Nelson was looking for jurors who were unbothered by what happened to George Floyd but who were disturbed by the Floyd protests.

Nelson's second peremptory strike was directed at Juror Number 4, a Hispanic man. I was concerned Number 4 was being removed because of his race. First Juror Number 1, a smart woman of Hispanic background, whose language capability was called into question, and now Nelson was using a peremptory challenge against this Latino man. So, in the first four jurors, two were Hispanic, and Nelson got one excused for cause and was now using a peremptory challenge against the second. I thought it was time to say something.

Schleicher rose to his feet and objected. This was our first opportunity to mount a *Batson* challenge. Nelson was able to give a race-neutral explanation, but at least he was on notice. We weren't going to tolerate racial bias in jury selection.

At the end of the first day of actual jury selection, three jurors had been seated. Two were men, and one was a woman. One was mixed race, but identified as Black, and two were white.

Jury selection was moving quickly. During jury selection, it's possible to pick up a bunch of jurors in one day or go all day without picking up any. At this rate we would have a fairly representative jury within a week or so.

I was feeling very good about our team. Steve and Christina were doing a wonderful job on jury selection. I was seated in the courtroom at the counsel table, a comfortable place for me. I was regularly giving input and feedback. Steve and Christina's questions were tight and impactful. They drew usable information from the jurors. We were finding out what we needed to know.

———————

The next day, another juror was up for *voir dire*, legalese for questioning. Juror Number 23 was an older white female who had limited life experience; she was primarily a homemaker dependent on her spouse. She had never met anyone who was addicted to illegal drugs, and she thought the protests against the COVID-19 restrictions—mask mandates, school shutdowns, etc.—led to some good, but that the protests against the treatment of George Floyd were unhelpful, except maybe for "drawing attention." We exercised a peremptory challenge.

By noon, we had four jurors—all acceptable to both sides. However, Nelson had already struck three people of color. Nelson had a race-neutral explanation for each one, but I was a little displeased. I told Steve that we needed to think about making a *Batson* challenge if the trend continued.

After lunch came Juror Number 26, an African immigrant. He was married, loved sports, worked in technology, and was fluent in multiple languages, including French and indigenous West African languages. He was well educated and thoroughly middle class, if not well-to-do. He was in middle management at the tech business where he was employed.

He expressed concern about serving on the jury for fear of his "personal safety." I think Nelson thought he had a good juror for Chauvin. It occurred to me that he might be right. In fact, the only thing Floyd had in common with Juror Number 26 was color.

Obviously, I didn't know Number 26, but all jury selection is guessing. I could see how a person like Juror Number 26 might be embarrassed by a person like George Floyd. He might resent being lumped together with Floyd just because of race. The guy was a mixed bag, but we didn't strike him and neither did Nelson. Now we had five jurors.

———————

When I drove to the courthouse on March 11, my car was driving a little funny. I stopped and found that my rear driver's side tire was flat as a pancake. Luckily, I was close to a gas station with an air hose. I jacked up my 2009 Pontiac G6, my green machine, and I put on my spare—that tiny little donut. Good thing I had started early that morning. I got to the courthouse only a few minutes later than usual.

The flat tire was not a bad omen. On March 11, the Minnesota Court of Appeals had reinstated the third-degree murder charge. Cahill had no choice: He had to allow the state to amend the complaint to include third-degree murder. Chauvin would be facing three charges instead of two; we would now have three chances to obtain a conviction.

The next juror up was an African American woman in her midthirties. Like George Floyd, and me for that matter, she was no African immigrant. She was a Black woman whose ancestors were kidnapped in Africa and forced into servitude in North America hundreds of years ago.

I found her frustrating. She appeared to be trying to get kicked off the jury for bias, though maybe she was just being candid, as the judge had instructed her to be. When Eric Nelson asked her whether she saw the Darnella Frazier video, and if so, how she felt about it, she said, "I can't unsee the video."

Regarding the property damage associated with the arson and vandalism, she said, "I feel like if that's what needed to happen to get the world's attention, then that's what needed to happen." This point of view is very difficult for some people to understand. She wasn't condoning the arson or vandalism, but she was channeling the despair, frustration, and rage that convulsed into explosive anger on the streets of South Minneapolis after the murder of George Floyd.

Three generations of trauma informed how she was feeling and what might justify expressing herself that way. Her perspective could be important. I thought her experience would serve the deliberations well, but she wasn't going to make it. She was under oath, she answered truthfully, and she got bounced. There's a certain irony that being Black alone might be perceived as lacking impartiality.

The next juror was a middle-aged white male. He seemed like a nice man, a hardworking fellow who seemed somewhat oblivious to America's complicated cultural landscape. He didn't seem to have any awareness of the world outside of his own life's bubble. We struck him.

One more important thing happened that day: I got my first COVID vaccination. The pandemic had been raging for nearly a year. More than half a million people had died in the United States by this point. Masking, social distancing, constant hand washing were the norm. Getting the first dose of Moderna's COVID vaccine gave me hope. This was the first hope I had that the pandemic that took my mom might one day come to an end.

––––––––

The fifth day of trial we started with six jurors; we were halfway there. By now Eric Nelson was asking the same questions of every juror. We knew what to expect from him at this point. We knew what type of person he wanted to seat and whom he wanted to excuse. He wanted people who would trust whatever explanation Chauvin offered. He kept asking, "Have you ever been a hundred percent convinced of something and then realized you were wrong?"

Eric Nelson struck Number 42. A young white woman, she was smart and aware of current events. I thought Eric would never keep her; he had eight strikes left. He could afford to excuse this juror. When he asked her, "Do you feel that you are serving a higher purpose?" I knew she was about to go.

All the jurors knew about what had happened to George Floyd. Even the most conservative pro–police officer juror disapproved of what Chauvin did to Floyd.

Juror Number 44 was a pleasant and congenial person. She had a few things that had happened in her life that were not appropriate for an on-the-record conversation. Both sides approached Judge Cahill for the private parley. Eric Nelson accepted Number 44, and after a few questions, so did we. That made seven. Eric Nelson and Steve questioned one more juror, Number 48. He was not acceptable to either side, and we ended the day.

After court finished for the day, our prosecution team went into the twenty-first floor conference room for our after-action meeting. We reviewed the week to come. We assessed the jurors who had been seated already. Then we reviewed social media. I was amazed at how closely the public was watching jury selection. I assumed they would consider it boring. Evidently, I was wrong. Each individual was fascinating, with the whole story, a whole life's journey.

Maybe someone won't make it on the jury and someone else will. Regardless, the process of assembling twelve people with diverse experiences is a fascinating study in human behavior.

Jury selection could have been going a heck of a lot worse. When my law partners and I picked the jury in the Lawrence Miles case, we deliberately exposed the jurors to the idea they might see evidence that fifteen-year-old Miles may have had a BB pistol, which resembled a gun. Lawrence was shot squarely in the back.

One elderly white juror volunteered, "Well, if the kid didn't have something that looked like it might be a gun, he wouldn't have been shot. It's the parents. The cop should be able to shoot'm."

I knew that juror had to go, but you never know how many others hold the same beliefs.

Steve and Christina were nervously optimistic that it was going well. No one had ever seen a Hennepin County jury this diverse before. We chalked it up to luck, and some excellent preparation.

We concluded our meeting and went home for the weekend. It was Friday. I was certainly tired. Moni had made dinner plans. I was looking forward to a quiet evening with my wife.

Week Two

The first juror was struck for cause almost immediately. She said she knew me, though I didn't recognize her, and that she had voted for me. She candidly admitted she could not be fair in this case. She was gone pretty fast.

The next juror was Number 52, a young man with an easy smile. He seemed like an approachable person who would readily engage with other jurors. Juror Number 52 was a really tall fellow, which we were looking for. Floyd was a tall man, an accomplished basketball player in his youth. Juror Number 52 reported that he liked sports, basketball in particular. He was probably close to the same size as George Floyd.

Floyd starred on the court in high school, and even played at the community college level. He probably could have gone much further with the right support. I thought Number 52 might identify with Floyd. He was also African American. I hoped the other jurors would see this large, relatable young fellow, and see that a man who resembled Floyd could be affable and someone to identify with. To my surprise, Eric Nelson did not use a peremptory challenge to strike him.

At this point we had nine jurors, six men and three women. We had a fairly diverse jury: five white people, three Black people, and a Latino man. Most of the jurors were young, which was something we were certainly happy to see. Steve and Christina were composing an excellent jury.

———

Day seven started with Eric Nelson making a motion, a request, of Judge Cahill to introduce evidence that in May 2019—a year before Floyd was killed—he had had police contact. Nelson argued that this demonstrated Floyd's history of drug use as well as a previous arrest. The apparent purpose of the motion was to show jurors that Floyd's death was partially his own fault.

There was a bodycam video of the May 2019 incident. It showed Floyd sitting in the passenger seat when an officer pulled over the vehicle. His hands were not immediately visible. The officer shouted, "Show your fucking hands." The officer got Floyd out of the car, but then ascertained that Floyd needed medical attention. Floyd got the treatment and was then released. No charges.

Matt Frank skillfully argued the May 2019 incident was just irrelevant and that Nelson was trying to shift fault onto the victim. The formal rules of evidence don't allow the introduction of prior bad acts just to prove that the victim or the defendant is a bad person who does bad things. A prior bad act can be introduced to prove things like habit, absence of mistake, modus operandi, common scheme or plan, or something else.

Nelson stated that the reason for wanting to use this prior police contact was to show that perhaps this incident with Chauvin was the time Floyd's luck ran out. The May 2019 and May 25, 2020, incidents were similar. Both times, as officers drew their guns and struggled to get Floyd out of the car, he called out for his mother, claimed he had been shot before and cried, and put what appeared to be pills in his mouth.

Both searches turned up drugs in the cars. In both incidents drugs like opioid pills were found.

Dr. Baker's autopsy report showed Floyd had fentanyl and methamphetamine in his system when he died. Nelson argued that in May 2019, Floyd received a medical intervention quickly enough to save him. However, on May 26, 2020, the paramedics didn't get to him in time, and he died of a drug-related incident.

Up to this point, Judge Cahill had held firm and said no to this motion. Well, this morning Cahill changed his mind. He found that the 2019 incident showed Floyd had a habit of taking drugs and then needing medical attention. He was going to allow it into testimony.

If the May 2019 incident was coming in, then we needed to deal with it. As a consolation prize, Matt Frank convinced Judge Cahill to instruct the jury that the May 2019 testimony could only be used as evidence of the effect of opioids on Floyd at the time of his death, not his character.

Erin Eldridge had a great observation. She said, "All this May 2019 incident shows is that Chauvin acted inappropriately. In the 2019 incident, Floyd got prompt medical attention and survived. In the May 2020 incident, he didn't, and he died."

Others chimed in, too. I thought, *YUP*. I am privileged to be part of a smart team. We got lemons, and we're about to make lemonade.

Though Cahill's decision made it easier for Nelson to throw dirt on Floyd, we had a way to turn it to our advantage, but we needed more. We needed a true and yet sticky story to help the jury see that the drug stuff wasn't an excuse. We began to play with the catchphrase, "no excuse for police abuse." We had to have a narrative that helped the jury see how irrelevant the drug stuff was to the issue of medical causation, and Floyd's drug use was no excuse for Chauvin's moral culpability.

We also discussed the importance of the narrative theme "in your custody is in your care." Still, to make "no excuse for police abuse" and "in your custody" more than slogans, we needed witnesses and documentary evidence to show the jury the legitimacy of the narrative theme. We needed a way to humanize Floyd. We needed to show drug addiction as a human experience that does not expel a person from compassion and respect. We needed to show Floyd in a sympathetic light, not as an out-of-control, six-foot-four-inch Black drug thug, which was what the defense was trying to project.

Our case didn't hinge on Floyd being a saint. All we needed to prove was that he was a human being, a person, who deserved far better than a knee on the neck for nine and a half minutes. We had a few ideas. The witnesses would be key here, and not just our spark of life witness, Floyd's brother Philonise. A person who was very special to Floyd at the end of his life would turn out to be a critical witness: Floyd's fiancée, Courteney Ross.

We were humming along and feeling pretty good about how everything was going. Then some big news broke that could have changed everything.

The headlines were everywhere: The city of Minneapolis had settled the civil rights lawsuit with the Floyd family. Eric Nelson insinuated that I had colluded with my son, Fifth Ward council member Jeremiah Ellison, regarding the timing of the announcement, because the circumstances sort of looked . . . well . . .

Nelson said he had evidence that my son and I collaborated on the timing of the announcement. According to Nelson, it was a strange coincidence that I was directly involved in the prosecution and Jeremiah was directly involved in the settlement negotiation. Nelson was prosecuting the prosecutor, a well-worn tactic.

I was insulted by the insinuation.

I hadn't played any role in the city's settlement with the Floyd family. In fact, the timing hurt the state's case; it gave Eric Nelson the chance to move for a change of venue, a continuance of several months, and to heap suspicion on the motives and tactics of the state and me specifically. The settlement certainly didn't help our case.

After ample discussion, Cahill rejected the ideas of a change of venue and a long continuance. Instead, he decided to call all the seated jurors back in to reinterview them on the issue of whether they had heard anything about the settlement announcement and whether that news impacted their ability to be fair and impartial. Cahill called the nine jurors one by one, and he did the questioning himself.

The first juror said, "Nope, it's the first I'm hearing of it." He noted his wife had said something, but he deliberately ignored it since the judge instructed the jurors to avoid the media.

The next juror answered, "I heard about the settlement. I heard the quantity was large. Over twenty million maybe." If the second juror was hoping to be removed, then he had said the magic words: "I felt strongly. The city obviously feels strongly. It will impact me a lot." And with that he was off the jury. We were down to eight jurors.

The next two jurors, Number 9 and Number 19, were not exposed to any of the developments in the news. Great, we were holding it at eight.

Then came juror Number 20, who said, "Yes, I saw the headline. The city agreed to pay out twenty million dollars." (Actually, it was $27 million.)

Judge Cahill asked, "What effect does that have on your ability to be impartial?"

Juror Number 20 said, "It was shocking to me. The city wanted to send a message. It swayed me a little."

With that admission, Judge Cahill removed Juror Number 20.

Next, Judge Cahill called Juror Number 44, who said, "I did see it. I just saw the headline."

Judge Cahill asked, "Does this affect your decision?"

"No, I'm not a lawyer. I'd say it has nothing to do with it."

I thought this was *awesome*. When Judge Cahill began his inquiry of the nine seated jurors, I worried that if too many reported they were no longer impartial, he might scrap the whole panel and order a change of venue or a lengthy continuance. I started to get the impression we were going to stay on track.

So overall we lost two; we were back to seven jurors.

During our noon break, the prosecution team had a conversation about *Sheppard v. Maxwell*, a case that set the standard for how judges should handle excessive pretrial publicity. *Sheppard* is the case the movie and TV series *The Fugitive* was based upon. Dr. Sam Sheppard, who always maintained his innocence, was a well-to-do Cleveland doctor who was accused of killing his pregnant wife. The Sheppard case stands as the epitome of an unfair, chaotic trial, poisoned by excessive pretrial publicity. It is what every judge with a high-profile case, including Judge Cahill, tries to avoid.

In the *Sheppard* case, one newspaper ran nearly 400 stories in six months, averaging more than one story in each issue. The trial took place two weeks before an election in which the judge and the prosecutor were candidates. Jurors were not sequestered and became celebrities because three weeks before trial the newspaper published the photos and names of all the jurors. The *Sheppard* jurors were subjected to newspaper, radio, and television coverage of the trial while not taking part in the proceedings. They were allowed to go their separate ways outside the courtroom, without adequate direction not to read or listen to anything concerning the case.

The judge did nothing to control the press and even contributed to a carnival-like atmosphere. The judge told one columnist that Dr. Sheppard was "guilty as hell." Even as they deliberated, jurors were allowed to phone their friends. The U.S. Supreme Court didn't like it. In an 8–1 decision, the Court upheld a decision by a federal district court that granted Sheppard a new trial, in which he was acquitted.

At the retrial, the judge limited the number of reporters allowed in the courtroom and banned interviews. The Supreme Court instructed the lower court to limit the reporters in the courtroom, insulate witnesses from press exposure, and ordered the lawyers and witnesses to avoid making extrajudicial statements.

State v. Chauvin was simply not comparable. Judge Cahill was keeping things in check. He issued a gag order early in the proceedings regarding any extrajudicial comments. Though he had rescinded that gag order, he warned all parties, including counsel, not to make any comments that could influence the jury. He reminded all lawyers of their professional responsibilities as attorneys and officers of the court not to say anything to undermine the process with extrajudicial statements.

He also ordered partial sequestration for jurors during deliberation. He used the number of peremptory strikes normally employed for first-degree murder cases so that counsel for the defense or state could excuse any juror who might carry a bias. Judge Cahill granted for-cause challenges more easily than usual in my opinion, excusing jurors suspected of being unable to be fair and impartial.

By interviewing all the jurors himself to ensure that no juror was influenced by the news, Cahill did his job to protect the jury from pretrial publicity.

At this point, we had five more jurors to seat, plus two more alternates. Juror Number 76 said the settlement news had no effect on him. He referred to the court as "Your Honor," and was mild-mannered and respectful at all times. When Judge Cahill asked him if he could put aside anything he had heard to decide the case, his answer was a definite "yes." Juror Number 76 described himself as a "quiet person who keeps to himself." And he said further that he had "mixed emotions" about receiving a jury summons. "It's like weight... carries a big weight on you as a person." And yet this man was excused for cause from serving on the jury.

In my opinion, it was essentially because of his race. I say essentially, but not exclusively. Juror Number 76 lived in the South Minneapolis neighborhood where Floyd was killed. He talked about how the community felt antagonized by Minneapolis police. He mentioned that police officers were known to drive through the neighborhood blasting the Queen song "Another One Bites the Dust" when somebody was shot. Still, he said he could put his opinions aside to judge the case on the facts presented.

Here are the words he got excused for: "As a Black man, you see a lot of Black people get killed and no one's held accountable for it and you wonder why or what was the decisions, and so with this, maybe I'll be in the room to know why."

I don't believe Judge Cahill or Eric Nelson moved to excuse him because of his race alone. It also had something to do with the fact that he lived in the area where Floyd was killed and had had negative experiences with the police officers who patrolled the Third Precinct. However, his race gave him a certain set of experiences. His experiences gave him a certain perspective on the world, and on the system of policing, which he reported honestly—without venom or malice toward anyone. Nelson and Judge Cahill made a leap because police had been biased against people like him. Therefore, he could not be fair and impartial toward them. Yet nothing he said indicated that he had an ax to grind against someone like Derek Chauvin.

I believe our team should have made a *Batson* challenge for this juror. It likely would not have prevailed, because Nelson could easily say, "Hey, this guy lived in the neighborhood." Still, the excusal of Juror Number 76 raised an important question about our justice system: Can a person who has been a witness to American racial policy be a fair judge of an actor within that system? I think Juror Number 76, as a witness and perhaps victim of historic racism, was as well qualified to judge an actor who perpetuates the system as a person who benefits from that same system.

The next juror, Number 85, was accepted by both sides. She was not bothered by the settlement. She was clearly smart and well educated. She said that she wanted to be on the jury. Juror Number 85 appeared to be a mixed-race person of African descent. It was not clear to me how she identified racially. Her accent indicated a suburban Minnesota middle-class upbringing. Anyway, at this point, the jury was back to nine.

When the day of court concluded, Judge Cahill informed us that the defense would be awarded three additional peremptory challenges and the state would be awarded one to deal with the recent pretrial publicity.

I thought this was a fair way to deal with the pretrial publicity. Judge Cahill was obviously concerned about pretrial publicity as a potential appellate issue. He took prudent steps to make sure Chauvin received a fair trial.

––––––––

On day nine, Juror Number 86 was excused quickly. She informed Judge Cahill that the circumstances of Floyd's death "hit too close to home." She meant that as a Black woman she identified too closely with Floyd to be fair and impartial. It was a good thing that she was so candid. She saved everyone a lot of time.

Juror Number 87 was the opposite of Number 86: She was quite certain of her ability to be fair and impartial. Her vocabulary, accent, and clothing indicated education, wealth, and access. She reported that her church was a very important part of her life, and she noted that her pastor took a literal approach to Bible interpretation. She noted in her questionnaire that she thought racial "discrimination is exaggerated," which she confirmed when asked. She was excused from jury service.

Juror Number 89 was a nurse, which we believed was helpful to our case. She understood medical facts and could distinguish them from medical nonsense, which was important for our narrative themes. She also appeared to be a very empathetic person. She exuded compassion and a nonjudgmental approach to life. I thought she could help fellow jurors understand Floyd's addiction issues as well. She was accepted by both sides as the tenth juror.

Juror Number 91 was the eleventh juror to be seated. She was a sixty-seven-year-old Black woman. She had a sharp mind and had the bearing of a leader. I wouldn't have been surprised to see her elected as foreperson of the jury.

Throughout jury selection, I kept an eye on Derek Chauvin. He was writing furiously, taking copious notes.

Thanks to my time as a criminal defense lawyer, I was well aware of the emotional toll that standing trial takes on a defendant. I knew something of what Chauvin and Nelson were going through. My clients couldn't sleep, couldn't eat, and were generally nervous as hell throughout the proceedings. Part of what Eric Nelson had to do was to keep his client calm. I had no idea what Chauvin was writing, but I wouldn't be surprised if Nelson told him to write simply to distract himself.

––––––––––

That Friday, after a drawn-out morning of arguing motions, we began the final stages of jury selection.

Juror Number 96 was called for questioning first. She had to go off-camera to talk about a prior incident in her life. From the state's perspective, nothing in her disclosure eliminated her from service. I appreciated her candor.

She disputed the idea that racial bias existed in the criminal justice system. Perhaps this was her experience. We decided to accept her because we felt other jurors could help educate her. In the end, there was nothing signaling that she would reject our narrative themes. We didn't need her to be smart on American racial history; we needed her to accept the idea that for the police, "in their custody is in their care" and "there's no excuse for police abuse."

Then a seated juror, Number 27, sent a note to the court. My suspicion was that he was going to try to bail. When I heard this news, I was worried. Maybe he had a family emergency; life doesn't stop simply because you're on jury service. It could have been a death in the family, or anything, but then it occurred to me if it were a death he would have simply said it was a death. It had to be something else. He could simply have a case of the jitters. Maybe he could be talked back into service.

It turned out that Juror Number 27's voice had been recognized even though his image was not televised. His coworker noticed he wasn't at work and had heard he was on jury service. He also heard his West African accent via Court TV and concluded that he was on the Chauvin jury. From there, word spread all over the company. Juror Number 27 was shook up by this, and began to fret about his safety. His wife, he said, was scared, too.

Cahill informed Juror Number 27 that if everyone who got a little nervous was allowed to get off the jury then no one would ever serve. Very true. Juror Number 27 stayed, and we had a full panel of twelve jurors plus three alternates.

Jury selection had gone really well for the state. Steve and Christina provided us with a solid group of people to sit in judgment of the facts in *State v. Chauvin*. The jury was racially balanced, six Blacks and six whites. It skewed young, though there were several folks in their fifties and sixties. It had an almost even number of men and women.

Steve and Christina had curated the single most diverse jury I had ever impaneled. It wasn't just luck. I knew that if we convicted Chauvin, many people would be taking some awesome jury selection work for granted. The greats make it look easy; it ain't.

Chapter 9

THE TRIAL

We wrapped up jury selection on March 26, 2021, but we had a busy weekend ahead. There were several witnesses to prepare, including the wild card, medical examiner Andrew Baker. We also had scheduled meetings with MPD personnel and on-scene witnesses, including Darnella Frazier. I was confident the witnesses would testify truthfully, confidently, and coherently.

However, witness Alyssa Funari presented a challenge. After we had served her with the subpoena, she simply wasn't responding to any of our calls for witness prep, and on the rare occasion that our victim-witness advocate contacted her, she told them things like, "Don't you all have enough people to testify? I don't want to do this."

So Bureau of Criminal Apprehension agent James Reyerson and I had to go to the job site of eighteen-year-old Ms. Funari to convince her to honor the subpoena. James and I asked for her at the front desk, and her manager escorted us to the employee lunchroom. She was preparing some ramen noodles, and she was noticeably pregnant.

I asked her how she was doing, and we chatted a little. I told her I knew she would have preferred to stay out of this whole thing, and I understood that she needed to think about her baby and her life, but we needed her truthful testimony.

She had been going into Cup Foods to get a cell phone charger on

May 25, 2020, when she came upon the scene of George Floyd pleading under the knee of Chauvin. I told her she might be nervous now, but one day she would be proud she had come to court to testify about what she had seen. She finally agreed that testifying was the right thing to do.

I arrived home that Friday evening to be alone with my thoughts for a moment. March 26, 2021, was a difficult day for me; it was the one-year anniversary of my mother's death. I knew that standing up for the life of an innocent victim like George Floyd was what she would have wanted me to do.

As I sat at my dimly lit kitchen table in my North Minneapolis condo, I gazed up at my mother's photograph. Next to her smiling face was the scripture: "Do justly and to love mercy, and to walk humbly with thy God."

I prayed for the strength to do that.

———

On March 29, 2021, the day of opening statements, a story broke in the early morning hours that a Chicago police officer had shot and killed a thirteen-year-old kid named Adam Toledo. Here was another reminder of the constant tension that continues to emerge between police and local communities of color.

It was also a reminder that the work my team and I were doing was important and could have an impact beyond the boundaries of Minnesota.

This would be a big day for the team. It always feels like the trial really begins at the point when opening statements are given. Of course, this trial had been going on for weeks. Jury selection was no warm-up act; we had to win it. It was a big step on the path to accountability. Now that it was all done, the jury and the world would hear our case via Court TV's live feed.

"All rise," said Gary Schaefer, Cahill's clerk. Everyone, including all fifteen jurors, stood up in unison.

Judge Cahill walked up the three or four steps to the top of the judge's bench and sat down. "You may be seated," he said. With that, we all took our seats. It's a solemn moment. I don't care if you're trying a drunk-driving case or a first-degree murder, it's a moment when even the steeliest person gets butterflies. In this case, the stakes couldn't have been higher. It felt like democracy, human rights, and the future of the nation were on trial. Yes, I had butterflies.

Judge Cahill read several preliminary instructions to the jury members. He talked to them about keeping an open mind, how to manage note taking, and how to assess credibility. He asked them to stay within a certain zone of the courtroom that would keep them off the Court TV cameras, and to remember to sit in the same seat every day.

I was the leader of the prosecution team, but I was not a trial presenter. I didn't need to be present inside the courtroom, and most days, I watched the trial on the livestream in our offices on the twenty-first floor. However, I wanted to be in the courtroom for the opening statements. On this day I wanted my presence to convey the seriousness of the moment.

I selected Jerry to do the opening statement. Jerry and Steve were the best public speakers we had. Jerry would do the opening, and Steve would do the closing, and then Jerry would do the rebuttal.

Jerry was well known for his ability to untangle complicated legal issues for jurors who would be encountering many such issues, including implicit racial stereotyping, heartbreaking and traumatic eyewitness testimony, complicated use-of-force testimony, and even more complicated medical testimony regarding cause of death.

Cahill turned to the state to make an opening statement. Jerry went to the podium, faced the plexiglass, and removed his mask.

With two sentences, Jerry established his own personality and our narrative theme. He also accelerated a roller-coaster ride of a trial that would last for eleven more days of testimony from thirty-eight witnesses.

"My name is Jerry Blackwell, and I apologize for talking to you through this plexiglass, but it's probably the least of the gifts that the pandemic has given us. You're going to learn in this case a lot about what it means to be a public servant and to have the honor of wearing this badge."

By apologizing for the plexiglass, Jerry called out the elephant in the room: the pandemic. It was weird, it was strange, and everyone knew it. Calling out the obvious truth demonstrated his earthiness and awareness. He followed that right up with saying that you're going to hear about "what it means . . . to have the honor of wearing this badge."

The state's entire case was not that *wearing* the badge was dishonorable, but that Derek Chauvin had *dishonored* the badge. We weren't prosecuting policing. We weren't putting policing on trial. As much as some protesters would have enjoyed that, it probably would have led to an acquittal. Plus, it's not fair or true, especially to officers trying to overcome the stigma of officers like Derek Chauvin. No, we were protecting the honor of the badge, and thereby restoring the honor and dignity that Chauvin had robbed from all good cops.

Jerry built on this theme. "It's a small badge that carries with it a large responsibility and a large accountability to the public. What does it stand for? It represents the very motto of the Minneapolis Police Department—to protect with courage, to serve with compassion—but it also represents the essence of the Minneapolis Police Department approach to the use of force against its citizens when appropriate. The sanctity of life and the protection of the public shall be the cornerstones of the Minneapolis Police Department's use of force. Compassion, sanctity of life are cornerstones, and that little badge is worn right over the officer's heart."

Here, Jerry alluded to Chauvin's betrayal of his badge and the honor it carried. "But you're also going to learn that the officers take an oath when they become police officers. They take an oath that 'I will enforce the law courteously and appropriately.' And as you will learn as it applies to this case, never employing unnecessary force or violence. And not only that, 'I recognize the badge of my office as a symbol of public faith and I accept it as a public trust to be held so long as I am true to the ethics of police service.'"

Now, Jerry was ready to tell the jury two things simultaneously: what happened and what they were about to see unfold in this trial. "On May twenty-fifth of 2020, Mr. Derek Chauvin betrayed this badge when he used excessive and unreasonable force upon the body of Mr. George Floyd, that he put his knees upon his neck and his back grinding and crushing him until the very breath, no, ladies and gentlemen, until the very life was squeezed out of him. You will learn that he was well aware that Mr. Floyd was unarmed, that Mr. Floyd had not threatened anyone, that Mr. Floyd was in handcuffs, he was completely in the control of the police, he was defenseless.

"You will learn what happened in that nine minutes and twenty-nine seconds, the most important numbers you will hear in this trial are 9:29, what happened in those nine minutes and twenty-nine seconds when Mr. Derek Chauvin was applying this excessive force to the body of Mr. George Floyd."

The "9:29" was something of a shock to people who had been hearing "8:46." And "8:46" was burned into the minds of many. Eight days after Floyd's murder comedian Dave Chappelle did a whole show entitled, "8:46," comparing it to the much shorter, but terrifying, thirty-five seconds of an earthquake he experienced. The duration of 8:46 originated from the Hennepin County attorney's initial complaint against Chauvin, based on Darnella Frazier's cell phone video of the incident, which began when Chauvin already had his knee on Floyd's neck.

When we obtained all the video in August 2020, it became clear through police body camera footage that Chauvin had his knee on Floyd's neck for about 9:29. Jerry pounded on that awful timeframe.

Jerry explained to the jury that they would hear Mr. Floyd saying, "Please, I can't breathe, please, man, please."

In this nine minutes and twenty-nine seconds you will see that as Mr. Floyd is handcuffed there on the ground, he is verbalizing twenty-seven times, you will hear in the four minutes and forty-five seconds, "I can't breathe, please. I can't breathe." You will see that Mr. Chauvin is kneeling on Mr. Floyd's neck and back.

You will hear him say, "Tell my kids I love them." You will hear him say about his fear of dying, he says, "I'll probably die this way. I'm through. I'm through. They're going to kill me. They're going to kill me, man."

You will hear him crying out and you will hear him cry out in pain, "My stomach hurts. My neck hurts. Everything hurts." You will hear that for yourself, "Please. I can't breathe. Please, your knee on my neck." You will hear it and you'll see at the same time, while he's crying out, Mr. Chauvin never moves. The knee remains on his neck. Sunglasses remain undisturbed on his head and it just goes on. You will hear his [Floyd's] final words when he says, "I can't breathe." Before that time, you'll hear his voice get heavier. You will hear his words further apart. You will see that his respiration gets shallower and shallower, and finally stops when he speaks his last words, "I can't breathe."

And once we have his final words, you'll see that for roughly fifty-three seconds, he is completely silent and virtually motionless with just sporadic movements. You're going to learn that those sporadic movements matter greatly in this case, because what they reflect, Mr. Floyd was no longer breathing when he's making these movements, you will learn about something in this case called an anoxic seizure. It is the body's automatic reflex when breathing has stopped due to oxygen deprivation. We'll be able to point out to you when you see the involuntary movements from Mr. Floyd, that is part of an anoxic seizure.

Not only that, you're going to learn about something that's called agonal breathing. When the heart has stopped, when blood is no longer coursing through the veins, you will hear the body gasp as an involuntary reflex.

We'll point out to you when Mr. Floyd is having the agonal breathing again, as a reflex, involuntary reflex to the oxygen deprivation. So we learned here that Mr. Floyd at some point has completely passed out. Mr. Chauvin continued on as he had, knee on the neck, knee on the back. You'll see he does not let up and he does not get up for the remaining, as you can see three minutes and fifty-one seconds.

During this period of time, you will learn that Mr. Chauvin is told that they can't even find the pulse of Mr. Floyd. You'll learn he's told that twice. They can't even find the pulse. You will be able to see for yourself what he does in response. You will see that he does not let up and that he does not get up.

Doesn't let up and you'll see he doesn't get up. The paramedic from the ambulance comes over, you'll be able to see this in the video, he checks Mr. Floyd for a pulse. He has to check him for a pulse you'll see, with Mr. Chauvin continuing to remain on his body at the same time, doesn't get up even when the paramedic comes to check for a pulse and doesn't find one, Mr. Chauvin doesn't get up. You will see that the paramedics have taken the gurney out of the ambulance, have rolled it over next to the body of Mr. Floyd and you'll be able to see Mr. Chauvin still does not let up, he doesn't get up.

They want to move the lifeless body of George Floyd onto the gurney; only then does Mr. Chauvin let up and get up and you'll see him drag Mr. Floyd's body and unceremoniously cast it onto the gurney. And that was for a total of four minutes and forty-four seconds.

The Trial

If Jerry Blackwell were teaching trial skills at a Continuing Legal Education course, he might tell you that cases are won and lost in opening statements. In *State v. Chauvin*, Jerry put on a master class on how to do an opening statement. Lawyers are not supposed to make arguments in an opening statement, but that does not mean that they cannot be persuasive. The lawyer making an opening statement needs to make an emotional connection with the members of the jury, share a narrative theme with the jury. Jerry did that, and we knew he connected. I could feel it.

Jerry gets full credit for his brilliant opening, but that is not to say we didn't give him ample feedback as a team. Good lawyers always rehearse the important parts of their cases, and Jerry Blackwell is nothing if not a good lawyer. One of the first things I did to help Jerry prepare was to study the opening statement in the state prosecution of Jeronimo Yanez, the killer of Philando Castile.

Veteran Ramsey County prosecutor Richard Dusterhoft delivered the opening statement for the state, and he delivered a perfectly standard opening statement. "The evidence will show...that on...the defendant..." It was short. Very short. It was delivered without verve or passion. It was deadpan and unemotional. Dusterhoft played the dashcam video of Yanez shooting into Philando's vehicle, but he never humanized Philando. He never talked about the spark of life witness who could discuss how wonderful Philando was. He never mentioned that Philando graduated from St. Paul Central High School in 2001 and served and fed the children in the exact same school district until he was shot to death by Yanez.

The state wisely called a witness to testify about Castile's work in the field of student nutrition and his career as a nutrition services assistant for both elementary and high school students. However, Dusterhoft never mentioned it in the opening statement.

The state introduced evidence that Philando received a promotion to a higher position at J. J. Hill Montessori Magnet School in

St. Paul but he never pulled those details into the opening statement, which I believe was a missed opportunity. Dusterhoft just said Castile announced to Yanez he had a gun in response to a warning and said that Castile was not pulling the gun out. Dusterhoft then explained that Yanez fired seven shots and hit Castile five times, including twice in the heart. "He didn't tell him to freeze," Dusterhoft said of Yanez. "Officer Yanez's actions led to Philando Castile's death."

On the other hand, Yanez's attorney, Paul Engh, said "[Philando] reached for it." Engh said Castile ignored two commands about not reaching for or pulling out his gun. Then Engh humanized Yanez, calling him "an exceptional human being" and son of a Mexican immigrant, who "will testify during the trial that Castile" reached for his gun. Engh stretched on with Yanez's story, and also stretched the rules by editorializing about how wonderful Yanez was as a person.

I took notes from Dusterhoft and Engh. Jerry would be doing a heck of a lot more than playing the gruesome video; he would be telling a compelling true story. More important, he would be telling it first. I knew Nelson would have a lot to say about Chauvin; after all, it was his job. According to our system, Eric Nelson was supposed to make the jury feel sorry for the killer and disgust for the killed. I did the exact same thing when I was a criminal defense attorney.

When Jerry finished his opening, Judge Cahill gave Eric Nelson the opportunity to make an opening statement on behalf of Derek Chauvin. Nelson approached the podium and addressed the jury in a scholarly tone. He kicked off his opening by discussing the importance of reason. I thought it was an odd choice. For human beings, emotion drives choice, not reason.

Nelson went right to work attacking Jerry's focus on the nine minutes and twenty-nine seconds. Eric noted there were more than 400 witnesses listed, more than 200 civilian witnesses, more than 50,000 individually marked pieces of documentary evidence. His point? The case was bigger than 9:29. *Fair point*, I thought. *Okay, there's a lot of stuff, but how much of it really matters?* I bet some members of the jury thought the same thing.

Nelson proposed that the consequential action in the case took place in four locations: inside Cup Foods, at the Mercedes-Benz, at squad car 320, and at the Hennepin County Medical Center where Floyd was officially pronounced dead.

I thought, *Eric just violated the law of three.* What's the law of three? If you want people to remember anything, never give them more than three items. Two is better than three, and one is best of all.

Anyway, embedded in Eric Nelson's opening statement was the implication of a few arguments: Use of force on Floyd was reasonable because he was high or drunk and out of control. Use of force was reasonable for Floyd because he was a physically large man. Next, Floyd died because he took drugs, had an enlarged heart, and had other comorbidities, and because the crowd distracted the officers. Finally, the use of force was taught to Chauvin, and therefore authorized within his training.

Within Nelson's opening, he started at Cup Foods with store clerk Chris Martin observing Floyd showing signs of being under the influence of drugs or alcohol. Eric noted that Martin recognized the twenty-dollar bill as a counterfeit bill. Consistent with his themes, Nelson noted that another young person at the store, Omar Kamara, had called the police and mentioned that the man who offered the fake twenty was drunk and six feet to six and a half feet tall.

Then, Nelson took the jury to the Mercedes-Benz, and he highlighted that Floyd had taken two Percocet tablets. The two people in the car with Floyd, Hill and Hall, reported that he couldn't be awakened in order to leave. Nelson noted the time as 8:09 when Lane and Kueng arrived, and observed that Floyd put drugs in his mouth to conceal them from the police. Nelson informed the jury that agents of the Minnesota Bureau of Criminal Apprehension found drugs in the Mercedes, which were a mix of fentanyl and methamphetamine. The pills were designed to look like Percocet.

Nelson mentioned that the officers asked Floyd, "What are you on?" and he answered, "Nothing."

Then Nelson turned the jury's attention to squad 320. Interestingly, he invoked witness Charles McMillan, who, he pointed out, was urging Floyd to get up and get into the car—even though it was obvious that Floyd could not get up. Nelson told the jury that when Chauvin arrived, he saw the struggle and asked the officers present whether Floyd was under arrest. When he received an affirmative response, Nelson noted that Chauvin and two other officers "couldn't overcome Floyd." Here's when Nelson emphasized that Chauvin was five foot nine and 140 pounds versus Floyd, who was six foot three and 223 pounds. Nelson noted that squad 320 was rocking because of the struggle, which caused the crowd to gather.

Nelson pointed out that the crowd started yelling at the officers, calling them names and distracting them. With a simple one-sentence phrase, Nelson mentioned that Chauvin used a knee to restrain Floyd. Eric justified the restraint because, according to him, Floyd was attempting to kick the officers.

Then Nelson returned to the gathering crowd and emphasized that witnesses of the scene were growing angry. Nelson singled out from the crowd two individuals as particularly aggressive: Donald Williams and Genevieve Hansen. Nelson must have read this line from his notes: "As the crowd grew in size, so did their anger." He said, "Officers perceived threat, causing officers to divert attention from the care of Floyd to the crowd."

Nelson, in defense of his client, said that Derek Chauvin "did exactly as he was trained to do" but noted, "It's not attractive." As Nelson transitioned to the Hennepin County Medical Center, he made no mention of the time the officers stayed on top of Floyd's person, or the number of times he mentioned his mother, declared he couldn't breathe, and cried out in pain. Nelson didn't mention the length of time Chauvin was on Floyd's neck with his knee, or how long Floyd was unconscious and unresponsive under Chauvin's knee.

As Nelson turned to the medical center where Floyd was pronounced dead, he again urged reason, and then launched into the medical evidence. He asked rhetorically, "What was Mr. Floyd's actual cause of death?" He then answered his own question: "The evidence will show Mr. Floyd died of a cardiac arrhythmia that occurred as a result of hypertension, coronary disease, ingestion of meth and fentanyl, and adrenaline flowing through his body, all of which acted to further compromise an already compromised heart."

Nelson accurately noted that Dr. Andrew Baker conducted the only autopsy and found some things but didn't find others. Dr. Baker found that Floyd's blood gas test revealed high carbon monoxide, and no petechial hemorrhaging, no injury to the neck muscles, no damage to Floyd's airway. However, Dr. Baker did find meth and fentanyl, a paraganglioma tumor which is known to secrete adrenaline, signs of coronary disease, an enlarged heart, swelling or edema of lungs, and numerous scratches and bruises.

Nelson's story was very different from the state's. He was clearly setting up all the themes we knew he would harp on. Would it be enough to raise reasonable doubt? I didn't know. We were all about to find out.

———

Shortly after Governor Walz assigned me the case in June 2020, I was in Detroit visiting my ninety-four-year-old father, Leonard Ellison, and my two older brothers, Leonard Jr. and Brian.

Brian is an ordained minister and a pastor. He picked me up from the airport, and as we often do, we stopped for a little lunch at the Big Boy, a local chain in Michigan.

After we made small talk with the hostess, a teenager wearing a COVID mask with rhinestones on it, Brian asked me to tell him what I could about the case. There was a lot I couldn't share, but there were some things I could.

As we were sitting in this booth of the restaurant, Brian held his chin, contemplating something. He said, "You say...none of them knew him, huh?" referring to the witnesses and Floyd.

"Nope. None of them knew 'm," I said, munching on French fries.

"So, why did they start yelling at the cops to stop?" Brian asked.

"They thought it was the right thing to do, I guess," I said.

"So, they stepped forward to protest what was happening to someone they didn't know? Someone they could've assumed the worst about? And took video of the cops as the cops were on top of him like that?"

"Yep."

"Wow. They could have been arrested or beaten themselves?"

"I suppose, yeah."

"Some cops still might retaliate. Ain't unheard of, ya know?"

"Yeah, true."

Then Brian said, "It's a modern re-enactment of the story of the Good Samaritan."

I paused. "Huh? Whaddaya mean, Rev?"

"You can't understand the story of the Good Samaritan," said Preacher Brian, "unless you understand that Jews and Samaritans considered each other heretics at the time. Both groups recognized Abraham as their father, they had their different beliefs, which led to conflict, including violence, destruction of holy sites, and more." Brian went on: "You can't understand the story without understanding that the injured man on the roadside and the Samaritan were in conflicting groups."

I started to pick up what Reverend Brian was laying down.

He went on: "So, as you know, a Samaritan saw an injured man lying on the roadside. Two men walked past the injured man, one man was a priest and another a Levite, both learned and moral men, trained in religion and law. Neither one of them helped. They had their reasons, but they didn't help. The Samaritan helped. He dressed the man's wounds, loaded him on the back of his donkey, and delivered the injured man to an inn. When he reached the inn, the Samaritan paid the innkeeper for the night and asked him to check on the injured man through the night. The Samaritan promised to reimburse the innkeeper for any extra expenses when he returned."

Brian repeated his point: "What these people, these bystanders, did: It's the story of the Good Samaritan.

"George Floyd, in the eyes of some people in this world, is the Other," Brian said.

Brian was right about this. Not more than a few days after Floyd's death, well-known pundit Candace Owens tweeted a harsh denunciation for the deceased George Floyd, which went viral. "We've turned George Floyd, a criminal drug addict, into an icon," she said. She wasn't alone. A chorus of critics illuminated Floyd's mistakes and addictions to justify what Chauvin did to him and protect the status quo—keep the wheel spinning.

He went on, "In the eyes of some, he's nothing but a big Black thug with a drug problem who tried to cheat the store with a fake bill. He's the ultimate Other, who is outside the circle of our compassion. But like the Samaritan, the bystanders never judged him. They did what they could to help him. They witnessed his martyrdom, and they tried to help."

Brian took another fry and thoughtfully continued. He said that Chauvin, Lane, Kueng, and Thao were like the Levite and the priest. They had the duty, the training, and ability to help the suffering man, but they didn't help. They caused the suffering. It was their job to protect Floyd, especially if he was on drugs, but they did nothing. Frankly, they did worse than nothing.

"Yeah," I said. "I see your point."

"The Samaritan didn't ask the injured man whether he had a criminal record, or whether he had been drinking alcohol or taking dope." Brian took a sip of coffee. "The Samaritan asked whether the injured man needed help, and that's all he needed to know."

According to something called the bystander effect, said Brian, what these people did was extraordinary. The reverend, my brother, said, "That's a miracle. That's what I call an amazing spiritual event, and it happened right there on video for the world to see."

I thought about it.

Months after talking with Brian, but well before trial, I proposed to our prosecution team that our case was really all about what the bystanders saw. I don't think I told them that Brian had sparked the idea, but I told them that the testimony of the use-of-force case with the officers, police trainers, and experts was just to confirm for the jury what the bystanders witnessed: unreasonable force. The testimony of the medical causation witnesses was really about confirming for the jury what the bystanders had witnessed, too: Unreasonable force substantially caused the death of George Floyd.

If we proved these two things, then we would prove unintentional murder in the second degree. All the prosecution team had to do was to convince the jurors to "believe their own eyes."

———

From the beginning of the trial, we focused on the crime itself—from the moment Chauvin put his knee on George Floyd's neck until the moment paramedics carried Floyd's lifeless body away. We could have started when Thomas Lane first encountered George Floyd, sticking a gun in his face. We could have started when Floyd was in the store, buying cigarettes with the fake twenty. We could have started when Floyd was a child, or when he woke up on May 25, or whenever. However, everyone—the judge, court reporter, all lawyers, witnesses, and jurors—were called together because of the nine minutes and twenty-nine seconds; the period of time Chauvin and company inflicted unreasonable force on Floyd with a lethal result.

We started it all by getting testimony from the people who had witnessed the crime, the bystanders: the ones who were so outraged that they protested with their voices, recorded videos, and uploaded them for the world to see. Some bystanders even called the police on the police officers who killed Floyd. We elected to start our narrative with the folks who saw it unfold: the bystanders. The folks who sacrificed themselves to save a man they didn't know.

The jurors and the bystanders had a lot in common: They were all randomly selected. Both the jury and the bystanders were a group of multiracial, multigenerational individuals of both genders, who didn't know one another or George Floyd. What the bystanders saw shocked and outraged them. We needed the bystanders to transmit their sense of disbelief to their fellow Minnesotans on the jury unanimously.

Judge Cahill instructed the jury that what the lawyers say isn't evidence. The evidence is the testimony and any exhibits, not lawyers' statements.

There are two parts to every witness's testimony: direct and cross. Whoever calls the witness does a direct examination first. On direct examination, the lawyer is supposed to ask open-ended questions, like, "What time did you arrive?" Leading questions, on the other hand, are generally reserved for cross-examination, when the lawyer asks the witness questions like "You arrived at six p.m., right?"

On direct examination, the witness is telling the story, and to be effective the lawyer conducting the direct exam needs to know every nuance of the case. Every question must have a point.

Since the state was responsible for proving the case to the jury beyond a reasonable doubt, we built a series of direct examinations designed to show that Chauvin intentionally used force that was unreasonable, and that this unreasonable force substantially caused the death of George Floyd.

On cross, Eric Nelson would try to show the opposite. Eric's job on cross would be to make the witness's testimony appear ambiguous, uncertain, dishonest, or otherwise untrustworthy.

A good direct exam has certain ingredients, and one of them is trial prep. Testifying in court is scary. The coolest person is likely to be nervous about it. A lot of things can go wrong.

Witnesses can forget. By the time the trial arrives, it might be years later. The situation the witnesses are testifying about was likely stressful, and stress can distort memory. The best thing a lawyer can do to prepare a witness is give them a chance to relax and tell it like it happened. That means familiarizing the witnesses with the whole process of testifying in court.

We start with the courtroom. We tell them where they will be sitting, where the judge and jury will be. Some witnesses need to visit the actual courthouse and courtroom. Some witnesses benefit from sitting on the witness stand before trial so they can understand the jury's perspective, how the witness chair feels, and what it will feel like answering a lawyer's questions. Courtroom familiarity helps the witness calm down and focus on the task at hand: giving effective testimony. We also go over terms of art, technical terms, or legal terms. The witness should know the questions that will be asked because it's important the witness isn't surprised by any of the questions on direct examination.

I always advise witnesses to be truthful, forthright, and direct. I tell them to avoid looking uncertain, unless they are genuinely uncertain, in which case it is okay to ask the lawyer to clarify the question. I tell the witness that the lawyer will ask one question for one idea. Experienced trial lawyers don't ask compound questions on direct or cross. This helps the lawyer get the testimony needed, and it allows the witness to give strong, concise, and confident testimony.

The prep is really designed to calm the witness down. They have the answers. They know what happened. They just have to be calm enough to tell it.

———

The first witness we called didn't believe her eyes at first.

Jena Scurry testified that she had been a 911 dispatcher for years, and with all her years of experience handling emergency calls, she saw something that seemed wrong. Something was weird. She glanced at the video showing the scene at 38th and Chicago. The video feed she was getting of that corner was from one of the city cameras. She had a bird's-eye view.

The officers weren't moving. One was kneeling on top of the handcuffed individual on the ground. She monitored other screens. When she looked back at the streaming video for 38th and Chicago, the officers were still on top of the arrestee. Way too long, from her experience. She thought the camera must have frozen. She thought the equipment wasn't functioning.

"My instincts were telling me that something was wrong. Something wasn't right," Scurry said. "It was an extended period of time… They hadn't told me if they needed more resources." She continued, "I don't know if they had to use force or not. They got something out of the back of the squad, and all of them sat on this man. So, I don't know if they needed to or not, but they haven't said anything to me yet."

She called a police sergeant about the manner of this arrest. Sergeant David Pleoger would testify later. Scurry said, "You can call me a snitch if you want to, but…" and went on to explain what she found so disturbing. Now, "call me a snitch if you want to" is telling, and I'm sure the jury understood the risk of retaliation from fellow law enforcement officers that Scurry was facing because she reported suspected misconduct. A self-interested 911 dispatcher might look the other way. Not Scurry. Matt Frank did the direct exam of Scurry, and he asked if she had ever felt the need to call a supervisor like that before. She said, "Never before."

If the jury wanted to believe Scurry, then the state had established that the officers used force, and that they used it long after it was necessary, which makes that force unreasonable. However, the jury was under no obligation to believe Scurry. Despite her being a trained professional and jeopardizing her relationships with police officers, and perhaps her career, the jury could still reject her testimony.

On cross, Eric Nelson emphasized the struggle inside the squad. He got Scurry to agree that she noticed squad 320 rocking back and forth when Floyd and the officers were inside struggling with him. She confirmed that the squad was moving around a lot due to officers struggling with a suspect. Nelson would use this to justify the officers' use of force.

Nelson scored his points on cross, but with Ms. Scurry, we established what the totally objective 911 dispatcher had seen and experienced. She was alarmed to the point of contacting her supervisor.

Alisha Oyler, twenty-three, who described herself as a shift lead at the Speedway gas station across the street from Cup Foods, was the state's second witness. On the evening of May 25, 2020, she was working the register, when she went on a smoke break. She looked out a large window facing 38th and Chicago, toward Cup Foods, where she saw three officers on top of the body of an individual on the ground. She didn't know the man on the ground, but what she saw was so shocking that she pulled out her cell phone and began filming.

She took seven separate videos. She had seen similar disturbing scenes before. When Steve Schleicher asked her to explain why she recorded her cell phone video, she said: "I always see the police, and they're always messing with people, and it's wrong, and it's not right."

Alisha's testimony was very helpful, especially when put together with all the other video footage. Her video added another important viewpoint for the jury because it showed the location of all four officers, Chauvin, Thao, Lane, and Kueng, next to squad 320.

Other videos, including Darnella Frazier's video, have excellent angles of George Floyd and Derek Chauvin, but not of the other officers. Oyler's video wasn't as good as the milestone video that Jena Scurry was looking at, but Oyler caught a substantial amount on her cell phone.

Alisha's testimony was not smooth, but it was effective. Perhaps she was a little disoriented because she had never been caught in such an important matter before, having to testify on national television, but she had come to court to testify about what she saw, and she did.

She recorded Floyd's murder, and we were able to introduce

probative video evidence because of her. In our prep session she was way better, but, hey, she was understandably very nervous. She was just an everyday person who saw a horrific thing, and she had the guts to come tell the jury about it. I was proud of her.

———————

Donald Williams II was just past thirty years old when he witnessed George Floyd's murder. He testified that he had gone fishing with his son and was just stopping in the corner store to pick up something. By pure coincidence, I knew Donald. He and my sons, twenty-seven and thirty-two, were on the same wrestling team twenty years ago at Fairview Park in North Minneapolis. Donald didn't stop wrestling after high school. In fact, he went on to become a professional mixed martial arts (MMA) fighter.

Williams testified that he recognized that the manner in which Chauvin was kneeling on Floyd's neck was known as a "blood choke." Donald also described from the witness stand that Chauvin was "shimmying to actually get the final choke in" on Floyd. He described Chauvin's arrest procedure as "torture." He called 911, or as he said, "called the police on the police," to report Chauvin because he believed he had "witnessed a murder." He also added that all the officers were involved, including Thao, who Williams said tried to intimidate him and taunted the bystanders.

As Matt Frank passed the witness to Eric Nelson, Williams, the tough MMA fighter, paused to wipe tears from his eyes. As I said, I knew this young man. He was no crier. He was just that emotional. Nelson asked Williams about his wrestling experience. Nelson asked whether Williams had ever seen anyone regain consciousness after losing it in a competitive wrestling match. Williams agreed that he had.

Nelson was trying to set up the argument that the officers had remained on top of Floyd because he might have regained consciousness and attacked them. I hoped no one on the jury would buy that the still-handcuffed Floyd would suddenly regain consciousness and spring back to attack the officers, but who knew?

Nelson clearly saw Williams as a witness he could use to promote his narrative of the angry mob theme, but it just came off as stereotyping to me. Nelson said, "You grew more and more upset."

Williams: "No, I was controlled and professional," given the circumstances.

Nelson pointed out that Williams called the officers "bum" or "bogus" or even a "pussy-assed bitch" thirteen times. He called Donald Williams "angry." Williams didn't take the bait and pushed back, saying, "You can't paint me out to be angry" and "I stayed within my body." Williams noted he stepped off the curb but returned to it when Thao commanded. Williams admitted that he raised his voice, but he needed to be heard. Nelson's line of questioning implied that Williams's objection to Chauvin's conduct was to blame, not Chauvin's actual conduct.

Our case was off to a great start. I felt that we were putting on a good case, and thanks to our witnesses, we were getting the truth out.

I was happy and proud that we were giving a voice to folks who so often don't get one. Donald Williams wanted to be heard. No matter what the jury decided, these regular folks, randomly selected by fate, got to share their truth. That was important to everyone on our team.

———

Judge Cahill opened the next morning with an important ruling; the judge resolved an issue that had me worried for a long while. Cahill announced that the underage witnesses could deliver their testimony off-camera. We had four witnesses who were eighteen or younger: Darnella Frazier, Alyssa Funari, Kaylynn Gilbert, and Judeah Reynolds. Cahill ordered that the audio of their testimony would be broadcast live, but the cameras would be aimed at the judge or lawyers.

The world was waiting to hear from Darnella Fraizer—the eighteen-year-old who was awarded a 2021 Pulitzer Prize Special Citation, along with the 2020 PEN/Benenson Courage Award presented by director Spike Lee, and received multiple scholarship offers at the age of seventeen. All of this was because she recorded and uploaded the video that went viral and sparked an international movement.

It is no exaggeration to say that because of the video she uploaded to Facebook in the early morning hours of May 26, 2020, at 1:46 a.m., Chauvin was now in court facing murder and manslaughter charges. However, her video also moved people to action, from Minneapolis to Frankfurt, from New York to Nairobi.

Her video was in stark contrast to the press statement released by the Minneapolis Police Department that same morning, which stated Floyd's death was the result of a "medical emergency."

Darnella testified that she and her little cousin, Judeah Reynolds, had taken a walk to the neighborhood store for snacks. She said her little cousin "really liked snacks." She denied that it was a dangerous neighborhood, as the police described it. She testified that she walked to Cup Foods "thousands of times." Darnella testified that when they walked up to the scene she saw Floyd facedown on the ground under the officers. She sent Judeah into the store because she didn't want her to see what was unfolding on the street.

Darnella testified, "I heard George Floyd saying, 'I can't breathe, please, get off of me. I can't breathe.' He cried for his mom. He was in pain. It seemed like he knew it was over for him. He was terrified. This was a cry for help."

Darnella told the courtroom that Floyd was "terrified, scared, begging for his life," and saying "I can't breathe," while Chauvin "just stared at us" with "this cold look."

Her testimony made me emotional, though I tried not to show it. She described for the jury how the bystanders tried to get the officers to help Floyd, but to no avail: "They definitely put their hands on the mace, and we all pulled back," Darnella said.

Eric Nelson's cross was focused on making Darnella look like she was motivated by money, fame, or glamor. When Jerry Blackwell re-examined Darnella he asked her about how she felt about the experience of watching Floyd die, and the aftermath. She spoke of her survivor's guilt, and how she saw her family in George Floyd. "When I look at George Floyd, I look at my dad, I look at my brothers, I look at my cousins, my uncles, because they're all Black." She continued, "I have a Black father. I have a Black brother. I have Black friends." The impact on her was personal: "I look at how that could have been one of them."

Darnella regretted not having done more to save the life of George Floyd. She felt regret for not physically engaging the officers, but then came the knockout testimony: "It's been nights I stayed up apologizing and apologizing to George Floyd for not doing more and not physically interacting and not saving his life," Darnella Frazier said. "But it's like, it's not what I should have done, it's what he should have done." When she said "what he should have done" she was looking toward Chauvin. No one on the jury could miss it.

Calling Darnella's cousin Judeah Reynolds, who was nine years old at the time, was controversial on our prosecution team. Some thought she was too young, and her psyche might be scarred by testifying. I consulted Vernona Boswell, Hennepin County attorney's manager of victim-witness services. On Vernona's advice, we took a lot of time to prep Judeah. Weeks before the trial, we took her into the courtroom, allowed her to sit on the witness stand, and walked her through her testimony. She was allowed to have a supportive adult, LaToya Turk, who stood near her while she testified. When the moment for her to testify came, she did great.

As I thought about Judeah, I couldn't help thinking about heroic children who face down difficulties. I knew Judeah needed to testify so that she could own a piece of justice. I had full confidence in her. When I explained my decision to the team, I told them about children in Birmingham, Alabama, in May 1963. It was called the Children's Crusade, and its purpose was to draw attention to the civil rights movement going on there. Most of the children's parents had either been arrested or had jobs that depended on staying within the good graces of the people who maintained the system of Jim Crow segregation.

Thousands of Black children ages seven to eighteen demonstrated peacefully around the city of Birmingham, and they were met with hostility by the police and white private citizens. Many of them were arrested and thrown in jail. These kids helped break Jim Crow in Birmingham. And why not? Weren't they segregated? Didn't they endure segregated education, housing, and transportation, like their parents? Even today, weren't kids like Judeah suffering the effects of police brutality?

Tamir Rice was twelve when he was shot and killed by a Cleveland police officer. Adam Toledo, thirteen, was unarmed, giving himself up for arrest, when a Chicago police officer shot him. I believed Judeah had a right to be part of her own struggle for justice.

Judeah's testimony was short but powerful. "I was sad and kind of mad," she said, explaining her thoughts on witnessing a police officer with his knee on the man's neck. "It felt like he was stopping his breathing and it was kind of like hurting him." I wanted the jury to see that if a nine-year-old kid could see the damage Chauvin was doing to Floyd, then anyone could, including academy-trained police officers. Nelson declined to cross-examine. He was wise to let it go.

Like Judeah, neither Alyssa Funari nor Kaylynn Gilbert were shown on camera.

Both these young white women were seventeen years old at the time they witnessed Floyd's death, and both testified that they were so outraged by what they saw, they recorded the incident with their cell phones.

Funari and Gilbert were just two buddies hanging out on Memorial Day. While Funari went into Cup Foods to pick up an auxiliary cord for her phone charger, Gilbert waited in the car. As Funari walked by the officers on top of Floyd, she heard him crying for a breath. "It was difficult because I felt like there wasn't anything I could do as a bystander," Funari said. "I felt like I was failing."

On Thao's bodycam video, which prosecutor Erin Eldridge played to support Funari's testimony, Funari can be heard saying, "He's not talking now!" She was responding to Officer Thao, who said, "If he's talking, then he's breathing."

Funari, visibly pregnant and wearing superlong eyelashes, said she heard Floyd say "he couldn't breathe and that his stomach hurt and that he wanted his mom." Floyd "looked like he was struggling," she said. "He looked like he was fighting to breathe."

Gilbert testified that when she saw the crowd gathering, she got out of the car to witness Floyd being murdered. Gilbert also pulled out her phone to record the officers on top of Floyd. Gilbert came closer to the officers who were on top of Floyd.

Gilbert was so close, she testified: "I saw [Chauvin] digging his knee into his neck more," referring to Floyd. "He was putting a lot of pressure into his neck that was not needed," she said. During our prep session with Gilbert, she told me that she wanted to be a lawyer one day. I told her she certainly could do it.

———————

Genevieve Hansen, twenty-seven, was a bystander, but not an ordinary one. She showed up for court all spit and polish in her dress uniform because she was an EMT-certified firefighter in the Minneapolis Fire Department (MFD). Hansen was a young white woman with a powerful sense of justice. She was taking a walk on her day off, and she happened by the tragic scene. She witnessed Floyd's condition and offered to treat him, but the officers denied her, and Thao in particular mocked her.

Hansen testified that Floyd's face was "puffy and swollen, which would happen if you were putting a grown man's weight on someone's neck." She testified to the jury, "I could have given medical assistance, and that's exactly what I should have done," but she never had the chance "because the officers didn't let [her] on the scene."

By the time Hansen arrived, Floyd wasn't begging to breathe or calling for his mother anymore. When she arrived on the scene Floyd "had an altered state of consciousness," because he was not responding to the "painful stimuli" of Chauvin's knee on his neck. She pleaded with officers to check Floyd's pulse and start chest compressions, but she was denied access to Floyd by the police.

When it was time for Eric Nelson's cross, he must have known that her testimony was powerful, because he really went after her.

> **Nelson:** "When you first arrived on scene, your own personal demeanor was much more calm."
>
> **Hansen:** "Correct."
>
> **Nelson:** "As you were there. Between 8:26 and 8:30, in those four minutes, you would agree that your own demeanor got louder, and more frustrated and upset."
>
> **Hansen:** "Umm... Frustrated? I'm not sure that is the word I would use."
>
> **Nelson:** "Angry?"
>
> **Hansen:** "More [like] desperate."
>
> **Nelson:** "You called the officers a bitch, right?"
>
> **Hansen:** "I got quite angry after Mr. Floyd was loaded into the ambulance. And there was no point in trying to reason with them anymore because they had just killed somebody..."

Nelson kept trying to press the narrative that the "crowd" was angry and included people swearing. Hansen replied, "I don't know if you've ever seen anyone killed, but it's upsetting."

Ouch.

Without Nelson's prompting, Judge Cahill disallowed the response on the grounds of argumentativeness. But it was too late: The jury heard it anyway.

———————

I was still working my way through the heavily fortified Hennepin County Government Center every morning, but it was not on my mind. I had become immune to it all, and it simply became a part of the scenery for me now. My focus this particular morning was the witnesses and the Floyd family.

I stopped in the Hennepin County grand jury room reserved for the Floyd family at eight-thirty a.m., as I usually did, to check in on them. Generally, one of the prosecution team members would join me. We stopped in to explain things and answer questions several times a day. My respect for the Floyds started high and grew.

This particular morning, Floyd family members were sipping coffee, talking to one another, and looking at their cell phones from time to time. Ben Crump and another Floyd family attorney, Tony Romanucci, were often with them in the grand jury room offering moral support, legal advice, and small talk. As always, Vernona Boswell was a fixture, always tending to the needs of the family. I walked in the door and saw everyone. I saw Ben and Philonise and shook hands and hugged them both. Ben asked me how I thought it was going.

I said, "So far fine, but I just don't know what the jury is thinking."

Ben nodded. "I hear you. But I appreciate how hard y'all are working. I haven't seen any AG or district attorney put this kind of hard work and care into the prosecution of a case involving a member of law enforcement." He reached his hand out to shake my hand once again. "Thank you. Please thank the team."

I let him know that I would relay his gratitude to the team. We hugged again, and I went to the eighteenth floor, ready for another day.

Chris Martin took the witness stand. He was the state's ninth witness since testimony had started. Chris was a tall, skinny, nineteen-year-old student. He wore a black hooded sweatshirt. He was eighteen when he sold Floyd the cigarettes at Cup Foods on May 25, 2020. Martin was a soft-spoken African American kid who had dreams. He had a job, and he aspired to go to college. He lived in an apartment above Cup Foods with his mom.

Martin's performance on the witness stand showed his intelligence. He testified that he had accepted the fake twenty-dollar bill in exchange for the cigarettes, and he noticed that it had a blue coloring he associated with a hundred-dollar bill. This tipped him off that it might be fake. He didn't say anything to Floyd at the time, but his employer directed him to go outside and ask Floyd to come back to deal with the fake bill. Chris approached Floyd while he was sitting in the Mercedes, still parked on 38th near Chicago Avenue. However, Floyd didn't come back in; therefore, his employer called the police.

Martin described Floyd's demeanor inside of Cup Foods. He testified, "[Floyd] seemed very friendly, approachable. He was talkative." Martin told the jury, "He seemed to just be having an average Memorial Day living his life. But he did seem high."

Matt Frank asked Martin to confirm video footage in which he appeared inside Cup Foods and outside as well. In describing the footage outside, Martin narrated how he and many other bystanders were horrified by what they saw happening to Floyd. He saw the officers, including Chauvin, on top of Floyd. He noted that he saw Floyd unconscious and unresponsive, and he saw Chauvin resting comfortably on top of Floyd, doing nothing to help Floyd.

Martin knew a few of the people assembled on the street, but not most. He knew his two coworkers and he knew Alyssa Funari, all of whom were calling on the police to stop the force and give medical assistance to Floyd. Martin testified that he had called his mother, who was in the upstairs apartment, and asked her not to come downstairs. He wanted to shield her from witnessing George Floyd's torture and death.

Martin identified himself and his coworkers on video footage in which the bystanders were begging, pleading, yelling, and cursing at the officers to stop what they were doing to Floyd. He and another coworker saw one of his coworkers get pushed in the chest by Officer Thao when he took a step into the street. Both he and the coworker escorted the other coworker back into the store to avoid any further provocation.

Martin came back to the scene after he escorted his coworker inside Cup Foods, and the video showed him standing there watching Chauvin on top of Floyd. He had his hands on his head, with a mystified look on his face. Frank asked him what was going on in the video. Martin told the jury that he was feeling "disbelief and guilt." Frank asked Martin why he was feeling guilty. Martin replied, "If I would have just not taken the bill, all of this could be avoided."

Frank asked Martin what happened next, and Martin said, "I was just kind of emotional, I went to the African American [referring to Donald Williams] on the curb, and said, 'They are not going to help him. This is what we have to deal with.'"

Judge Cahill sustained an objection from Nelson. I didn't understand why.

A few minutes later the video showed the emergency medical vehicle arriving, and it showed Martin approach his mom, who was standing at the door in the same building as Cup Foods. The video showed her talking to the officers, and it looked like she was giving them a piece of her mind. Finally, Frank asked Martin whether he continued to work at Cup Foods, and Martin replied, "No. I didn't feel safe."

After Martin shared what he knew, defense counsel Nelson had his turn on cross-examination. "You made the decision after Floyd handed you this counterfeit twenty-dollar bill that you weren't going to call him out on it?" Nelson asked. "Was that in part because you felt maybe he's under the influence?" Nelson was obviously trying to get Martin to testify that he was scared of Floyd, all part of the narrative that Chauvin's use of force was reasonable. Martin didn't cooperate.

"I thought that George really didn't know it was a fake," Martin said. "So I thought I'd be doing him a favor."

Nelson was able to introduce the idea that Floyd was high, but Martin also said he wasn't violent or threatening. He tearfully admitted that he felt guilty about ever calling the police. It was a brave admission. A number of witnesses stated they felt guilt, because they mistakenly believed that if they would have done something differently, Floyd wouldn't have been killed.

Charles McMillan may have been the hardest witness for me to watch. A Black man of sixty-one years, balding with a light beard, McMillan may have been the first person to notice that George Floyd was suffering under the weight of the three officers. He also might have been the last to talk with Derek Chauvin. McMillan appeared on the scene shortly after Floyd was arrested and marched across 38th Street toward squad 320.

At trial, McMillan wore white-framed plastic glasses, a green suit, and a lighter-colored shirt and tie. He looked ready for church. Erin Eldridge conducted the direct exam of McMillan, and she used video extensively. She ran the tape and paused it, all the while asking McMillan to authenticate his voice on the tape.

Erin Eldridge asked about the moment McMillan stopped on the corner where Floyd was being arrested to tell Floyd to "git up 'n git ina car, man" and "you cain't win, man." Erin Eldridge asked McMillan why he used those words. McMillan replied on the witness stand, "To help him." Apparently, he thought those words would persuade the officers, including Chauvin, to allow Floyd to get up and get a breath. But McMillan's words did not work.

As he delivered his testimony to the jury, he choked up more than once. He was a man who knew how to survive on the streets. He was savvy and had had his own run-ins with the criminal justice system and policing, but all of that didn't stop his tears.

Erin ran the portion of the video in which Floyd said, "Please, I can't breathe." McMillan confirmed that he was the one on the video saying, "You got him down. Let him breathe at least, man. At least let him breathe and get off his neck, man."

As Eldridge was playing the video of Floyd dying—again, McMillan broke down on the witness stand. He dropped his head into his hand; he palmed his forehead and began to weep. McMillan pulled four facial tissues from the box on the witness stand, and sobbed, "Oh—my—God." Judge Cahill called a break for Mr. McMillan to collect himself.

Charles McMillan was a somewhat reluctant witness. Weeks before trial, we were having our prosecution team meeting, and Josh Larson, who led our fact witness subcommittee, was giving his report. Josh would just check down the list of fact witnesses, report on whether the witness had been served with a subpoena, and when the witness's prep session was scheduled. As we were approaching the trial date of March 8, there were a few folks we didn't exactly have a handle on, like Alyssa Funari.

Josh reported that McMillan wasn't exactly excited about testifying and mentioned that McMillan had a lawyer named Will Walker.

I knew Will Walker. I told the team that I would call Will and get him to help us secure McMillan's presence for prep and trial. Will and I were not in law school at the same time; I was leaving when he was coming in. However, Black law students are so few in number that we all pretty much know one another. Will is a charismatic guy with a huge smile. He's a trial lawyer and a proud dad. People are attracted to Will; maybe that's why he makes a lot of money. He is one of those people who always looks like he's having fun.

When I got Will on the phone, he was helpful as usual, but he told me that McMillan wasn't feeling super great about participating. Lawyer to lawyer, I told Will that we needed Charles. There really was no other option. We would subpoena him, and we would have the judge send the sheriff out to greet him if necessary.

McMillan did show up, and his testimony before the jury was

explosive. Shortly after Floyd was taken away in an ambulance, Chauvin's body camera video showed him responding to Charles McMillan, who took issue with him kneeling on Floyd's neck. Chauvin responded to McMillan by saying, "That's one person's opinion, we had to control this guy because he's a sizable guy. It looks like he's probably on something."

With that response, McMillan got Chauvin to give the only explanation he ever gave as to why his knee went down on George Floyd's neck that day.

———

The next series of witnesses were members of law enforcement, but they weren't use-of-force experts. They were the witnesses who showed up at the scene of Floyd's death. Even though these witnesses were not use-of-force experts, they were cops, and they had gone through academy training. The cumulative effect of the police officers, the police executives, and the use-of-force experts was to convey one simple idea to the jury: Chauvin (and Thao, Lane, and Kueng) knew better, they just didn't do better.

Lieutenant Jeff Rugel was the first law enforcement officer witness we called. He was head of the MPD's business technology unit, and he knew police body camera footage. The state wanted to introduce video because, carrying the burden of proof beyond a reasonable doubt, we needed the right witness to do it. Rugel authenticated the footage from both Kueng's and Thao's body-worn cameras.

The state showed the jury footage from Chauvin's body camera as he and Thao drove toward Cup Foods in their squad car. Rugel's questioning allowed us to show the footage from Chauvin's body camera, which gave Chauvin's perspective as he walked up to Kueng and Lane as Floyd was being restrained.

A segment of Chauvin's bodycam video revealed both of his hands wrapped around Floyd's neck, although briefly. This was minutes before Chauvin's knee landed on Floyd's neck. Rugel testified that Chauvin's body camera, which was attached to the front of his shirt, had somehow gotten knocked off his uniform and then slid underneath squad 320. This likely happened during the arrest. Though Rugel was a fairly technical witness for the state, he was impactful for the case and the family. The video showed multiple points of view, and we wanted the jury to know that we were showing them everything; nothing was being withheld from them. Unfortunately, in order to do this, we had to put the family through a tough day. They had to watch Floyd die multiple times. The day ended after the jury viewed each segment of body camera footage entered into evidence.

———

Now, it was time for Courteney Ross, Floyd's fiancée. She had met him at the Salvation Army shelter, where Floyd was a security guard. Courteney went there to talk to the father of her son about his upcoming birthday. When her son's father didn't come down to the lobby of the secured building, she got upset. That's when Floyd approached her and said, "Sis? You okay, sis?" She told him why she was there and why she was upset. He asked if he could pray with her. "That was just Floyd," she said.

When asked about losing his mother, she described Floyd as a mama's boy. She said that when he came back from his mother's funeral in Houston, "he seemed like he was broken...He was devastated. He loved his mom so much and I knew that. He talked about her all the time."

Matt Frank was skillful at balancing Courteney's testimony between too little and too much. He gently directed her to topics that needed to be presented in a way that humanized Floyd.

Matt asked her about Floyd's addiction to opioids next.

"Both Floyd and I, our story, it's a classic story of how many people get addicted to opioids. We both suffered with chronic pain. Mine was in my neck; his was in his back. We both had prescriptions." She rolled her necklace between her fingers as she spoke. "We got addicted and tried really hard to break that addiction many times."

Matt Frank asked her how long this struggle went on for them. She responded, "Addiction, in my opinion, is a lifelong struggle. So, it's something we dealt with every day. It's not something that just kind of comes and goes. It's something I'll deal with forever."

There were people who would never forgive George for having a drug problem, but Courteney Ross helped make his struggle with addiction a little more understandable, more human to the jury. Ross's testimony about their shared struggle with opioids was raw and honest. She couldn't hold back the tears, much like other witnesses.

On cross, Nelson probed Ross about Floyd's drug use. He asked where they purchased drugs, including opioids. She testified that Morries Hall was a source. Hall was with Floyd on May 25, 2020, when he died in the custody of the police.

Hall, represented by counsel, informed Judge Cahill outside of the hearing of the jury that he intended to invoke his Fifth Amendment right against self-incrimination. He was never called to testify.

Eric Nelson had been pounding on the drug stuff from the beginning. I felt like Ross helped us get out in front of these arguments by showing the jury that Floyd was not violent, and it was the knee on the neck that killed him, not drugs.

When paramedic Seth Bravinder took the witness stand, he testified that Floyd appeared dead when he and his partner had arrived at the scene. "I didn't see any breathing or movement," he said.

Bravinder, a paramedic for Hennepin County, and his partner, Derek Smith, were on duty when they got the call to respond to 38th and Chicago Avenue. Bravinder and Smith transferred Floyd's body from the street surface to the gurney to the ambulance soon after arriving, he testified.

The video footage showed that Chauvin didn't get off Floyd until the paramedics tapped Chauvin on the shoulder to get him to move. As they loaded his body on the gurney, Floyd was visibly not responsive. Floyd had no control over his head and arms, and they flopped around as he was loaded in the emergency medical vehicle. Bravinder testified that they continued to try resuscitating Floyd. They saw no signs of breathing or movement by Floyd when they arrived, and they were never able to detect a heartbeat as they got him to the hospital at Hennepin County Medical Center. Nothing was successful.

The state called several witnesses to show that the scene investigation was conducted according to standard protocols, and that Floyd was dead before he arrived at the hospital. One of those witnesses was Captain Jeremy Norton, who served the people of Minneapolis in the fire department for twenty-one years. He rose as high as battalion chief. He responded to the scene on May 25 after paramedics had already removed Floyd from the scene.

He testified that he visited the scene at 38th and Chicago Avenue, and then proceeded to the rig a few blocks away, where paramedics said, "He was an unresponsive body on a cot." The LUCAS machine was pumping his chest to "breathe for him." In the absence of these actions, the patient would have been pulseless, unresponsive, not breathing, and "for all practical purposes dead."

Erin Eldridge, conducting the direct examination, asked, "Did anyone ever find a pulse?"

Norton said, "No, ma'am."

David Pleoger, a law enforcement professional with twenty-seven years of service, was a particularly important witness for the state because he was the supervisor of Chauvin, Lane, Kueng, and Thao. He knew the rules and regulations officers under his supervision had to follow; it was his responsibility to supervise these officers and to conduct a force review.

Based on Pleoger's review, he thought the restraint should have ended earlier than it did. Pleoger was not particularly forthcoming or helpful to the state, but he was honest. He told the jury that the force against Floyd should have ended when Floyd was no longer offering up any resistance. We thought he made a critical point for the jury.

Pleoger testified that he received a call from a dispatcher, Jena Scurry, on May 25, 2020, at about eight-thirty p.m. Pleoger paraphrased her words as "she didn't mean to be a snitch" and that she was concerned about how officers were treating a suspect.

Scurry's call prompted him to call Chauvin, and the call was recorded. Chauvin said, "I was just going to call you. Had to hold the guy down. He was going crazy. Wouldn't go in the back of the squad." Pleoger, permissible within the policy, talked to Chauvin off camera. Schleicher followed up by asking what the conversation was after the audio was cut.

According to Pleoger, Chauvin told him that he was trying to put Floyd in the car, he became combative, and after struggling with him he suffered a medical emergency. Chauvin did not tell him that he used his knee on Floyd's neck or back.

Pleoger talked to all four officers, including Lane and Kueng, when he arrived on the scene. None of them talked about knees on the neck or the length of time that force took place. He learned that Floyd had been taken to Hennepin County Medical Center (HCMC).

Pleoger directed Officers Lane and Kueng to secure the suspect vehicle and to interview any witnesses. He then directed Thao and Chauvin to travel to HCMC. Pleoger asked Chauvin to also interview witnesses. Schleicher then played a recording of Pleoger and Chauvin's exchange. Pleoger asked Chauvin to find witnesses, but Chauvin is recorded saying: "I could try, but they are pretty hostile."

Pleoger drove to HCMC and inquired about Floyd. A nurse said he was doing bad or poorly. At that point, he talked with Chauvin again, and this was the first time Chauvin told him that he kneeled on Floyd or kneeled on his neck. Still, Chauvin didn't tell him for how long the kneeling on the neck took place.

Pleoger then testified that it was at this point he learned that Floyd had "passed away," and this definitively converted the episode into a "critical incident," which triggered another set of protocols. With a critical incident, the officers become suspects. Chauvin was directed to go to City Hall room 108, where he would be interviewed by other police officers.

———

MPD Sergeant John Edwards was next to testify. Edwards is a young Black man, with braids on top of his head and shaved sides. This stylish hair style was a contrast to his conservative demeanor and his conventional ensemble, a gray suit with a white shirt and light-blue tie with darker blue diagonal stripes. His glasses, skin tone, and goatee reminded me of Malcolm X.

Edwards was calm and well composed. He offered short but responsive answers. Edwards made it clear he was currently on leave. He didn't say how long he had been on leave, but I wondered whether the protests, civil unrest, and arson prompted his decision.

On the witness stand he was professional but not at all excited to be there. Edwards was hard to judge. He was polite but clipped. Edwards didn't have any particularly surprising testimony. He was really a caretaker of the scene. We needed him to explain that he had received the scene from Pleoger and then handed it off to the Bureau of Criminal Apprehension agent.

Edwards's testimony took a long time, even though all he really did was set the scene. He described how he directed Officers Lane and Kueng to turn on their body cameras, set up yellow crime tape, and directed other officers to canvas the neighborhood. He concluded his testimony by explaining how he had gathered whatever information he could, which wasn't anything.

Right about the time Edwards was wrapping things up and handing them off to the BCA agent, homicide investigator Lieutenant Richard Zimmerman was called to the scene.

Lieutenant Zimmerman is a likable guy. He had been on the

Minneapolis police force since 1985, and his confidence and experience came through on the witness stand.

Zimmerman's testimony was courageous. Here's how that questioning went:

Matt Frank: "Based on your review of the body-worn camera videos of the incident and directing your attention to that moment when Mr. Floyd is placed on the ground...what is your view on that use of force during that time period?"

Zimmerman: "Totally unnecessary."

Matt Frank: "What do you mean?"

Zimmerman: "Well, first of all, pulling him down to the ground facedown and putting your knee on a neck for that amount of time is just uncalled for. I saw no reason why the officers felt they were in danger, if that's what they felt, and that's what they would have to feel to use that kind of force."

Matt Frank: "So, in your opinion, should that restraint have stopped once he was handcuffed and prone on the ground?"

Zimmerman: "Absolutely."

Zimmerman said kneeling on a person's neck "can kill 'em." He was unequivocal: Once a suspect is handcuffed, "the threat level goes down all the way," and officers "need to get them out of the prone position as soon as possible because it restricts their breathing."

Coming from one of the most senior officers on the Minneapolis police force, this testimony was very helpful for the state's case.

———

I have known Medaria "Rondo" Arradondo, chief of the MPD, for decades. He's always been the consummate professional. He is well-mannered and diplomatic. Rondo carried himself much more like a businessman than a cop.

When Rondo made chief, I called him to congratulate him. I even set up an appointment to meet face-to-face to discuss collaboration. He was always happy to work together. He was popular in the community. The MPD had a bad reputation among many Black residents of Minneapolis, but Rondo was the exception. When he came on board, there was a sense that if anyone could fix it, it would be Rondo.

When John Harrington and I organized the working group on police-involved deadly force encounters, Rondo was one of the leaders in the community we tapped. Though super busy, Rondo made time to contribute to the twenty-eight recommendations and thirty-three action steps aimed at reducing deadly force encounters with law enforcement in Minnesota.

Rondo did not waste time after news of the May 25 video came to public attention. Within a day after Floyd's death, Rondo fired Chauvin, Thao, Kueng, and Lane and called for an FBI investigation. Rondo didn't mince words either. He condemned Chauvin's conduct and labeled Floyd's death a "murder."

When the state decided to call Chief Arradondo, his identity as chief was as important as his testimony. We wanted to convey to the jury that they could convict Chauvin without insulting the institution they rely on to protect and serve them. If the chief opposed Chauvin's conduct, then they could, too.

From the beginning the prosecution was trying to restore honor to the badge, as Jerry Blackwell had said in the opening statement. Arradondo helped the state make good on that promise. In fact, Rondo testified that Chauvin violated department policy, training, and ethics by continuing to kneel on Floyd's neck after he was no longer resisting, and certainly after he was "no longer responsive."

Nelson's cross-examination was focused on his themes. Nelson wanted to establish that Rondo might know how to run a department, but it had been a long time since he'd done hands-on policing. He got Rondo to admit that he had not made an arrest in many years.

Nelson cherry-picked a segment of Kueng's body camera video in which Chauvin's knee, at that moment, appeared to be on Floyd's shoulder blade. Rondo acknowledged it, but it didn't shake his conclusions.

Inspector Katie Blackwell's testimony was crucial for the state. She was the commander of the MPD's training division at the time of Floyd's death. She helped us show the jury that Chauvin knew better; he just didn't do better. Blackwell and Chauvin had known each other for decades. They were community service officers together.

The trial revealed how dramatically their careers had diverged. She was a commander, who had acquired a number of promotions, advanced degrees, and certificates. Chauvin started as a patrol officer, like Blackwell, but he had not advanced. Nineteen years after starting with Blackwell he had received no promotions and was on trial for murder.

Blackwell testified that the Minneapolis Police Department trained officers to use their arms to carry out neck restraints, instead of using the knee as Chauvin did. She showed the jury that MPD officers, including Chauvin, "were taught about positional asphyxia." MPD policy, she testified, required officers to move suspects onto their sides "as soon as possible" once they are "under control."

Sergeant Ker Yang bolstered Blackwell's testimony. Yang is an MPD crisis trainer who explained to the jury that listening is key to crisis intervention and that officers are trained to "de-escalate" when "it is safe and feasible."

The state also called Lieutenant Johnny Mercil, who was the MPD's use-of-force policy and training expert. He was part of a series of MPD officials who testified about the department's training and use of Chauvin's force against Floyd.

Mercil gave off a strange vibe, however. His answers seemed forced and unwilling. I thought he was going to turn on us and attempt to justify Chauvin's actions, but he didn't. Weeks later I would see behavior from Lieutenant Mercil on video that might explain why he had been minimally cooperative. He was caught on body camera video making disparaging remarks about protesters in the days following Floyd's murder.

Despite Mercil's lack of candor, he could not deny that Chauvin failed his official training. Mercil testified that Chauvin had received better training than he showed Floyd on May 25. He helped the state show the jury that Chauvin knew better.

All officers testified that Chauvin was trained to use the least amount of force to get control of a suspect, and to de-escalate his restraint once Floyd, or any suspect, was under control. Chauvin didn't do that. He carried on the force for several minutes after the force was unnecessary.

Like Mercil, Officer Nicole Mackenzie seemed reluctant to serve as a witness. We called her because she was the MPD's medical support coordinator when Floyd was killed. She was professional, well prepared, and knowledgeable on the stand, but she was also terse, perhaps because she was nervous. She had been called by both the state and the defense.

The state called her to show the jury that Chauvin had medical training in CPR, which he could have used to assist Floyd. She also testified that the MPD had a policy of rendering emergency first aid to people who needed it, which included George Floyd. Mackenzie testified that the policy of the duty to render emergency aid included first aid and calling for emergency medical services.

The duty to render emergency medical aid is binding on all police officers. Mackenzie testified that Chauvin had a CPR card, which was kept on file. That card proved Chauvin had the medical training to be aware of the dangers of mechanical asphyxia. Mackenzie said the police officers were trained, both in the academy and in-service training, to give a person CPR immediately after failing to find a pulse. She also testified that MPD does not teach "if you can talk, you can breathe." She directly refuted what Thao and Chauvin were barking at the bystanders on the scene as they were pleading for the officers to allow Floyd to breathe.

Steve Schleicher asked her to explain why it's wrong to believe that if you can speak you can breathe. She replied, "Because there is a possibility that someone could be in respiratory distress. And still be able to verbalize it. Just because they are speaking doesn't mean they are breathing adequately."

Schleicher asked Mackenzie if the presence of a hostile crowd could excuse an officer from giving emergency medical aid. Mackenzie replied, only "if an officer was being physically assaulted."

Nelson would later call Mackenzie in the defense case to testify about excited delirium, the controversial diagnosis often associated with people who suddenly die in police custody.

After Mackenzie got off the witness stand, Judge Cahill adjourned for the day. I headed to the twentieth floor to check in with the Floyd family.

I saw Philonise, who would be getting on the witness stand within a day or so as the state's spark of life witness. Philonise was always smiling, despite having to watch testimony centered on the death of his brother. Other than his wife and brothers, perhaps no one could know the pain he was carrying. As the leader of the Floyd family, Philonise likely had to carry everyone else's pain as well as his own.

———

It was Wednesday, hump day, and the weather was overcast. We had been in court for nineteen days at this point, including jury selection. I was still energetic, and the team was feeling strong as well. However, I didn't feel as confident as I had when we began. March 8 seemed like a long time ago.

When I saw Ben Crump that morning, I pulled him aside. I asked if he could arrange for Gwen Carr, the mother of Eric Garner, to speak to the prosecution team after the close of evidence that afternoon. Garner was killed by a New York police officer who placed a prohibited choke-hold on him during an arrest. That arrest resulted from Garner being accused of selling single cigarettes from a pack. I thought that a talk with his mother would keep the team uplifted. Ben said he would see what he could do.

On the eighth day of trial evidence, the state started off by calling to the witness stand Sergeant Jody Stiger of the Los Angeles Police Department (LAPD). Stiger was one of our two use-of-force experts. Seth Stoughton, who would testify last, would be the state's expert on the legal standards for police officer use of force. Stiger was our "hands-on" guy.

In federal courts in Minnesota, and probably every state in the United States, experts are often called to help juries understand scientific, technical, or other specialized information. These witnesses must be qualified as experts, usually by means of laying out their education, experience, background, research, or written works like books, articles, and lectures.

Jody Stiger is a cop and lawyer. He is also a Black man, and a national expert on use of force by police. He had spent twenty-seven years in law enforcement when he took the stand in *State v. Chauvin*. He had worked numerous assignments such as patrol, gangs, undercover narcotics officer and tactics, and use-of-force instructor for in-service and basic recruit training. He is also the lead tactics instructor at Rio Hondo Police Academy. Finding an amazing expert like Stiger is one of the reasons why I recruited Steve Schleicher in the first place.

Steve was an essential team member, in part because he had prosecuted members of law enforcement before. Steve recommended that we get two experts: one practical guy with recent experience with street cops, and one legal expert who was well versed in the law.

Stiger was the epitome of practicality. According to his résumé, which he presented to the jury through testimony, he had also developed and managed reality-based skills training for department personnel for six years and trained over 5,000 officers.

Stiger described for the jury how he also conducted use-of-force instruction for in-service officers—cops on patrol every day. He is also a certified FBI Rangemaster. Part of Stiger's duties include review of hundreds of use-of-force incidents and vehicle pursuits as well as providing his insight and recommendations to command staff. In other words, Stiger knows policing, including the proper use of force.

After laying out his credentials, Steve Schleicher asked Stiger questions about the video footage of Chauvin on top of Floyd. According to Stiger, while Floyd was prone and handcuffed, "no force was reasonable in that position." Floyd was "not attempting to resist, not attempting to assault officers, kick, punch," said Stiger. Chauvin's body weight on top of Floyd handcuffed in the prone position could "cause positional asphyxia and could cause death." Stiger said, "My opinion was that the force was excessive."

Stiger also showed the jury that Chauvin was inflicting gratuitous pain on Floyd. He pointed out how the video footage showed Chauvin applying a "pain compliance" procedure by pulling Floyd's wrist into the handcuffs, which could be heard tightening with each click of the cuffs.

Stiger said the technique is normally used to inflict pain in order to make the suspect comply with the officer's lawful commands, but Floyd was not offering any resistance. So the use of the pain compliance technique was just causing unnecessary torment, Stiger told the jury.

Schleicher anticipated defense counsel's "the crowd did it" argument and asked Stiger about it. Stiger testified that he did not recognize the crowd of onlookers during Floyd's arrest as a threat "because they were merely filming, and most of it was their concern for Mr. Floyd."

During cross-examination, Nelson asked Stiger if the crowd "calling you names and saying you are a fucking pussy [echoing Donald Williams] can be perceived as a threat?" Stiger agreed that folks shouting and yelling expletives could be seen as a threat.

Our next law enforcement witness was Special Agent James Reyerson of the Minnesota Bureau of Criminal Apprehension (BCA). Reyerson was the case agent assigned to the Floyd case, responsible for the entire case file.

The BCA routinely investigates police use-of-force incidents in Minnesota. The agency drew criticism for its troubled and controversial investigations of other police-involved deaths, especially the case of Justine Ruszczyk Damond in 2017.

The BCA performed well in the death of George Floyd, and Reyerson was a valued member of the team. With his testimony, the state wanted to make sure the jury saw everything and understood where it came from. So, much of Reyerson's testimony was about introducing pieces of evidence like the fake twenty-dollar bill (which, by the way, looked real to me), certain videos for various places, and other materials collected from Floyd. He also identified a glass pipe and a business card, which came from the Mercedes. Reyerson had submitted these for testing. He also had squad 320 and the Mercedes SUV Floyd was driving for processing at the BCA crime lab garage.

Reyerson testified that he had supervised the additional search of the Mercedes SUV in which pills were found. He ordered that these pills be tested. Reyerson testified that he had collected video from Cup Foods and Dragon Wok, the restaurant across the street from Cup Foods.

Then, things got interesting with Nelson's cross-examination. Nelson asked Reyerson whether in a videotape clip it sounded like Floyd had said, "I ate too many drugs"?

At first, Reyerson said, "No." Following this, Nelson played the short clip again and asked, "Did it appear that Mr. Floyd said, 'I ate too many drugs'?"

This time, Reyerson said, "Yes, it did."

I was watching via livestream on the twenty-first floor. I smacked my forehead. *Oh, crap!* All of us watching remotely thought it was a tricky, underhanded move. But there it was: Eric got our witness to adopt his assertion, saying that Floyd admitted taking "too many drugs."

Eric wrapped up his questioning and just two minutes later, Matt approached the podium. We watched, on the edge of our seats.

Matt wasn't going to let that trick slide. He asked Reyerson whether he had heard any of the conversation or line of questioning by the police officers right before the video clip. He said he had not. Matt Frank played a longer clip of that same section of the video.

Matt Frank asked, "Is there a discussion about drug use by the officers in attempting to talk to Mr. Floyd?"

"Yes."

"Having heard it in context, are you able to tell what Mr. Floyd is saying there?"

"Yes." Agent Reyerson leaned into the microphone. "Yes, I believe Mr. Floyd was saying, 'I ain't do no drugs.'"

When Reyerson came back to the prosecution team, he was a little embarrassed, but he had done his best. Sometimes crazy stuff happens.

Nelson was still fighting for Chauvin, and he had some more ammunition to argue that maybe Floyd died as a result of "too many drugs."

———

A series of forensic folks got on the stand to round out the day.

McKenzie Anderson, a BCA forensic scientist who processed Floyd's SUV and the officers' squad car, tested eight stains positive for Floyd's DNA, including seven bloodstains.

Breahna Giles, another BCA chemical forensic scientist, testified that pills were found inside Floyd's Mercedes SUV, and these pills contained fentanyl and methamphetamine.

Susan Neith, a forensic chemist, testified that the three pills found inside the SUV and squad car contained a fentanyl concentration of less than 1 percent and a methamphetamine concentration of 1.9 to 2.9 percent. She put these tiny percentages of fentanyl and meth in perspective because, she testified, "the majority of time" she examines samples that contain "90 to 100 percent methamphetamine."

It was good to be done with witnesses for the day. I went down to the eighteenth floor where the trial was actually taking place. I just wanted to be present for the team for moral support.

We all headed up to the conference room on the twenty-first floor to review the day. Rather than starting with how direct examinations went, what witnesses were coming up, and what the media landscape looked like, we did something a little different. The team was doing well, but we needed some inspiration.

Ben Crump came through for me, and we were graced to have a Zoom call with Eric Garner's mother, Gwen Carr.

I wanted the team to hear from Ms. Carr because I wanted them to understand we were carrying the hopes of many people who had lost loved ones to excessive force at the hands of a police officer and who never saw their day in court.

I wanted our eyes firmly focused on prosecuting one case, *State of Minnesota v. Chauvin*, but I wanted our team to keep in mind that there were bigger social, political, and historical forces at work.

Everyone on our team knew who Eric Garner was, though they might not have known his mother. Ms. Carr's voice, a mix of New York and Southern accents, had a powerful effect on the team. She was the epitome of dignity. She thanked the team for their hard work and reminded them that her son never got his day in court.

The Richmond County grand jury, which sits in Staten Island, considered charges against New York City officer Daniel Pantaleo, who had killed Eric Garner with the prohibited chokehold. Garner pleaded, "I can't breathe," as Pantaleo choked him with enough force to trigger a lethal cascade of events, ending in a fatal asthma attack.

The medical examiner who performed an autopsy on Eric Garner testified that Garner's death was a homicide, meaning death at the hands of another due to the officer's use of force, despite other comorbidities including high blood pressure and chronic asthma. Dr. Floriana Persechino, a veteran forensic pathologist, said, "The chokehold is a significant initial factor of the [lethal] cascade."

Unfortunately, the grand jury refused to indict Pantaleo.

Everyone was grateful for Ms. Carr's time. After the meeting, my friend Neal Katyal said, "It was so spellbinding to listen to her and hear her say, 'You're giving me something my son and I never got, a day in court.'"

That night, I felt fatigued, maybe for the first time. We had one of the most critical parts of the case coming up in the morning: medical causation. I had complete faith in Jerry Blackwell's ability here, but I was still nervous. What would Eric Nelson come up with on cross for the next few witnesses?

Fortunately, our next witness would prove to be more impactful than I ever imagined.

———

By this point we had presented the Good Samaritans—the bystanders who courageously spoke up for George Floyd, and who showed up for court almost a year later to testify about what they saw. Almost all of them cried on the witness stand, and yet through their tears, they found the strength to tell their stories—all for a man they didn't know.

Then came the use-of-force witnesses, who had testified that Chauvin was trained better, he knew better, he just didn't do better. His decision to stay on top of Floyd's neck, back, and legs for several minutes after he was subdued violated MPD policy.

Now, it was time to prove medical causation. Essentially, it was time to show that Chauvin and company's knee on the neck, back, and legs for nine minutes and twenty-nine seconds was the substantial cause of Floyd's death.

We had a strong team assembled for the task, including Jerry Blackwell, who could probably convince anyone he was a trained doctor given his grasp of medical topics; Lola Velazquez Aguilu, from Medtronic; Corey Gordon and Mary Young from Blackwell Burke; and Erin Eldridge, assistant AG. We also had the help of Keystone Strategy, a consulting firm that dedicated itself to helping us find the right experts.

We would prove our case of medical causation in two ways. First, we would prove our case affirmatively, and then we would prove it negatively by sequentially showing that every defense explanation for Floyd's cause of death was wrong.

For this we had Dr. Martin Tobin, who turned in an amazing performance. Dr. Tobin literally wrote the book on breathing, *Principles and Practice of Mechanical Ventilation, Third Edition.* Jerry Blackwell had a copy by his side for months before trial began and at the lectern with him during his direct exam.

Tobin is an Irish American, and he has a discernible Irish accent to prove it. On the witness stand he showed that he was a master teacher. When he reached for his own chest to demonstrate the mechanism of breathing, all the jurors mimicked him. Judge Cahill had instructed them they didn't have to track Dr. Tobin's demonstration though they could if they found it useful.

Tobin, seventy-one, is a critical care physician, pulmonologist, and academic with forty-six years practicing and teaching pulmonology. He is a recognized expert in acute respiratory failure, mechanical ventilation, and neuromuscular control of breathing.

Jerry Blackwell took twenty-five minutes to qualify Dr. Tobin as an expert. He then asked Tobin what materials he reviewed to prepare to offer an expert medical opinion. Dr. Tobin testified that he reviewed all the medical records, and a large number of videos, witness statements, and medical information. He then did his own research.

Blackwell asked Tobin to testify as to his expert opinion "to a reasonable degree of medical certainty," which is just legal lingo. Dr. Tobin testified that in his expert opinion Floyd "died from a low level of oxygen," which led to damage to his brain, and pulseless electrical activity (PEA) arrhythmia, causing his heart to stop.

Low oxygen is sometimes referred to as hypoxia or asphyxia. The cause of Floyd's low level of oxygen was shallow breathing—he had been taking small breaths that weren't able to carry the air down to the essential areas of his lungs, which get oxygen into the blood and get rid of the carbon monoxide.

Dr. Tobin explained that the compression of Floyd's neck and chest into the hard pavement stopped the expansion and contraction of his lungs. If a person's lungs can't expand, they can't take in oxygen and oxygenate the blood, and the person dies from low oxygen.

Tobin used graphics that showed the jury exactly where each officer was positioned on Floyd's body and where each of their knees was positioned.

With the use of the graphics, Tobin testified that the combination of Floyd's body being in the prone position, being handcuffed behind his back, and the hard pavement on the street had the effect of squeezing Floyd's chest and neck. He also testified that the effects of handcuffs were extremely important.

Using the video, Tobin showed Chauvin gripping Floyd's left arm and pushing Floyd's arm upward behind his back, inflicting pain.

Tobin described the pressure from Chauvin on Floyd's neck and back and Kueng on his back, against the hard street, operating like a vise and preventing Floyd from breathing.

Tobin did an amazing job of calculating the number of pounds on Floyd's neck. He testified that Chauvin pressed 86.9 pounds onto the neck of Floyd, who tried to push himself off the pavement with his fingertips.

Tobin, narrating the video, slowed it down so the jury could see Floyd's eyes widen in an instant. Tobin testified that this was Floyd's last conscious moment. "One second he's alive, and one second he's no longer," said Tobin.

Watching the video, Tobin said, "That's the moment the life goes out of his body." When Tobin precisely identified the moment that George Floyd died, we all sensed that this was one of the most dramatic moments of the trial.

Tobin testified that Floyd did not die of a fentanyl overdose.

On cross, Nelson attacked Dr. Tobin's diagnosis by highlighting Floyd's health risks and comorbidities. For example, he posed questions to Dr. Tobin about Floyd's use of tobacco, implying Floyd had impaired lung function because he was a smoker. Nelson inquired about the effect of drugs like methamphetamine and fentanyl in Floyd's blood, as well as the presence of a paraganglioma in his body, which secreted adrenaline. Nelson also inquired about Floyd's substantial blockage of his coronary artery.

According to Tobin none of these things was a substantial factor in Floyd's death, but Nelson put them in front of the jury.

Nelson then proposed an alternative theory of death by overdose. Nelson asked Tobin whether the partially ingested pills containing fentanyl would cause respiratory depression to occur within five minutes. Using military time, Nelson asked Tobin "if any amount of fentanyl were ingested at 20:18, wouldn't the peak respiratory depression occur at 20:23?" Tobin agreed with Nelson's assertion, assuming what Nelson said was accurate.

Eric's approach on cross-examination, for the most part, was to lean into Tobin's testimony rather than try to directly refute Tobin. For example, he argued that a police officer could not possibly be expected to know all that the learned Dr. Tobin knows with limited time and medical knowledge.

Nelson argued, with leading questions, that while, "If you can talk, you can breathe" is not correct, Officer Chauvin wouldn't necessarily know that. He also tried to get Tobin to agree that many of Tobin's measurements were based on assumptions. Dr. Tobin did not accept this entirely but had to agree somewhat.

Ultimately, Eric's cross-examination gave defense-oriented jurors something to go on. Nelson's argument was essentially this: "Doctor, you're not a police officer. Officers are not medical experts, like you, and can't be expected to know all you know. You've had the benefit of time. Chauvin didn't have time."

Would jurors buy it? I didn't know.

With Dr. Tobin's testimony, the jury had the truth about what caused Floyd's death: low oxygen caused by compression of Floyd's neck and back due to the officers' unreasonable force. While Chauvin was the one on trial, Dr. Tobin showed that all the officers had killed Floyd. Their combined weight contributed to squeezing Floyd's body to the point where he could not get enough air to oxygenate his blood and expel carbon monoxide.

The main purpose of the rest of our witnesses was to strengthen Tobin's conclusion and refute red herring explanations for the cause of Floyd's death. The first red herring explanation was overdose.

Daniel Isenschmid, forensic toxicologist for the NMS Labs in Pennsylvania, who has handled "tens of thousands" of tests per year, was next up. Isenschmid testified that his lab had tested the hospital blood and urine of George Floyd. According to him, the notable findings in the hospital blood were the presence of fentanyl, the breakdown product, norfentanyl, and methamphetamine.

Isenschmid testified that methamphetamine at 19 nanograms per milliliter in Floyd's blood would be consistent with a prescription dose; a "very low level," he said. This was critical testimony because it was a direct refutation of methamphetamine causing the death of Floyd.

He testified that fentanyl was found in the amount of 11 nanograms per milliliter, and he found the breakdown product, norfentanyl, in the amount of 5.6 nanograms per milliliter. The significance of the norfentanyl was that it showed that Floyd didn't die due to a fentanyl overdose. It is present only when the body has had a chance to metabolize, or break down, fentanyl. If a person who ingests fentanyl lives long enough to metabolize it and produce norfentanyl, then they didn't die from the fentanyl. In fentanyl overdose deaths, norfentanyl is not found because the body of the user never had a chance to metabolize the substance.

Ultimately, Isenschmid testified that the fentanyl and methamphetamine in Floyd's system did not contribute to his death.

We called Dr. Bill Smock as a witness to refute the argument about excited delirium, the controversial diagnosis associated with in-custody deaths. Smock testified that he believed in excited delirium, but that it did not apply to Floyd.

Smock testified that Floyd did not exhibit delirium. He was oriented to time and place, could recite his name, telephone number, and address. He could articulate his own needs and respond appropriately to questions. He was not particularly excited. He was not overheated. People with the diagnosis of excited delirium often take off their clothing and complain of being hot. Floyd didn't exhibit superhuman strength. The officers subdued him and kept him that way.

Dr. Smock carried an impressive résumé as a legal forensic medicine specialist, surgeon, and former emergency room doctor. His experience as an emergency room doctor allowed him to testify that he had previously witnessed excited delirium, and what he saw from Floyd was not that. Most important, Smock testified that Floyd died from a lack of oxygen and not a fentanyl overdose, which he was well familiar with as an ER doc.

The next witness we called was forensic pathologist Dr. Lindsey Thomas. She was a smart, well-spoken, well-informed witness who, I believed, accurately identified Floyd's cause of death: low oxygen caused by compression of Floyd's neck and back, or in another word, asphyxia.

She broke down exactly what was on the death certificate: "Subdual" means he was subdued, "restraint" means he was restrained, "neck compression" means that the pressure on the neck, along with the subdual and restraint, caused the death.

Dr. Thomas testified there was "no evidence" indicating that Floyd "would have died [on May 25, 2020], except for the interactions with law enforcement." Thomas testified that the numerous videos of Floyd's arrest she had reviewed showed no signs of death from a fentanyl overdose. Fentanyl overdose deaths, Dr. Thomas said, presented as the person progressively growing "very sleepy" and then "peacefully stop[ping] breathing."

While she was not the medical examiner on record for this case, we wanted the jury to hear a clear explanation of Floyd's cause of death from a highly experienced medical examiner. Dr. Thomas had actually trained the medical examiner on record, Dr. Andrew Baker.

Dr. Baker made some comments that left us uncertain about what he might say on the stand.

A medical examiner's job is to determine cause and manner of death. Unless a medical examiner reviews all the circumstances surrounding the person's death, including what is contained in the tissues of the body, then the medical examiner is limited to the body and the toxicology.

In an interview on June 1, 2020, Dr. Baker made a point of saying that he didn't see petechiae, which are tiny reddish spots containing blood that appear in skin or mucous membranes as a result of localized hemorrhage. This concerned me since Dr. Baker told investigators that the absence of petechiae points away from a finding of asphyxia. The truth is that the absence of petechiae does not disprove asphyxia. Petechiae are simply a marker of increased venous pressure in the head.

Dr. Thomas helped the jury understand the cause of death by gathering all the facts that were important before offering opinions that the whole world was going to rely on.

We knew what Dr. Andrew Baker's final conclusions in his report were, but we didn't know what he was going to say on the witness stand.

After Dr. Thomas concluded her testimony, we hoped Dr. Baker would testify consistent with his report, but we could not risk it.

We all knew that Dr. Baker's testimony might determine the outcome of the entire case. One witness's testimony could make the difference. As the only medical professional who had conducted an autopsy of George Floyd, examining his physical body, we knew he would have credibility.

Would he use it to illuminate or confuse? Up until now, he had done both, in my opinion, and I will confess some anxiety around his anticipated testimony. Jerry Blackwell, however, didn't seem nervous to me. Jerry seemed ready and confident for the battle ahead.

Anticipating Dr. Andrew Baker's testimony made me anxious. The anticipation kept me up the night before, something that never happens to me.

Right after Floyd's death, Baker's comments were sparking controversy. I don't know what his intent was, but the comments he made regarding Floyd's death caused confusion and doubt in the national dialogue about what had killed Floyd.

When county attorney Freeman said "there is other evidence that does not support a criminal charge" against the officers involved, and the whole city reacted, he was operating on preliminary conversations he'd had with Baker. Baker was saying things like "if [Floyd] were found dead at home alone and with no other apparent cause, this could be acceptable to call an overdose."

To many people, Baker's June 2020 comments were just one of the first signs of the old pattern repeating itself: unarmed African Americans being killed in police custody while the system protected the officers from accountability. Baker seemed almost eager to supply reasons for Floyd's death that would justify the use of force against him or offer alternate theories for what killed him.

Baker's early comments explained why Ben Crump and the Floyd family had sought two independent autopsies, both of which concluded on May 31, 2020. Ben Crump had already arranged for Dr. Michael Baden and Dr. Allecia Wilson to conduct independent medical examinations of George Floyd when my office took over this case. Their preliminary findings concluded that Floyd died of asphyxia due to neck and back pressure.

They found that the pressure on his neck and back interfered with his breathing and blood flow to the brain. According to the independent medical examiners, the officers' weight on Floyd's back, the handcuffs behind his back, and the prone positioning all contributed to inhibiting Floyd's ability to breathe. They said Floyd died at the scene, and that no other cause of death was present. Finally, they concluded that the toxicology findings might be helpful in determining the circumstances of Floyd's death but were not a cause or contributing cause of death.

Baker's interviews with investigators on June 1, 2020, record him saying that he did not view the video before conducting the autopsy. One might think that the video might give him insight into how Floyd died, but Baker told investigators, who generated handwritten notes, that he didn't want to bias himself. When I read Baker's notes from June 1, I wondered why an ME would want to close himself off from relevant evidence.

As noted above, Baker had told the investigators that "if [Floyd] were found dead at home alone and with no other apparent cause, this could be acceptable to call an overdose."

This struck me as a highly speculative comment, and not what I would expect from a seasoned medical professional, unless that professional had an agenda. This speculative comment really began the rumor mill that Floyd died from a fentanyl overdose, which was never true. In sort of an ass-covering follow-up statement, the investigator's notes state that Baker said, "I am not saying this killed him."

Baker told investigators in the same June 1 report that Floyd's comorbidities might well have contributed to his death. For example, Floyd's untreated hypertension would tend to lead "to death quicker" because of an increased need for oxygen, according to notes taken during that interview. "Certain intoxicants" could exacerbate the problem, the notes also say.

By June 6, 2020, twelve physicians penned a piece entitled, "George Floyd's Autopsy and the Structural Gaslighting of America" in *Scientific American* magazine. The doctors decried the ways the "weaponization of medical language emboldened white supremacy with the authority of the white coat. How will we stop it from happening again?" While not attacking Dr. Baker directly, the authors critiqued how his work was used to write the criminal complaint against Chauvin. "All under the cloak of authoritative scientific rhetoric. They took standard components of a preliminary autopsy report to cast doubt, to sow uncertainty—to gaslight America into thinking we didn't see what we know we saw. In doing so, they perpetuated stereotypes about disease, risky behavior, and intoxication in Black bodies to discredit a victim of murder."

As if channeling the physicians who wrote the *Scientific American* piece, Hennepin County commissioner Angela Conley got her dander up when Andrew Baker's contract came up for renewal before the Hennepin County Commission. Commissioner Conley voted no on Baker's contract. Her reasons were the autopsy report's mention of "potential intoxicants in his system," which she said criminalized him even in death.

"Why would this be listed?" said Conley. "The community lost trust in the system. That report was ultimately the catalyst of an insufficient [third-degree] murder charge by the county and later upgraded to [second-degree] murder by the State." Conley, Hennepin County's first Black member, continued, "Baker's report gave the very reason not to trust these processes that haven't brought justice in the past." She added, "With a good conscience, I can't approve this today."

I called Conley and thanked her for her concern and passion. I also noted that while Baker offered, in my opinion, comments that invited speculation and confusion, he said the truth in his autopsy report in the end: Floyd was a homicide victim and died as a result of his heart stopping because of law enforcement subdual, restraint, and neck compression. He was giving us the bare minimum, but it was enough.

When Baker spoke with the FBI on July 8, 2020, he again confirmed his conclusion that "cardiopulmonary arrest complicating law enforcement subdual, restraint, and neck compression" was what caused Floyd's death. He stuck by his determination of homicide.

At that point, Baker refused to give a "but for" answer to the question of "but for the action of the officers, George Floyd would have lived?" Baker told FBI investigators that he did not know if Floyd would have lived but for the actions of the officers. He could not predict what would have occurred. Baker also noted in the FBI report that Floyd's heart was "larger than it should be."

Baker told the FBI agents he did not know which officers were positioned on parts of Floyd's body and could only identify Officer Chauvin. Despite not knowing where the officers were positioned, he told the FBI agents, "There was no relation to Floyd's cause of death by Lane's position."

Regarding the fentanyl and the meth, Baker told the FBI agents that an individual can develop a tolerance to opioids, but Baker said he did not know Floyd's tolerance to fentanyl. Though not a toxicologist, Baker considered the amount of fentanyl in Floyd's blood as high. He did not have any information on when Floyd may have ingested fentanyl. However, he did note fentanyl was a respiratory depressant that slowed down the brain's drive to breathe.

Baker told FBI agents that he found arteriosclerosis, which is hardening and narrowing of arteries. Under questioning, Baker agreed that Floyd did not appear near death in the video leading up to his arrest and the subdual and restraint. However, Baker refused to offer an opinion about when Floyd became critical or near death.

Instead, Baker shared that he did not believe the prone position was any more dangerous than other positions, based on an article or a journal that he had read. Baker claimed to be unaware of the autopsy findings of Dr. Baden or Dr. Wilson, who provided the opinion that Floyd died of low oxygen in a report on May 31. Baker told FBI investigators he did not know when someone's heart disease would become lethal.

Baker told FBI agents that he could not determine whether the cause of death was compressional asphyxia, because there was no autopsy evidence that the blood or air supply was cut off. At the end of the FBI report, Baker returned to his speculative assertion that if Floyd had been found dead in his bed with the level of fentanyl in his blood that was present for this autopsy, it might be classified as a fentanyl fatality.

Dr. Baker was hard to pin down. On the one hand, he was clear that Floyd's death was a homicide connected to the actions of the officers. On the other, he appeared to invite speculation around meth and fentanyl, the enlarged heart, the arteriosclerosis, and whatever.

It was no wonder Eric Nelson made use of the doubt Baker seemed to be insinuating. In his August 28, 2020, court filing, Nelson picked up the bread crumbs that Baker appeared to be dropping. Nelson wrote, "Combined with sickle cell trait [and] his pre-existing heart conditions, Mr. Floyd's use of fentanyl and methamphetamine most likely killed him." The purpose of this court filing was to seek (unsuccessfully) a dismissal of the charges against Chauvin. "Adding fentanyl and methamphetamine to Mr. Floyd's existing health issues," wrote Nelson, "was tantamount to lighting a fuse on a bomb."

Months before trial, I joined a prep meeting with Matt Frank and Jerry Blackwell involving Dr. Baker, and I left the meeting more worried than when I had walked into the prep room. In the December 2020 meeting, Dr. Baker confirmed his autopsy report findings from May 2020: Floyd died as a result of "cardiopulmonary arrest complicating law enforcement subdual, restraint and neck compression."

However, his flow and demeanor seemed a little off. Dr. Baker seemed unnecessarily argumentative with us. I got the impression that he knew he had the power to screw us and wanted us to know it. He showed us a series of photos that appeared to show Floyd did not have the telltale signs of asphyxia.

Baker emphasized that he found Floyd had no petechial hemorrhages, which are small pinpoint hemorrhages generally seen in the lining of the eyes (common signs of asphyxia). Baker showed us pictures of Floyd's neck muscles, which didn't show signs of bruising or injury.

At the end of his presentation, he showed us a photograph of a male college student, young and unhandcuffed, with gym weights loaded onto his back. He was surrounded by other guys apparently ready to attend to the young man lying prone on the padded surface.

It was exactly what he threw out to the FBI agents at their July 8, 2020, meeting with him. Baker then said something like, "Medical research exists showing that lying prone isn't necessarily dangerous." Perhaps not an exact quote but something very close.

Baker was referring to a Canadian law enforcement study on the use of prone positioning during arrests. He noted this study found no fatalities among about 3,000 arrests. "A prone position is not in and of itself more dangerous than other positions," he said, according to the medical literature. The Canadian government paid for the research.

For me, Dr. Baker wasn't signaling scientific neutrality; he was signaling, but not explicitly expressing, sympathy for the defense. We could not rely on him at trial. I started thinking about how we were going to manage Dr. Baker.

Finally, he told us he knew the individual whom the defense intended to call as an expert medical examiner, Dr. David Fowler, and that he was a personal friend.

In fairness to Dr. Baker, he has a right to befriend anyone he wants, including Dr. Fowler. However, we were a little shocked with what we learned about Dr. David Fowler.

The fateful morning came, and so much of our case was hanging on what Dr. Baker was going to say on the witness stand. Strategically, we had decided months before that we would need to tuck his testimony in the middle of the medical experts, Drs. Tobin, Smock, and Thomas. After Baker, we would call the cardiologist Dr. Jonathan Rich.

We would essentially surround him with straightforward and truthful witnesses, and then hope he blended with the team. He, of course, was perfectly free to go rogue if that was what he believed, but the world would be comparing what he said with what the other highly trained doctors said. He had his professional reputation to consider.

So, April 9, a Friday, on day ten of testimony, the state called Dr.

Andrew Baker—the Hennepin County chief medical examiner, who performed the official autopsy on Floyd's body. Dr. Baker looked the part of a medical examiner. He sported a gray suit, white shirt, and purple tie. Clean-shaven with brown plastic-frame glasses, Baker reminded me of Christopher Reeve's Clark Kent.

For all the buildup and worry, things went well. Jerry Blackwell conducted the direct examination of Baker. It went better than I had expected. Baker stuck to his report and, ultimately, homicide. He didn't offer conjecture or speculation. He testified that he stood by his autopsy finding that Floyd's death was a homicide caused by "cardiopulmonary arrest complicating law enforcement subdual, restraint and neck compression."

He said Floyd's heart disease, fentanyl intoxication, and methamphetamine use were contributing causes but not direct causes because they "did not cause the subdual or the neck restraint." He said he did not believe the neck compression he saw in the videos (which left no visible injury) could have restricted air or blood flow to Floyd's brain, but that it contributed to physiological stress, increased adrenaline, and elevated blood pressure. Baker conceded that a pulmonologist, like Dr. Tobin, was better qualified than he was to offer an opinion about whether Floyd could breathe, and how much air he could take in given the subdual, restraint, and neck compression.

When Baker's testimony was complete, Judge Cahill made the unorthodox decision to invite the witness, Dr. Baker, back into his chambers. He told us that he wasn't talking about the case, but only catching up with an old friend.

We gathered up our stuff and headed up to the twentieth floor to debrief with the Floyd family. They had all shared our nervousness about Baker's testimony, but they agreed that it had gone well enough.

We ended the long day, after a grueling four weeks. Even though Eric Nelson certainly made his points with the jury, we got ours in, too. I didn't let myself speculate on whether we were winning or losing, but I did allow myself to feel proud of our team.

As I walked toward my car in the basement of the Hennepin County Government Center to go home, I thought, *We are putting on a good case.* It was Friday night, which is Date Night in the Ellison-Hurtado household, and I wanted to see Moni's welcoming face.

Little did I know, more shit would hit the fan Sunday afternoon.

————

Sunday, April 11, 2021, all hell broke loose in Brooklyn Center, a majority-minority Minneapolis suburb that shares a border with the city. Twenty-year-old Daunte Wright was shot and killed by Officer Kim Potter during a traffic stop. Potter had pulled her 9mm Glock when she says she intended to pull her taser.

The Chauvin trial wasn't even over, and here we go with another unarmed Black person shot and killed. I would have thought that officer-involved shootings of unarmed Black men would slow down, at least for a while.

The shooting sparked protests. Governor Walz again implemented a curfew to help curb any violence. The National Guard was deployed to create a non-police presence. When peaceful protesters at the Brooklyn Center police department refused to disperse, police fired tear gas, rubber bullets, and flash-bangs into the crowd.

After six days and nights of protests, more high-profile activists came to the Twin Cities, such as Maxine Waters, chairwoman of the congressional committee that I once sat on, the House Financial Services Committee. I know Auntie Max, as she is known, well and she shows up wherever injustice rears its head, ready to confront it.

Others who came back were Ben Crump, Rev. Jesse Jackson, and Rev. Al Sharpton. Together, they organized a funeral for Daunte Wright that highlighted the injustice and sense of siege that the Black community so often feels when tragedies like this occur.

I called Brooklyn Center mayor Mike Elliott, a friend and political ally. Mike was a new mayor, and he was doing his best in a completely new and volatile situation. He asked me to come out to Brooklyn Center to help him figure out how to calm the city.

How could I say no? It's true…I could have easily said no because I already had my hands full with the Chauvin trial, and a smarter person would have said no. Nevertheless, I said, "Sure, Mike, I will be there." I got into my gray Jeep Compass and headed to Brooklyn Center, about fifteen minutes from my house.

When I arrived, I saw a line of Black teenagers and young adults about twenty-five yards away from a fully outfitted line of police in riot gear. My first thought was *How can we de-escalate this?* Mike and I went to talk with the kids. I am not sure what I said, but I tried to tell them they had every right to be angry and heartbroken. I said that I understood how they might feel targeted because of their race and color. I then shifted gears to remind them that I was in the middle of the Chauvin trial, and they could trust me to pursue justice.

Little did I know then that Hennepin County attorney Mike Freeman and Washington County attorney Pete Orput would ask me to take the Potter case weeks later. I wasn't thinking about that.

I just wanted to avoid anyone getting hurt, including police officers, and I wanted to minimize the chances for a mistrial in Chauvin's trial, which I am sure Eric Nelson would be asking for bright and early Monday morning.

Somehow, the crowd began to disperse. They would probably be back out the next day and the following one, but for now, things were calm. I checked in with the mayor, who told me what had happened.

Veteran officer Kim Potter pulled Wright over for a traffic violation, possibly for an air freshener hanging from the rearview mirror. After pulling him over, Potter found that the driver had a warrant for his arrest. When officers tried to handcuff him, Wright tried to squirm back into the car. Potter then pulled out what she claims she thought was her taser and shot Wright with her gun.

When things seemed to calm down enough, I headed home to get ready for the final days of the Chauvin trial.

Later, I heard that protesters had gathered again on Sunday night outside the Brooklyn Center Police Department. Some of the demonstrators threw things at the cops, and the officers responded with chemical agents and 40mm crowd-dispersing plastic projectiles.

As expected, Eric Nelson made a motion for a mistrial and a motion to sequester the jury first thing in the morning. Judge Cahill asked the jurors what they had heard and cautioned them to avoid the news. Then he took arguments from both sides and ruled against Nelson's motions.

The jury was called back into the courtroom, and we continued by calling to the stand Dr. Jonathan Rich, a medical expert in cardiology. Rich was a youngish fellow who clearly was passionate about cardiology. He made a great witness because he appeared super informed and likable. Rich testified that despite the coronary artery blockage in Floyd's heart, the heart can create new paths for blood to circulate, and he saw nothing to suggest that a cardiac event played a role in his death.

He also testified that he saw no evidence to suggest that a drug overdose caused Floyd's death. He explained to the jury that Floyd was not frail and on death's door since the heart can counteract stenosis, arterial narrowing, by making new pathways. He said Floyd's heart was fairly strong, and that he would not have died but for the compression of his body, which restricted his oxygen intake.

The trial really felt like it was winding down when Philonise Floyd, younger brother of George Floyd, took the stand. Philonise was being strong for the family, but I could see in his face the difficulty of reliving his brother's death, over and over, on video. He was wearing a blue suit, a light blue shirt, and a stylish tie. He looked nervous, but as he spoke about his family with his warm Southern accent, his nerves calmed down.

He lit up talking about how he and George would play video games together. I think he brought a smile to everyone's face when he said,

"George, he used to make the best banana-mayonnaise sandwiches… because George couldn't cook. He couldn't boil water…"

A photograph was shown of George and his mother, Cissy. George must have been about three years old in the photo. Philonise couldn't stop the tears when he talked about his brother, and everyone watching was right with him. He kind of made me wish that I had the pleasure of knowing his brother Perry, as they called George, a man I came to know all about, as well as his mother, Cissy, a Southern Black woman, like my own mom.

Spark of life witnesses are somewhat unique across the states. Many jurisdictions do not allow a witness whose only contribution is to humanize the deceased crime victim. In Minnesota, courts allow the state to call a witness or two who will testify to who the victim was as a person, since in a murder case, he or she cannot be there.

It's a little dangerous because it's not supposed to be character evidence, which would allow the defense to offer testimony to rebut the victim's reputation for good character. Spark of life testimony usually isn't cross-examined, because for defense counsel, it doesn't matter. However, it means a lot to the crime victim's family.

Philonise testified about the close relationship between his brother, Perry, and their mother. He talked about growing up in public housing in Houston, playing video games, and how he liked sports. "People would attend church just because he was there…he was a person that everyone loved around the community. He just knew how to make people feel better." It was beautiful and emotional. I was glad the Floyd family got a chance to share a bit of why they loved George Perry Floyd, and why his loss was devastating to them.

The state's final witness was Seth Stoughton, a law professor and former police officer. Stoughton is the co-author of *Evaluating Police Uses of Force* with Jeffrey Noble and Geoffrey Alpert. Stoughton is an expert on the *Graham v. Connor* standard and testified to the jury as a use-of-force expert. Using the "reasonable officer" standard, he testified that Chauvin's level of force was disproportionate to the circumstances. "No reasonable officer would have believed that this was an appropriate, acceptable, or reasonable use of force."

The Defense Case

After the prosecution rested its case on April 13, following eleven days of testimony and a load of video evidence, it was the defense's turn. Since the state carries the burden of proof, the defense can win simply by poking holes in the state's case.

Nelson chose to call witnesses, and they fell into two groups. One group was the May 2019 group. This is the group Nelson hoped would show to the jury that Floyd had a habit of being in trouble with the police. I'm sure Nelson would disagree with this characterization, but I really couldn't see any other point. The second group were his expert witnesses, Barry Brodd, a use-of-force expert, and medical examiner Dr. Fowler.

Shawanda Hill, who was in the Mercedes with Floyd when police arrived, didn't fit in either category, but she helped Nelson argue that Floyd's sleepiness could have been a sign he was overdosing even before police arrived on the scene.

First, Nelson called Scott Creighton, a retired MPD officer who pulled Floyd over in a May 2019 traffic stop. He testified that Floyd was "unresponsive" to commands to show his hands, and that Floyd's "behavior was very nervous, anxious." Of course, Creighton had a gun pointed at Floyd during the incident, which might account for nervousness. Nelson asked Creighton twice about Floyd swallowing drugs, but Creighton said he didn't see Floyd take any.

On cross, Erin brought out that officers gave Floyd contradictory commands, with Creighton telling him to put his hands on the dashboard and another officer telling him to put his hands on his head. Erin also got Creighton to admit that another officer threatened to use a stun gun on him, while Floyd pleaded not to be shot or beaten up.

Next, Nelson called Michelle Moseng, also retired. Moseng was a Hennepin County EMS paramedic who helped Floyd after his May 2019 arrest. She testified that she provided medical help to Floyd in connection with the May 2019 incident. Moseng said that Floyd told her he had been taking multiple opioids about every twenty minutes. "I asked him why and he said it was because he was addicted," said Moseng. She said Floyd's blood pressure was very high, and he was at a risk of stroke.

On cross, Erin asked Moseng about Floyd's other vital signs like respiratory output, pulse, heart rate, EKG, and heart rhythms. She testified that they were normal.

That was all for the May 2019 witnesses.

What concerned me about these witnesses is that they could feed a stereotype and diminish the likelihood of a fair evaluation of the case. On cross-examination, however, Erin Eldridge brought out a critical point. In the May 2019 incident, Floyd took drugs and got into medical trouble. Instead of having three officers kneel on him, he got medical help and Floyd survived. I hoped her excellent cross landed.

Nelson's third witness was Shawanda Hill, the passenger in Floyd's SUV, and Floyd's sometime girlfriend. Hill is an African American woman in her forties. Her hair was dyed bright red, and she was wearing a brown leather jacket. She was obviously nervous.

She testified that Floyd was dozing off while sitting in the car after leaving Cup Foods. She said that he woke up briefly after Cup Foods employees ("the little boys," she called them) approached, but then took a phone call. She testified that he was sleeping when she tried to rouse him when she told him "the police is here." Hill described Floyd's behavior: happy, normal, talking, and alert.

On cross, Matt Frank asked Hill if Floyd had any of the symptoms or signs of medical distress. She said no and did not consider his sleepiness a problem.

At this point, Nelson entered the real heart of his case. If Nelson could get just one juror to believe that Chauvin had acted reasonably, then he could prevent Chauvin from being convicted. He called veteran use-of-force expert Barry Brodd, who had served as an expert witness in other high-profile police excessive force cases such as the killing of Laquan McDonald.

Brodd looked like a cop's cop—fit and tough, with his silver white hair and beard. His ears sort of stuck out, giving him the appearance of a Vulcan from *Star Trek*. Barry Brodd brought a lot of credibility to the witness stand, nearly thirty years of policing experience. He was a former police officer and expert on self-defense.

Brodd defended Derek Chauvin's use of his knee to pin Floyd down by the neck during his arrest, contradicting Pleoger, Arradondo, Blackwell, Mercil, Stiger, and Stoughton. Brodd testified that Chauvin was acting with objective reasonableness and was justified when he handcuffed Floyd and placed him in a prone position. He testified that the knee on the neck didn't qualify as force because no pain was inflicted. I thought I heard audible gasps from the jury at this testimony.

Brodd testified that Chauvin was following Minneapolis Police Department policy and current standards of law enforcement. He referenced the standard in *Graham v. Connor*, the 1989 Supreme Court case in which the justices ruled that an officer's use of force must be "objectively reasonable," but that "police officers are often forced to make split-second judgments—in circumstances that are tense, uncertain and rapidly evolving—about the amount of force that is necessary in a particular situation."

Steve's cross was brilliant, though. He got Brodd to admit that while Floyd was handcuffed, prone on the ground, he was no threat to the officers.

David Fowler was the last important witness of the defense. While Brodd's job was to testify that the force was reasonable, Fowler's job was to testify that the officer's use of force wasn't the cause of death.

Fowler, a white South African immigrant, took the stand and laid out his considerable credentials. Fowler was the chief medical examiner at the Maryland Office of the Chief Medical Examiner from 2002 to 2019. When Fowler took the witness stand on April 14, 2021, day thirteen of testimony, it was clear that he was confident and well qualified.

Before Fowler gave his opinion on the cause of death of George Floyd, he testified to his vast experience and esteemed record in forensic medical examinations. He graduated from the University of Cape Town in 1983 and did a year of general medical and surgical internship, followed by a year of pediatric pathology at the Red Cross Children's Hospital in Cape Town. He then completed a five-year full-time training program in forensic pathology at the University of Cape Town, where he earned his Master of Medicine in forensic pathology.

As Fowler laid out his credentials, I wondered, Could Black students attend the University of Cape Town—or any university in apartheid South Africa—in 1983? Apartheid, the system of racial subordination, did not end until 1989. I remember watching Nelson Mandela's release from prison on television, marking the end of apartheid.

Of course, I had no idea where Fowler stood on the issue of South African apartheid. For all I knew, he was indifferent or opposed to it. However, as I watched Eric Nelson set forth David Fowler's credentials, my mind connected to my years on the campus of Wayne State University, opposing the prevailing system of racial injustice in South Africa. I wondered if any of the jurors were thinking the same thing.

Fowler had an impressive background, but we were well aware that Fowler was being sued by the family of a nineteen-year-old college student named Anton Black. Black was an African American teen who died in 2018 after being restrained and pinned to the ground by three white police officers, sort of like Floyd.

As chief medical examiner, Fowler signed the report that said the teenager's death was due to his heart issues, bipolar disorder, and stress associated with his struggle with law enforcement officers. It sounded remarkably similar to Dr. Baker's determination. Fowler's report in the Anton Black case noted "no evidence was found that restraint by law enforcement directly caused or significantly caused or significantly contributed" to the September 15, 2018, death.

The Black family's civil complaint accused Fowler of concealing evidence and protecting the officers. The ACLU accused him of "creating false narratives about what kills Black people in police encounters." Unfortunately, the Minnesota Rules of Evidence precluded us from asking Fowler about Anton Black, but it would have been interesting.

Fowler testified that he had reviewed medical, police, and ambulance records, as well as toxicology reports and video footage, among other information in the George Floyd case.

Fowler said he would have classified the manner of Floyd's death as "undetermined" rather than "homicide." He testified, "In my opinion, Mr. Floyd had a sudden cardiac arrhythmia...due to his atherosclerotic and hypertensive heart disease...during his restraint and subdual by the police."

"Restraint" and "subdual" were the exact words Dr. Baker used in the autopsy report of George Floyd, and the same concept Fowler used in excusing police officers in the death of Anton Black. I suspected that this was more than mere coincidence, given that Baker in his December 2020 meeting with the state made a point of telling us about his friendship with Fowler.

In Fowler's determination, both the drugs fentanyl and methamphetamine contributed to Floyd's death. Additionally, exposure to vehicle exhaust (while he was lying under the knee of Derek Chauvin) could potentially have contributed by causing increased carbon monoxide in his bloodstream or even carbon monoxide poisoning.

One last potential witness remained: Derek Chauvin. Judge Cahill wanted Nelson to ask Chauvin a few questions to make certain that he was knowingly waiving his right to testify. Cahill noted on the record that Chauvin appeared to understand that he was waiving a known right after having a fair and full opportunity to talk with his counsel. Chauvin made it clear that he understood his rights, and that he freely and knowingly decided not to testify in his own defense, exercising his Fifth Amendment right.

So, after Fowler's testimony was over, the defense rested. The prosecution had a right to call a rebuttal witness. We only called Dr. Tobin back for a moment to contest the carbon monoxide claim. He testified that the oxygen saturation report from Hennepin County Medical Center did not support the claim put forth by the defense.

After Tobin's rebuttal, that was it. We had said everything; there was no need to do anything further.

With that, testimony ended in *State v. Chauvin* on April 15, after twenty-five days of trial and thirteen days of testimony.

As we assembled around the conference table on the twenty-first floor, I could see a slow smile breaking over Steve Schleicher's face. Josh Larson started pulling off his tie. Lola Velazquez Aguilu was smiling ear to ear.

I doubt anyone thought we had the case in the bag, but we had exposed Fowler, rebutted him, too. I remember Keaon Dousti said something like, "Carbon monoxide poisoning!" and we all laughed. It was a great release of anxious energy after a long battle.

―――――

It was a Thursday afternoon, but it felt like Friday. I was tired, but I still had tons of energy to carry on. We used the remainder of the afternoon talking with the judge about jury instructions—the legal instructions that Judge Cahill would be reading to the jury after closing arguments ended, which would be the coming Monday.

A large portion of the jury instructions are boilerplate—important boilerplate—but instructions that are read in every criminal case. For example, the instructions contain sections on the presumption of innocence, proof beyond a reasonable doubt, statements of lawyers and judges, and more. Still, there are more contested parts, and these more controversial sections are what Sundeep Iyer, Neal Katyal, and Matt

Frank and defense counsel Eric Nelson all went back into Judge Cahill's chamber to discuss.

Our team took this matter seriously. We were really focused on this important but often overlooked aspect of the case.

After the closing arguments of all the lawyers, Judge Cahill would read the instructions and give each juror a copy of them to refer to. The jury instructions included an explanation of the charges and the affirmative defenses that the defendant might rely on to legally excuse their conduct.

If the jury agreed unanimously that the state proved the case, then it would be their duty to convict. If the jury unanimously agreed the charges were not proven, then it was their duty to acquit. But, of course, the jury can hang, meaning they cannot come to unanimous agreement. This was a huge worry for me, because it takes only one juror to hang the jury. Then we would have a mistrial.

I was painfully aware of all the things that could go wrong if the jury did not get accurate instructions, and so I was particularly gratified with the amount of work Sundeep, Neal, and Matt were putting into the jury instructions.

As the day concluded, the prosecution team once again retired to our twenty-first-floor office space. Before we started our regular end-of-day meeting, we had a special guest. Neal Katyal had invited the former U.S. attorney general Eric Holder to talk to us via Zoom.

I was honored our team was getting an encouraging word from Holder, the first African American to hold the position of U.S. attorney general. He was the AG under President Obama when I was in Congress. I well remember voting no when a highly partisan Republican House conference voted to hold him in contempt of Congress for refusing to hand over privileged documents. It was pure politics. The DOJ's inspector general refused to prosecute him, of course, and later cleared him of any charges of wrongdoing. Holder knew how to walk through the fire. He also knew something about trying to build a positive culture between police departments and local communities.

As AG, he led a DOJ that prosecuted more than 300 individual officers for misconduct and opened twenty pattern or practice investigations into police departments across the country. Holder's DOJ enforced fourteen agreements to reform law enforcement practices at agencies both large and small.

In the course of his service, America's 18,000 police departments saw decreases in the number of cases of excessive force, and greater equity in the delivery of police services.

Given Holder's record, he knew what he was talking about when he told our team on the eve of closing arguments that "I am incredibly proud of the job you're doing." He said that we put on a "seamless prosecution" and commended the police officers who had testified.

This was the type of boost the team needed and deserved. No matter what the jury decided, the former United States attorney general could see from across the country that they had put on a quality case.

Chapter 10

SUPERHUMANS EXIST IN COMIC BOOKS

Judge Cahill told the jury members to pack a bag because on Monday, April 19, they would be sequestered during their deliberations until they rendered a verdict.

On April 16, 2021, a Friday, we weren't in court. It was an eventful day anyway. We all showed up in our jeans and t-shirts at the Hennepin County grand jury room on the twentieth floor. We were going to run through the closing arguments.

We all gathered around the big U-shaped table in the grand jury room. I played the judge to start us off. "Ladies and gentlemen, the parties have rested and now it's time for each party to offer a closing argument should they elect to do so. Mr. Schleicher, do you wish to give a closing argument?"

Steve got up and gave us what sounded like a pretty good argument. He said he still needed to work on it a little more, and we all gave him some feedback. Then somebody jumped up, maybe Josh Larson, and gave a defense closing argument, giving a passable impression of Eric Nelson. Even though it was off the cuff, it was an argument that some people might find convincing. I thought, *I hope the jury doesn't buy that stuff.* I knew it only had to be one person to save Chauvin from accountability.

Jerry gave a great rebuttal. Like Steve, he has a solid and ear-catching style of delivery. In the middle of his presentation, he said something like, "The defense has tried to argue that George Floyd died of an enlarged heart. But it's not that George Floyd's heart was too big; it's that Derek Chauvin's heart was too small."

When I heard that line, I said, "Dude, that's a mic drop line if I ever heard one."

Jerry Blackwell said, "Yeah, okay. Let me see what I can do."

We worked on Jerry's and Steve's closings a little longer. They hit our themes of "in your custody is in your care," "believe your eyes," "Chauvin put his pride before policing," and others. Then I left the meeting.

After this, across the news came the story of the bodycam footage involving thirteen-year-old Adam Toledo. He was the seventh grader who was shot in Chicago weeks before, as the Chauvin prosecution was getting underway. The video shows Toledo running away from the police through an alley with a wooden fence on the right side. The officer yelling for him to stop and show his hands is audible. Toledo is running along a fence that is to his right. He gets to a doorway, steps in, then turns around with his hands up and clearly visible. The officer shoots him in the chest, killing him.

At that moment, when Toledo turns and raises his hands in response to officer commands, nothing appears to be in his hand. Chicago police said a gun was visible in Toledo's right hand as he was running away. As I watched the video, I couldn't see it, but when I slowed it down, a gun is visible in Toledo's right hand. It appears that he throws it through the door of the wooden fence. However, no gun is in his hand when the officer shoots and kills him while his hands are up.

After I saw this news report about Adam Toledo, I stood up and went back to my office to make some calls. Over the weekend, we just continued grinding. We had work to do before Monday morning when closing arguments would begin.

Closing Arguments—April 19, 2021

The best lawyers can weave complicated facts, arcane law, and raw emotion into a logical, smooth, and compelling fabric. I've also seen lawyers ramble on endlessly, perhaps confusing, boring, and offending the jury.

I recruited the best lawyers because the urgency of the moment demanded nothing less. Now, Steve and Jerry would get their chance to show how good they were. Steve would deliver the main closing, and Jerry would deliver the rebuttal.

Of course, Eric Nelson would have his turn and he would muster all his persuasive ability to convince the jury that, though sad and tragic, the death of George Floyd simply wasn't Derek Chauvin's fault.

Steve didn't start his closing argument at the closing argument. He started communicating the trial themes during *voir dire*, jury selection. I knew that whoever conducted *voir dire* had an edge on closing because that lawyer probably had the best chance of developing a rapport with the jurors. Steve began exposing the jury early because jurors tend to decide who they think should win during jury selection and opening statements.

I don't believe you can win a case with a great closing, because by the time you get to closing you've either already won or lost.

Finally, the fateful moment came. I was in the courtroom, along with Steve Schleicher, Jerry Blackwell, and Matt Frank. Chauvin walked in with his lawyer, Eric Nelson, and some family members. He wore a light gray suit, a dark blue shirt, and tie. I noticed that he had, for the most part, said nothing. I wondered, as we sat there waiting for the judge, what he would have said.

Philonise and other Floyd family members were present as well. They sat in the back of the courtroom, and it was ironic to me that the Chauvin and Floyd families sat only a few feet away from each other in the courtroom, yet they seemed a million miles apart.

At nine-thirty a.m., Judge Cahill came out, everyone stood up, he climbed up the steps to the bench, and he ordered everyone to be seated.

Judge Cahill turned toward the jury and began reading the instructions. The jury listened thoughtfully even though Cahill was reading in a clipped manner: Judge the facts; the defendant is presumed innocent; remarks of the attorneys are not evidence. He, as judge, had no opinion.

He informed the jury about the three counts in the complaint, but first he defined critical terms. When he defined "cause," he made it clear that even if the jury found other causes might have contributed to Floyd's death, Chauvin is responsible if his actions were a "substantial causal factor." This is the idea that the defendant must take the victim as he finds him.

Then, Judge Cahill read the elements of the counts one, two, and three. He also read the instruction on liability for crimes of another. We asked for this instruction because Chauvin had committed the crime in a group. If the jury found, for example, that Kueng really caused Floyd's death by pressing on his chest, then Chauvin is still guilty as an aider and abettor. Our theory was that it took all of them to do it.

Judge Cahill read the *Graham v. Connor* instruction, the one defense that worried me the most:

No crime is committed if a police officer's actions were justified by the police officer's use of reasonable force in the line of duty in effecting a lawful arrest or preventing an escape from custody.

The kind and degree of force a police officer may lawfully use in executing his duties is limited by what a reasonable policer in the same situation would believe to be necessary.

The defendant is not guilty of a crime if used force as authorized by law.

To prove guilt, the State must prove beyond a reasonable doubt that the Defendant's use of force was not authorized by law.

Judge Cahill told the jury to rely on their common sense to evaluate credibility of the witnesses, and this included the expert witnesses as well.

As requested by Chauvin, Judge Cahill read the instruction that Chauvin had the right not to testify. The defendant sometimes asks the court not to mention it. Chauvin elected to have it.

Judge Cahill instructed the jury on the issue of the May 6, 2019, incident, saying that it was not character evidence, but only evidence of the effect of opioids on George Floyd.

Then it was time. Judge Cahill said, "Mr. Schleicher, you may proceed."

Steve rose, walked toward the podium, and said, "May it please the court, and counsel," nodding toward Eric Nelson. Then he began.

Steve started slowly and solemnly. He struck a serious tone as he began, focusing on the humanity of George Floyd: "Members of the jury, his name was George Perry Floyd, Jr....to George Floyd, Sr. and Larcina Jones Floyd, 'Cissy' the matriarch...George Floyd's mom. Mom of the house. Mom of the neighborhood."

I decided to sit in the courtroom for closing arguments. Steve Schleicher started with a tempered, calm tone of voice, and he focused on Floyd's humanity. His family, the people who loved him, childhood, adolescence, into his twenties. "George Floyd was surrounded by people he cared about and who cared about him. Throughout his life...into his adulthood."

Then Steve revisited how Floyd died.

George Floyd died, face down on the pavement. Nine minutes and twenty-nine seconds. During this time George Floyd struggled, desperate to breathe. To make enough room in his chest to breathe.

So desperate to breathe. But the force was too much.

The force was too much with unyielding pavement beneath him. As unyielding as the men who held him down. For nine minutes and twenty seconds. Twisting his fingers.

To give his chest and give his lungs enough to breathe. As he used his knuckles to breathe. So desperate to breathe he pushed with his face, to lift himself. To open his chest to give his lungs room to breathe. The pavement tearing into his bare skin. Lacerating his knuckles So desperate to breathe, he pushed with his face.

Steve's pacing was intense. It was powerful. Methodical.

George Floyd losing strength. Not superhuman strength.
    Superhumans exist in comic books.
    Not superhuman strength. Not superhuman, only human.
Just a man crying out. A human being.

Here, Schleicher was mocking the absurdity of an imaginary drug-induced George Floyd who might have needed to be physically suppressed by three officers due to his superhuman strength. This was where Schleicher transitioned to Floyd's humble effort to comply with officer demands.

While he was surrounded in life with people who loved him, for nine minutes and twenty seconds, he was surrounded by strangers.
    But he did say his final words, 'Mr. Officer.' He pleaded with Mr. Officer. George Floyd's final words were "Please, I can't breathe." He said those words to Mr. Officer. But Mr. Officer did not help. Mr. Officer continued to twist his knees, to shimmy, to twist his hands, to twist his fingers."

Schleicher began using our "pride before policing" theme.

Staring down horrified bystanders who watched this unfold.
    The motto of the Minneapolis Police Department is to "protect with courage and serve with compassion." Facing George Floyd that day did not take one ounce of courage and

none was found. All that was required was a little compassion. But none was shown.

This was a call about a counterfeit twenty-dollar bill.

What George Floyd needed was some oxygen. Because people need that. People need that. He heard him, he just didn't listen. He begged until he could speak no more. Beyond the point that he had a pulse. When the ambulance arrived, the defendant continued. He would not get up, he would not let up.

He was not responsive, and the defendant had to know. Beyond the point he had a pulse. He would not get up. He would not let up.

You saw the video. After a paramedic tapped him and then he got up. After they lifted him on the gurney. You can see... There was nothing there. He was completely limp.

The defendant was on top of him for nine minutes and twenty-nine seconds.

Now Schleicher transitioned to Dr. Baker and medical causation.

The medical examiner would find the cause of George Floyd's death was cardiopulmonary arrest complicating law enforcement subdual, restraint, and neck compression. What you saw the defendant and the other officers doing killed him. The medical examiner ruled his death a homicide.

What they did to George Floyd killed him. It was ruled a homicide.

Here, Schleicher confronted one of our biggest concerns: the general public sentiment to resolve doubts in favor of police. Despite some folks in the police abolition community, most people want to believe in and support members of law enforcement. We were asking them to convict Chauvin which, despite the facts, may have been difficult for them.

It may be hard for you to imagine a police officer doing something like this. Imagining a police officer committing a crime is not the way we think of police officers.

Remember jury selection. We talked about bias and setting preconceived notions aside. Imagining a police officer committing a crime is difficult to set aside.

Even the bystanders, after they saw what they saw, Genevieve Hansen called the police, Donald Williams called 911, to complain about the police. Judeah, nine years old, suggesting calling the police on the police...

Our expectation is that the police are going to help. And with good reason. Because policing is a noble profession. To be very clear: This case is called *State of Minnesota v. Derek Chauvin*; this case is not called *State of Minnesota v. The Police*.

It is a profession with rules and standards. Nothing is worse for a good police officer than a bad police officer, who doesn't follow the rules, who doesn't follow procedure, who doesn't follow training, who ignores the policies of the department, who doesn't follow the motto of the department, "To protect with courage, to serve with compassion."

Chief Arradondo took the stand and he told you.

There's more to policing than putting handcuffs on people and taking them away.

He didn't follow the rules.

This is not an anti-police prosecution. It's a pro-police prosecution.

Again, on the theme of pride over policing.

This started over a fake twenty-dollar bill. But George Floyd died for something far less valuable than that.

His ego, his pride. The kind of ego based on pride. He was not going to let these bystanders tell him what to do. The bystanders were powerless. The defendant chose pride over policing.

Schleicher faced Floyd's addiction issues head-on, just as we had in trial.

You've heard about addiction.
But George Floyd is not on trial here. Defense claims he was noncompliant.

Steve then explained how George Floyd was terrified about getting into the tiny, confined space of squad 320. Steve played the video of Floyd saying he had anxiety. In the video Schleicher shared, Floyd's voice is audible: "I'm claustrophobic."

You don't get to meet the police on your best day.
There is a whole range of humanity. Officers train for that.
He knew better; he just didn't do better.

At this point, Steve began to take the jury through the charges as stated in the jury instructions. Steve skillfully used video evidence to demonstrate Chauvin's indifference, his cruelty, and his culpability.

A reasonable officer follows the rules. Officer after officer after officer got up on that stand and told you that this conduct violated the training—

Schleicher was citing Pleoger, Blackwell, Mercil, Zimmerman, Arradondo, Stiger, and Stoughton on this use of force. Given all these officers' accumulated criticism of Chauvin's use of force, would a reasonable police officer have used this force against Floyd? Numerous officers, including the Minneapolis Police Department's chief and the longest-serving member, said no.

Steve talked to the jury for about an hour and a half. I was proud of his closing. I thought it should be enough, but who knew? It wasn't a simple matter of excellence. If that was all there was to it, then we'd win hands down. However, it was about the jurors. How did they see the evidence? Where did their emotions lie? We would know soon.

After a fifteen-minute break, Eric Nelson stood to address the jury one last time. He would not get a rebuttal, as the state did. He had to say whatever he was going to say right now. In truth, history was on Eric's side. Charging a police officer with a crime for conduct against a civilian while on duty was a rare event. Taking one to trial—even with video—is an even rarer event, and obtaining a guilty verdict is even rarer still. It had only been done once before in Minnesota. Eric and Chauvin, despite the evidence, had reason to believe.

Eric started, "Thanks, jury, for diligence and attention, on behalf of Mr. Chauvin." Then Nelson launched into an explanation of perhaps the two most important ideas in American criminal law: the presumption of innocence and proof beyond a reasonable doubt.

"Defendant doesn't have to prove his innocence. The burden is on the state. Proof beyond, ordinarily prudent men and women, would use in their most important affairs, highest standard of proof."

Nelson appealed to the jury to conduct an honest assessment of the case. His tone was quite measured and calm. He was clearly trying to counteract the hot emotions that Schleicher conjured with his soaring oratory and heartrending video evidence.

Then Nelson went into the *Graham v. Connors* analysis, carefully laid out in the jury instructions. He posed a question to the jury based on *Graham*: "What were the facts known to the officers at the precise moment the force was used?"

Nelson was prodding, steady, and rational. Not too many quotable lines. He talked for hours, but essentially, he asked the jury to consider all the matters that officers had to consider in the moment on May 25, 2020, as Floyd was not complying with officers' demands, and bystanders were gathering and creating a distraction. He noted that Chauvin had to consider the assessment of threats, such as the crime rate in the area, the scene security, and the unpredictable nature of people.

Nelson was well into his presentation when he began to explain why Chauvin didn't get off Floyd, even after he became unresponsive, but then he began building the case. He pointed out that the clerks at Cup Foods reported the person passing the bad twenty as a large person.

Nelson seemed to be arguing that instead of focusing on the nine minutes and twenty-nine seconds, the jury's focus should be on the longer period of time before the 9:29 started, considering the prior sixteen minutes and fifty-nine seconds.

Nelson pointed out that the 911 dispatcher, Jena Scurry, heard sounds of a struggle in the earlier period. Officers Lane and Kueng were so frustrated by Floyd's resistance to getting into the vehicle they concluded that attempts to get him into the car were futile. Nelson seemed to be arguing that since Floyd was difficult to deal with earlier, Chauvin's use of force was justified during the 9:29 due to the surge of adrenaline he was experiencing. He added that Floyd was unpredictable and might re-emerge as a threat, even after losing consciousness.

Nelson turned to the medical evidence. He argued two theories: Chauvin, with rudimentary first aid training, could not be expected to know what a doctor knows. Alternatively, they were wrong.

Nelson referenced the point in Dr. Tobin's testimony when he identified the moment Floyd experienced an anoxic seizure. Nelson argued that Chauvin didn't know that Floyd was experiencing an anoxic seizure, as a trained pulmonologist might who had unlimited time to study video.

Nelson turned to the bystanders. He argued that reasonable officers are aware of their surroundings, including potential threats like Donald

Williams, a mixed martial artist, and Genevieve Hansen, a Minneapolis firefighter who walked up behind Chauvin and startled him.

Nelson argued it was the bystanders who caused Chauvin not to pursue CPR because the bystanders made the environment unsafe. Nelson asked the jury a rhetorical question: "When do we stop CPR? When it's not safe. Difficulty of performing CPR when confronted with a loud crowd, they made it difficult to focus, more difficult to assess the patient. Distraction can do harm to a patient."

Nelson jumped back to *Graham* analysis and the reasonable use of force. Citing the defense expert, Barry Brodd, Nelson argued that "you can use non-deadly force to physically manage a person." To bolster the position that the knee-on-the-neck technique was within departmental standards, he cited the testimony of Lieutenant Johnny Mercil, Derek Chauvin's actual use-of-force trainer.

Nelson argued that Mercil testified that the knee-on-the-neck technique was not unauthorized. "The knee on the neck can be used depending on the level of resistance. No strict technique; you need to be fluid." Nelson continued, "Mercil testified that a suspect can resist through their word. If you're fighting with the subject and they become compliant you can continue force.

"Talking about using force affects the officers' judgment. MPD teaches that you can hold a person in the prone position until the situation is safe. Simply because someone is not resisting doesn't mean you can't use force."

At this point, I sensed that Nelson was getting tired of listening to himself talk. He apologized to the jury for being "long-winded." But he pressed on. Nelson argued that "use of force is incredibly difficult to analyze.

"You have to look at it from the totality of circumstances. Officers make mistakes in highly stressful situations.

"The use of force was an authorized use of force, and this is reasonable doubt. The reasonableness of the use of force is very difficult."

As Nelson began to wind down his closing argument, he said of Floyd's death, "It's tragic.

"But just because something happened to the person, it's not the natural result of the defendant's act." Here Nelson was trying to argue that one of Floyd's health challenges caused his death, not the knee on the neck.

"Hypertension, stenosis, enlarged heart, arteriosclerosis, controlled substances. I submit that the testimony of Tobin, Isenschmid, Smock, Thomas, Rich, fly in the face of reason and common sense."

Finally, Nelson turned to Dr. Baker, who, he pointed out, "is the only person who performed the actual autopsy. No evidence of asphyxia, petechiae, subcutaneous hemorrhage, no finding of injuries to the structure of the neck. No fracture. No evidence of asphyxia. His heart was enlarged.

"Dr. Baker's testimony is that Floyd's death was a multifactorial process. His heart simply couldn't handle it.

"It is preposterous that this does not come into play."

And then, suddenly, Judge Cahill announced thirty minutes. Lunch break. I got up to stretch my legs, and I wondered to myself how long Nelson was going to continue. I didn't find anything Eric said particularly compelling, which wasn't his fault. He had to argue the case he had with the defendant he had. Nonetheless, there was nothing in his closing that I found concerning or a point we couldn't answer.

Even though Nelson argued for well over two hours, I was surprised that he never tried to humanize Chauvin. Never mentioned his years of service, his time in the military, his family, or even his mom. Maybe he thought he couldn't because if Nelson tried to argue that Chauvin has good character, it might open the door for us to introduce his eighteen prior force complaints. The fact is the jury never got to know Chauvin. Maybe they didn't need to. Maybe Chauvin's status as a police officer was enough.

It was time for Jerry's rebuttal, and as a master orator, he knew how to intrigue the jurors.

> While you've heard hours of discussion in closing, it's not complicated. Excessive use of force and medical caution.
>
> It's so simple a child could understand it. In fact, a child did understand it. When the nine-year-old girl said, "Get off of him." That's how simple it was.
>
> Your common sense. Why was it necessary to continue applying deadly restraint to someone handcuffed, defenseless, not resisting, not breathing, and going on and doing it for three-plus minutes before the ambulance shows up, and then continues doing it? How is that a reasonable use of force?
>
> You can believe your eyes, ladies and gentlemen. It was what you thought it was. It was a homicide.
>
> And you didn't get the whole truth. Notice that when Nelson talks about a reasonable officer he never mentions the part about Mr. Floyd not moving, not conscious, not having a pulse.
>
> You didn't get the whole truth. Notice how the analysis cuts off not moving, didn't have a pulse, and didn't get up when EMTs come up.
>
> Verdict means truth. You didn't get the whole truth.
>
> Remember how safe they told you the prone position is? Here are all the Canadian studies. Not one of those subjects had a knee on the neck. None of them measured oxygen intake.
>
> Excited delirium? Not one witness said it applied to Mr. Floyd.
>
> Nelson said that Baker said "homicide" was a medical term. But *homicide* means "being killed at the hands of another."
>
> Neither Dr. Fowler nor Dr. Baker could calculate the amount of oxygen that Mr. Floyd was not getting into his body, but Dr. Tobin could calculate it. He said laying Mr. Floyd in the

prone position reduced his oxygen by 24 percent, the weight on his back reduced it by 43 percent. Dr. Tobin said no person could have survived.

Jerry attacked the claim that Floyd died as a result of opioid overdose.

Does not fit the description of a fentanyl death. There was so little meth that it was below therapeutic levels, minuscule amounts.

The pills. Mr. Nelson wants you to think about—what he might have had in his mouth in the photo in the car. It was just as likely chewing gum. He was chewing it in the store. But why are we bothered with that when we know what was in his bloodstream. One pill was found in the car, but not in his bloodstream.

Between the three medical examiners, [their combined] 15,000 autopsies, [they] testified that they never saw a pulseless person come back, break handcuffs, and rampage the city.

But the largest departure from the evidence: You were told that Mr. Floyd died because his heart was too big. Now, having seen all of the evidence, having heard all of the evidence, you know that the reason George Floyd is dead is because Mr. Chauvin's heart was too small.

Chapter 11

THE VERDICTS

The morning after closing arguments, I couldn't figure out what to do with myself. Judge Cahill had given his final instructions to the jury late in the afternoon the day before, and only a few hours had gone by before day broke on the morning after. I slept restlessly that night and got up earlier than usual even though I'm an early riser, getting up for the first of the Muslim prayers called fajr.

It was Tuesday morning, and I was, like everybody else, waiting on the jury's deliberation, which was all anyone could do. I headed downtown to the courthouse. I threw on a suit—just in case the jury had a question. I was sure that the jury would take days if not longer. I jammed a tie in my pocket and walked out the door, collar open.

When I got to the Hennepin County Government Center, the site of the trial, the fortress was still up. Razor wire all around the complex. Badges and vetting—everything for everyone. Armored personnel carriers, MRAPs, National Guard, and lots of cops.

I hopped on the elevator, mask on, and went upstairs. I figured I'd be alone. I was wrong. Josh Larson was there. Jerry Blackwell was there. I greeted them, shared some small talk, sat down at my desk and opened my laptop. Then I logged on to a Zoom call with members of the prosecution team. The meeting was about messaging. We knew—come rain or come shine—we were going to have to tell the public something after the trial ended.

We discussed three statements: one if we lost on all counts, another if we split verdicts, and one if we convicted on all counts. We didn't know. As much as everyone was telling me about how obvious the guilt of Chauvin was, we didn't know what the outcome would be. We saw the trial in the beating of Rodney King in 1991, and we saw the jury's verdict of not guilty. In 2018, we saw the not guilty verdict in the killing of Philando Castile, the elementary lunchroom supervisor whose murder was streamed on Facebook.

History was on Chauvin's side. We went over the statements and talked back and forth about what to add and what to cut. Our media team was on the call along with Lola Velazquez Aguilu, Steve Schleicher, and John Stiles. After about an hour or so, I got up from my seat and walked into the hall to get coffee.

I ran into James Reyerson, the case agent from the Bureau of Criminal Apprehension. James said, "Did you hear?"

"Hear what?"

James said, "I got friends across the country saying the verdict is in."

"No it ain't. They would call us first." That's when I started seeing the signs. Security personnel were kind of scurrying and moving about.

Maybe the verdicts were in. It was only Tuesday, April 20, 2021, and the jury had gone out late the evening before.

I phoned two law enforcement friends who I thought might know. I reached one and left a message for the second to call me ASAP.

First guy: "Yes, Mr. AG, this is information we have. Verdict is in."

Of course, I hadn't heard a word from official sources, but I wasn't surprised. Judge Cahill had made it very clear that he wasn't doing anyone, least of all the state, any favors. However, my friend was sure that a verdict was in.

As we were still on our Zoom call, I texted Lola Velazquez Aguilu on her cell phone: **Better start coming down.**

Be there in 15. Is that gonna be okay?

I wrote back: **Awesome. Drive safely.**

263

Lola was one of the big brains behind our case, including her amazing work on our medical case. Then I texted Steve Schleicher, our leader on the use-of-force case. He acknowledged and started moving toward the Government Center, where in a few minutes the jury would let us know what they thought.

Then the court's clerk called. It was official. Our team was assembled, and we were ready to go. Everybody was nervous, tense. We all made small talk and guesses about what the quick verdict meant. But no one really knew. We hoped, but we didn't know.

The case agent from the Minnesota Bureau of Criminal Apprehension, James Reyerson, was on hand. He knew the case better than anyone as the lead investigator. He even threw on a tie—not his normal attire.

So many of the cases of police violence against Black people have ended with acquittals or no charges at all. Breonna Taylor, Mike Brown, and Eric Garner's cases never made it past the grand jury. I reminded the team that they did a great job getting the case to the jury. No matter what the outcome, I was proud of them.

The verdict in the case of the assault on Rodney King made a lifelong imprint on me, ending in an acquittal of all the police officers who savagely bludgeoned him on video. No. History was on Derek Chauvin's side.

Matt Frank said, "It's about that time." We headed down. My heart began to beat palpably in my chest. With every step I took I came closer to the outcome of this trial, which all had begun last Memorial Day when George Floyd begged for his life and met his final end under the knee of Derek Chauvin.

As we boarded the elevator and pressed the button for the eighteenth floor, I wasn't sure I was eager to receive the news. Would the family of George Floyd receive vindication? Would another African American person be denied justice? Step by step we made our way into the courtroom. More than 23 million people were watching and waiting for the verdict to be announced on live television in only a few minutes.

Strangely, the courtroom was pretty much the same as the way we had left it only a day before. All outfitted with plexiglass and everything—everyone separated from everyone else. We sat. We made small talk. We looked at our watches. We waited for what seemed like an hour, but it was only half that. My heart. I could feel it beating in my chest. I could hear it when suddenly the court's clerk walked in, and then the court deputy, and then the jurors. They all filed in, one by one.

We all stood. Solemn and attentive.

There was Derek Chauvin, standing up straight as a rod, and his two lawyers, Eric Nelson and Amy Voss, a young woman with a law degree who Eric never let utter a word in open court. I couldn't tell what emotion was registering with Chauvin—I assume it was fear. Eric Nelson was by his side.

The four lawyers for the state were me, Matt Frank, Steve Schleicher, and Jerry Blackwell. We stood next to one another in two rows: me and Jerry at the front, Matt and Steve behind us. If any of them knew what was about to happen, they never let on.

Judge Cahill entered the room. Stone-faced and impassive—not his usual look. He was usually very expressive: He smiled broadly, and maybe even laughed, or he scowled and occasionally yelled. He wasn't a typical stoic Minnesotan.

Judge Cahill opened an envelope. The courtroom was silent. He announced that he would read the verdict. And then the words came fast:

Count 1: Unintentional second-degree murder while committing a felony: *Guilty*

Count 2: Third-degree murder perpetrating an imminently dangerous act: *Guilty*

Count 3: Second-degree manslaughter, culpable negligence, creating an unreasonable risk: *Guilty*

When I heard Judge Cahill read the verdicts, there was something surreal about it. I felt a rush of relief. I looked at Jerry, and we shared a fist bump. I looked over at Steve, and he seemed to be suppressing a smile. I don't know. Matt asked the court to revoke Chauvin's bail and order him into custody. He was no longer "innocent until proven guilty." He was just guilty.

I looked over at Chauvin. I knew his life would change dramatically. I took no joy in it.

We walked out of the courtroom that had been such a big part of our lives the past few weeks. I allowed Eric Nelson and his assistant to walk out ahead, and there, on the eighteenth floor, we walked right into Philonise, Ben Crump, and the whole family.

They were victorious. They were happy. They were relieved. They were grateful.

They accepted a phone call from President Biden; he is a man who knows loss. He lost his son, his wife, and his infant daughter, and this pain is impossible to calculate and impossible to understand unless you've been through it. That's why I believe he was so tender and kind to George Floyd's daughter, Gigi.

The Floyd family held a press conference that afternoon. Philonise went to the microphone and said, "I feel relieved today that I finally have the opportunity to hopefully get some sleep. A lot of days I prayed and I hoped and I was speaking everything into existence, I said, 'I have faith that he will be convicted.'"

He continued, "We have to always understand that we have to march, we will have to do this for life. We have to protest, because it seems like this is a never-ending cycle...I'm going to put up a fight every day...I get calls, I get DMs, they're all saying the same thing, 'We won't be able to breathe until you are able to breathe.' Today, we are able to breathe again…Justice for George means freedom for all."

My team, along with Hennepin County attorney Mike Freeman, also held a press conference after the trial. I wanted to make sure my entire team was on camera. They deserved that recognition.

My voice broke a few times. I was full of emotion, but I wanted to make one thing very clear: "I would not call today's verdict justice… because justice implies true restoration, but it is accountability, which is the first step towards justice. And now the cause of justice is in your hands…I urge everyone to continue the journey to transformation and justice. It's in your hands now."

As I write this, the George Floyd Justice in Policing Act has yet to be passed. It has passed the House twice but died in the Senate.

There is still so much work to do.

In December 2021, Chauvin pleaded guilty in federal district court to willfully depriving George Floyd of his constitutional rights, resulting in Floyd's bodily injury and death. Pursuant to a plea agreement, Chauvin admitted that he used unreasonable and excessive force to kill Floyd, and he agreed that he acted willfully and in callous and wanton disregard of the consequences to Floyd's life. Chauvin also pleaded guilty to willfully depriving John Pope, fourteen years old at the time of the offense, while acting under color of law, of his constitutional rights, resulting in Pope's injury.

Chauvin was sentenced to twenty-one years in prison for his federal civil rights crimes against Floyd and Pope. By agreement, Chauvin's state and federal sentences ran concurrently. Chauvin is now serving his sentence in a federal facility, outside of the state of Minnesota.

Lane, Thao, and Kueng went to trial before Judge Magnuson on federal civil rights violations and were found guilty on February 24, 2022. Lane held Floyd's feet, Kueng sat on Floyd's back, and Thao stood guard and prevented anyone from helping Floyd. In July 2022, Judge

Magnuson gave Thao three and a half years; Kueng, three years; and Lane, two years, recognizing that Lane was a rookie and had asked Chauvin whether they should turn Floyd on his side. Kueng made no statement at sentencing, but Thao had plenty to say: He quoted the Bible and talked about his Christian faith, all to argue that his prosecution for his role in Floyd's murder was evidence of government "corruption" and that God would get revenge on the people who prosecuted him. He offered no apologies to the family of George Floyd. He did, however, instruct prosecutors and the Floyd family that they need to follow his example and "turn to God."

Before the state court trial, Lane pleaded guilty to the charge of aiding and abetting manslaughter in the killing of George Floyd in state court. He was sentenced to three years in prison, to be released in two years. The state trial of Thao and Kueng was originally slated to begin in June 2022, but Judge Cahill moved the trial to October 2022. Both Kueng and Thao accepted plea deals. Kueng pleaded guilty to manslaughter and received a sentence concurrent with his federal sentence. Thao, who was also found guilty of federal civil rights charges at trial, waived his right to trial and asked Judge Cahill to find him guilty of manslaughter and sentence him concurrently with his federal sentence.

But there is still so much work to do.

My office prosecuted the case of Officer Kim Potter, who killed Daunte Wright by pulling her handgun instead of her taser. She was convicted of first- and second-degree manslaughter. We asked that she be sentenced to seven years and two months. She was sentenced to two years in prison.

There is still so much work to do.

On March 15, 2022, Cook County State's Attorney Kim Foxx announced that Officer Eric Stillman would not be charged in the killing of thirteen-year-old Adam Toledo.

There is still so much work to do.

George Floyd's daughter Gianna was six years old when her dad was killed on the street in Minneapolis. She was seven years old when she delivered her victim impact statement to the court. She is a beautiful child. She has an amazing smile. When asked what she would say to her daddy if she could talk to him again, her response was "I miss you and I love you."

There is still so much work to do, and it is in your hands.

———

Perhaps the final verdict in the George Floyd case wasn't delivered by the jury. Perhaps the final verdict would be delivered by the electorate, not the jury. It was not long after the resolution of the Chauvin cases that I realized that the officer-related prosecution would be an issue in my 2022 campaign for reelection.

Could a prosecutor like me get reelected after prosecuting and convicting police officers like Derek Chauvin, Kim Potter, and the others? My reelection would be a kind of referendum on whether a prosecutor would have to run a political risk if he or she pursued justice against a person who wore a badge. If I were defeated, the word would go out: Prosecute a police officer at your political peril. If I prevailed, then prosecutors could have a little more confidence that prosecuting a police officer was not a choice between keeping a job and pursuing justice without fear or favor.

Usually, the issues in attorney general races involve consumer protection and representing state agencies. In my 2022 reelection campaign, there were three issues: crime, crime, and crime. Though my opponent, Jim Schultz, had no experience in the criminal justice system and no trial experience, about forty local county sheriffs and the Minnesota Police Peace Officers Association, which boasts 10,000 members, endorsed him. Under my leadership, lawyers at the Minnesota attorney general's office prosecuted dozens of serious felony cases, including homicide cases and sexual assault cases. We never lost. None of that mattered.

Schultz's endorsers, a group calling itself Minnesota for Freedom, spent over $1.5 million in political ads accusing me of being "anti-cop forever, cops know it" and supporting "convicts." The ads were clearly misleading and untrue. Some scenes depicted in the ad show the burning of the Minneapolis Police Department's Third Precinct, which I publicly condemned. Another scene from the ad depicted a carjacking scene, in which a person was pulled out of a vehicle. The scene wasn't even from Minnesota at all. It was from an incident that had occurred in Miami, Florida. Another attack ad featured a fictional imprisoned individual on a telephone call explaining, "I want you to know why inmates support Keith Ellison. Keith Ellison supports us." The ad ends with the quip, "Keith Ellison, the criminal's choice for attorney general."

The ads were so bad that an interfaith group of sixty-seven leaders called on Republican attorney general candidate Schultz to "rebuke and demand recent ads steeped in race- and fear-based dog whistles" come down. The interfaith leaders described the attack ads as "racist."

The election came down to the wire. In fact, one week before Election Day, which was November 8, 2022, a KSTP/survey USA poll projected that Schultz had taken the lead in the Minnesota AG's race, with a lead of 49 percent to 42 percent, and 9 percent undecided.

I didn't know if the poll results were accurate or not, but I knew that if equal justice was to prevail, I had to find a way to win. I simply could not allow the lesson to be that prosecuting a cop is political suicide.

We poured everything we had into the race. We raised more money, we knocked on thousands of doors, and we joined the other statewide Democratic candidates on a statewide tour. We were knocking on doors in the Riverside Plaza, a complex of six buildings and 1,303 units. With the help of my brother Tony Ellison, a lawyer from Boston; Keaon Dousti, who took leave from his official duties to run the last leg of the campaign; and Mayor Jacob Frey, a tireless campaigner, we knocked on every single door in the complex. We knocked on doors and helped voters until 7:50.

One of the last voters to show up at the polls at the Brian Coyle

Center, the local polling spot for Riverside Plaza, was a twenty-year-old single mom, Destiny. I don't even remember her last name. I can only remember that she had a beautiful baby, still in the stroller, who was crying for changing. Mayor Frey, Keaon, and I saw her coming into her apartment building from the Minnesota cold and heading for the elevator. "Hey, umm, have you voted yet?" said Mayor Frey. "No. I am not sure it really matters," she said. That began a conversation in which Destiny, barely more than a teenager, got a lesson in civics, voting law, and how every vote mattered. But we really couldn't convince her until Keaon said, pointing to me, "This is the guy who led the prosecution of the cops who murdered George Floyd." Destiny said, "What? Really? Okay! Where do I vote?" Mayor Frey, Keaon, and I helped Destiny with the stroller, and this twenty-year-old voted for the first time. And without a minute to spare. She very well could have been the last voter to cast a ballot at Precinct W-6 P-03 1620 at the Brian Coyle Center.

Then we got into our cars and drove to the downtown St. Paul Hotel to wait for the votes to come in. The beginning of the evening was fine. The metro precincts came in early, and we were well ahead. And then the night wore on, and my lead began to narrow. And narrow. The Associated Press declared Governor Walz the winner of his relection bid. I was thrilled for him. Later, Secretary of State candidate for reelection Steve Simon's win was announced, and I was happy for him. But then more time passed, and my lead began to get slim. I got worried. Was I about to lose? I thought the nerves could show in my mood. "Are you okay?" and "It's going to be fine," my friends were saying. At midnight, my campaign told me that I should relax. While we were sure to win, it was still too close for the Associated Press to call—only 21,000 votes separated me and Schultz. I decided to go to speak to the people gathered at the election night party in the ballroom.

I took the stage with my Mónica holding my hand, and I told the volunteers, "Thank you . . . Millions of dollars were spent to sow division, hate, and fear, and we overcame it."

We overcame it. The next day, the AP and the Minnesota secretary of state declared me the winner. I didn't sleep. I ruminated all night. Should I have declined the Chauvin case? Can a prosecutor charge, prosecute, and convict an officer and survive reelection? The voters said yes.

But so much more needs to be done.

ACKNOWLEDGMENTS

This book is about a lifetime of working to stop deadly force encounters between police officers and the people they are entrusted to protect and serve; therefore, there is no way I can acknowledge everyone who contributed to the effort. However, I must acknowledge those who helped me to hold the former officers who killed George Floyd accountable. Without any doubt, I will leave out some people who left an indelible mark on me and my journey. I apologize in advance, and I thank them for contributing to my experience, which informs *Break the Wheel*.

Special thanks to Philonise Floyd, Rodney Floyd, and the entire Floyd family. Beautiful, dignified, and strong, they showed the world how to stand tall and strong under the most difficult of circumstances. Special thanks to super lawyers Ben Crump and Tony Romanucci, and special thanks to all the witnesses who testified, especially all the young people. People like Darnella Frazier, Alyssa Funari, and Judeah Reynolds confronted officers on the street as they were killing Floyd even though they were afraid of doing so, then returned to court a year later despite their fear to recount what they saw, proving that courage is doing the very thing that you're afraid to do. Special thanks as well to police officers and medical witnesses.

I thank my entire staff at the Minnesota attorney general's office, but I especially thank the amazing professionals who worked directly on the cases involving the murder of George Floyd. Special thanks to John Keller, David Voigt, Matt Frank, Erin Eldridge, Zuri Balmakund,

Natasha Robinson, Dionne Dodd, Ann Chambers, Jillian Sully, Eric Miller, John Stiles, and Keaon Dousti. The prosecution of the Floyd case was a joint enterprise with the office of the Hennepin County attorney. Special thanks to my friend Mike Freeman, as well as Joshua Larson, Jean Burdorf, and the amazing Vernona Boswell. The lawyers of Blackwell Burke were indispensable. Special thanks to Jerry Blackwell, now Federal District Court Judge Blackwell, as well as Corey Gordon, Mary Young, Tony Atwall, and Des Hinds. Thanks to the brilliant lawyers of Hogen Lovells, including the remarkable Neal Katyal and his team: Sundeep Iyer, Nathanial Zelinsky, Danielle Stempel, Victoria Joseph, Harrison Kilgore, Johannah Walker, Dana Raphael, Patrick Vencia, and Darryl Williams. Special thanks to Steve Schleicher, former Minnesota assistant AG and current partner at Maslon LLP. Thanks to my friend and confidante Lola Velasquez-Aguilu of Medtronic. Much appreciation to the FGS team: Michael Feldman, Nedra Pickler, Peter Garder, Sydney Walley, Willie "My Man" Robinson, Sophia Boyer, and Galia Slayden. Also major thanks to the folks at Litigation Insight: Merri Jo Pitera, the amazing Christina Marinakis, Adam Wirtzfeld, Keith Pounds, Adam Bloomberg, and the always ready Bret Eltiste. And a very special thank-you to Lily Wolfenzon of Keystone Strategy.

Only one person put up with my 5:00 AM trips from our bed to our dinner table (my writing desk), which I occupied for nine months. Only one person patiently listened to my proposed passages, rephrasings, and rewrites. That person is Mónica Maria Hurtado, my wife and partner. In fact, when the events that form the content of this book were unfolding, it was Mónica who stood firm. She read the threatening hate mail, endured the protest marches at our home, and stayed up with me as I worried, planned, and awaited verdicts. I thank my entire family, who have been with me through thick and thin (sometimes very thin). I thank all of the activists who organized and led marches and demonstrations and raised awareness, among them the leaders of the Black Lives Matter movement and activists like Toshira Garraway, Michelle

Gross, Eli Darris, and others. I thank the activists who taught me the importance of grass-roots advocacy—people like Chris Nissan, Mel Reeves, Kimberly Washington, and Garmez Parks—and elders like Spike Moss, Mahmoud El-Kati, and Tyrone Terrell. Finally, I thank the folks who believed in telling this story, especially Matt Latimer and Sean Desmond.

INDEX

Index

Index

Index

ABOUT THE AUTHOR

Keith Ellison was sworn in as Minnesota's thirtieth attorney general on January 7, 2019. From 2007 to 2019, Keith Ellison represented Minnesota's 5th Congressional District in the U.S. House of Representatives, where he championed consumer, worker, environmental, and civil and human-rights protections for Minnesotans. He is the proud father of four adult children: Isaiah, Jeremiah, Elijah, and Amirah. He is the first African American and the first Muslim American to be elected to statewide office in Minnesota.